FLEECED

FLEECED

How Barack Obama, Media Mockery of Terrorist Threats,
Liberals Who Want to Kill Talk Radio, the Do-Nothing
Congress, Companies That Help Iran, and Washington
Lobbyists for Foreign Governments Are Scamming Us . . .
AND WHAT TO DO ABOUT IT

DICK MORRIS
and EILEEN McGANN

HARPER

An Imprint of HarperCollins*Publishers*
www.harpercollins.com

HarperCollins books may be purchased for educational, business, or sales promotional use. For information, please write: Special Markets Department, HarperCollins Publishers, 10 East 53rd Street, New York, NY 10022.

Library of Congress Cataloging-in-Publication Data is available upon request.

ISBN: 978–0–06–154775–1

08   09   10   11   12   DIX/RRD   10   9   8   7   6

To Blanche and Gene Morris,
93 and 97—the Energizer bunnies,
still going strong—and to Doll and Bill

CONTENTS

FLEECED

INTRODUCTION

FLEECED: Stripped of money or property as a sheep is stripped of fleece; obtained by unfair or unjust means; plundered; deprived of money or belongings by fraud or hoax; swindled

FACT: The mainstream media in America is distorting the news to deliberately downplay terrorism. The Society of Professional Journalists has actually recommended that reporters "avoid using word combinations such as 'Islamic terrorist' or 'Muslim extremist' "!

FACT: Even when terrorists are caught targeting high-profile facilities in New York City like the Brooklyn Bridge and JFK Airport, *The New York Times*—along with the rest of the national media—works overtime to convince us that the threat was artificial and overblown.

FACT: If liberals win the White House and Congress in 2008, they plan to kill conservative talk radio by requiring stations to balance their content by broadcasting extreme liberal opinions and forcing stations to install liberals in top management positions.

FACT: Barack Obama says he will double the capital gains tax rate. This could trigger a sell-off in both the stock market and real estate market between election day and the first of the year.

FACT: Barack Obama claims to be fiscally responsible. But he has publicly proposed tax increases that will amount to more than $1 trillion over the next ten years. If the Democrats win the White House, Americans making $100,000 or more could be paying almost 60 percent of their income in taxes.

FACT: The Do-Nothing Congress is still doing nothing. The U.S. Senate and House of Representatives held roll-call votes on less than a third of the workdays between January 1 and March 31, 2008.

FACT: The three major presidential candidates of 2008, all senators, have virtually stopped doing their Senate jobs. Hillary Clinton, Barack Obama, and John McCain were present on only five of the twenty days of Senate roll-call votes in the first three months of 2008.

FACT: Under our very noses, foreign companies like Shell, Repsol, Siemens, Hyundai, BNP Paribus, and others are helping Iran's repressive regime stay in power, even though it is developing nuclear weapons. And it's our state pension funds that invest in these companies, enabling them to come to the ayatollah's aid.

FACT: Credit card companies made $30 billion in profits last year by charging interest rates that would make Mafia loan sharks blush. And they collect a hidden fee of 2 percent on virtually everything sold in the nation—a fee that's then folded into the cost of almost everything we buy.

FACT: One third of all cardholders pay interest rates above 20 percent, and late fees and other penalties have tripled in the last ten years.

FACT: Hedge fund billionaires—like George Soros—make astronomical incomes each year and pay only the lower capital gains tax rate on their income. Hedge fund employees pay less in federal taxes than other Americans: on average, they pay only 15 percent of their income in taxes, while other Americans pay up to 35 percent. And it's the Democrats—yes, the Democrats!—who are protecting them.

FACT: EADS (European Aeronautics Defense and Space), the French company that owns Airbus, recently won a huge U.S. defense contract, beating out Boeing and costing Americans tens of thousands of defense jobs. So now our tax money is going to create *their* jobs.

FACT: Lobbyists and lobbying firms close to the presidential campaigns of Hillary Clinton and John McCain were paid millions of dollars to lobby for EADS and to use their influence to steer the contract away from the American company.

FACT: Each year, foreign governments, including Venezuelan president Hugo Chávez, spend millions of dollars lobbying our Congress and trying to persuade the American public of the validity of their often troublesome positions.

FACT: While record numbers of homeowners were forced into foreclosure, Angelo Mozilo, the former CEO of Countrywide Financial Corporation—one of the largest providers of subprime home mortgages—was paid $100 million in 2006. When he was forced out in 2008, he left with a pension and retirement package estimated at more than $60 million.

FACT: Countrywide announced a $1.2 billion loss in the third quarter of 2007 and another $422 million in the fourth quarter. By the end of the year, the price of the company's stock fell by 80 percent. During the same time, Mozilo received a $1.9 million annual salary and $20 million in stock awards and sold $121 million in stock. He told Congress that his shares had grown in value by 23,000 percent.

FACT: Countrywide subprime loans for 120,000 homes were in foreclosure at the end of 2007, and the company laid off 12,000 workers.

FACT: The FBI is investigating Countrywide for alleged securities fraud for misrepresenting its financial position and the performance of mortgage loans in securities filings.

FACT: Bill Clinton is a partner in a global investment fund with the emir of Dubai, one of the United Arab Emirates (UAE) states. His recently released tax returns suggest that his income from involvement with the fund could be as much as $15 million.

FACT: Hillary Clinton says that the United States should retaliate against Iran if it attacks the UAE, Kuwait, or Saudi Arabia. No other president, presidential candidate, or senator has ever suggested that we go to war under these circumstances.

Is it any wonder that Americans feel fleeced at every turn?

And it could get even worse. If the Democrats win the 2008 presidential election, you'd better hold on to your shirt. Because, without a doubt, you're going to be fleeced! There's no question that federal taxes will go up—income taxes, Social Security taxes, capital gains taxes, and estate taxes. Spending will go way up, too, and the size of the bureaucracy will likely swell. About the only thing that might go down is your morale.

Our presidential candidates spread the message of optimism, of the "audacity of hope." Yet unnoticed in this inspirational rhetoric are plans to pass the largest tax increase in history; to introduce rationing to our health care system; to weaken our defenses against domestic terrorism; to cripple our efforts to reform education; to let criminals and crack dealers out of prison; and to send our economy into a downward spiral.

Once the Democrats' health care programs are implemented, it will mean the beginning of socialized medicine in the United States. If a politician like Hillary Clinton should ever have her way, the government will even garnish the salaries of workers who don't have health insurance. Big government and big brother will be on patrol.

There's more to be concerned about: Democrats will be pouncing on social and cultural issues, too. One of their first priorities will be to reinstate the Fairness Doctrine. They won't be happy until they destroy talk radio by requiring a liberal response to every conservative program. Imagine a policy that would require ABC Radio to give Alan Colmes a three-hour daily talk show to offer a contrasting view of Sean Hannity's opinions. Or compel Fox News to offer an hour a day to Rachel Maddow to disagree with Bill O'Reilly. No thanks. But that's what they want.

The first chapter of this book describes in great detail what you can expect from a Barack Obama presidency—in short, how we'll all be fleeced by spending and taking policies and plans for bigger and bigger government.

This book is really about the far too many ways Americans are routinely fleeced by our politicians, banks, credit card companies, mortgage companies, foreign countries, and domestic corporations that are trying to set the agenda for our Congress and executive branch, and labor unions who fatten the coffers of the union treasury by luring members into questionable investments.

We'll name the worst offenders and suggest some practical ways to turn the tide.

Here's a good example of how credit card companies are fleecing consumers. Twenty or thirty years ago, every state had laws prohibiting usury. Only Mafia loan sharks collected interest rates of 20 or 30 percent. But Supreme Court decisions stripped the states of their power to regulate credit card interest—and the political clout of the companies has stymied congressional attempts at regulation. So while the six credit card companies that monopolize the industry post annual profits of $30 billion, tens of millions of us are chasing our tails, trying in vain to repay our credit card debt. It's not that we owe too much: The average balance is only $13,000. It's that we can't repay the principal while we're trying to keep current with the 20 to 30 percent interest. In the meantime, the credit card companies use the slightest pretext to impose penalty charges, which have tripled in the past decade.

This plastic fleece hampers our economy. It reduces our buying power and makes debtors of too many of us. But Congress won't act because its members are on the take, receiving millions in contributions from the credit card companies—money they receive by overcharging us!

As we identified many of these critical problems that cry out for national attention, one thing became quite obvious: the White House and Congress appear to be AWOL. They're not doing very much.

Who's calling the shots instead? Big media, big business, big government, big labor, and big lobbyists. And their self-serving agendas are doing nothing to help the ever-increasing number of American people who are losing their homes, paying credit card interest rates higher than 25 percent, and finding their jobs outsourced to foreign countries.

Consider this: Three banks that suffered huge losses because of the subprime mortgage disaster gave huge rewards to the stewards of their downward spiral:

Merrill Lynch CEO Stan O'Neal left the company with $161 million—after the company's stock crashed by 80 percent.

Citigroup CEO Charles Prince left with $68 million—after the company's value dropped by $64 billion.

And Countrywide CEO Angelo Mozilo pocketed more than $100 million—after the company's shares slumped from $45 to $5 a share. Countrywide was eventually sold for about one sixth of what its market value had been only a year before.

Where were Congress and the White House during all this?

Nowhere.

Isn't it time for our senators and congressmen to stop fleecing us and start doing something for us, instead of spending all their time raising money for their own campaigns and patting the backs of the special interests? Is it any surprise that only 14 percent of Americans approve of the job that Congress is doing—or, that is, *not* doing?

Things are getting worse as they do nothing. There were 45 percent more foreclosures—at stages from the dispatch of the first default notice to bank seizure of property—in January 2008 than a year earlier. Three states led in the mortgage mess: Texas, with 14,669 foreclosures; Florida, with 10,334; and California, with 9,354.

And the foreclosures aren't likely to stop anytime soon.

We hear a lot of concern from the presidential candidates about the mortgage crisis. They have a lot of ideas, they say. But unfortunately that's all they are—ideas. The fact is that the three senators who dominated the race through much of 2008—Hillary Clinton, John McCain, and Barack Obama—all but quit their day jobs in January 2007, when they announced their candidacies for president. Since then they've rarely shown up in the Senate, have paid little attention to their responsibilities as senators, and have done almost nothing to solve the very problems they claim to be so concerned about. All they've done is talk about how they'll solve the mortgage crisis when they get to the White House. We need a lot more than just talk.

Yet, for all their absences, they haven't completely lost contact with the Senate. Even though they don't show up for work, they faithfully pick up their paychecks. That's $165,000 a year—for doing nothing.

Can you imagine telling your boss that you wanted to spend your next two years campaigning full-time for a more important, higher-paying job—but you still expected to be paid for your current job, which you'd be completely ignoring?

It wouldn't work. And it shouldn't work for members of Congress, either. If they don't want to do their jobs for two years, they should resign. Why on earth should the taxpayers subsidize their irresponsibility? It's one of the reasons we feel fleeced.

It's time for some accountability. Do your job, senators, or resign.

By the way, it's not as if their working conditions are onerous. Apparently, Congress has never heard of the five-day work-week—or the eight-hour day. Those annoyances are for other people—not them. So far this year, they've scheduled votes an average of only about 1½ days a week. And by days, we don't mean anything like a normal workday. Congressional voting days sometimes last no more than a few minutes.

Nice work if you can get it.

What kind of leadership can we expect from Washington if its most prominent leaders won't even set foot in the place?

During her last Senate campaign, Hillary Clinton hoodwinked the voters of New York into believing that she wasn't really going to start running for president as soon as the votes were counted. She repeatedly said that she was interested only in being the best senator she could possibly be. But she's actually turned into the worst senator she could possibly be—that is, an invisible one.

While no one is minding the store, there's been a marked increase in foreign bailouts of American banks and companies. When Citibank ran into trouble, the Abu Dhabi Investment Authority—a sovereign wealth fund with assets estimated to be as high as $875 billion—jumped in and invested $7.5 billion in Citigroup. And one of Abu Dhabi's smaller funds, Mubadala Development Company, recently bought stakes in the Carlyle Group and Advanced Micro Devices. Abu Dhabi is the capital of the UAE, the oil-rich country that includes seven states, including Dubai.

Dubai is everywhere. In recent years, Dubai-based firms have bought Barneys, the upscale clothing store; the Essex House Hotel (now the Jumeirah Essex House) in New York City; the Travelodge hotel chain; Loehmann's, the discount woman's clothing store; and Madame Tussaud's, the legendary wax museum. The state of Dubai has a stake in Daimler-

Chrysler, the German carmaker, and recently entered the gambling business when it purchased a 10 percent stake in the MGM Mirage hotel and casino in Las Vegas. Through its purchase of the Doncasters Group, a British engineering firm, Dubai now owns several plants in the United States that produce military equipment. It also holds a stake in Airbus, the recent winner of a huge Pentagon contract. It has invested in HSBC, one of the major banks hit hard by the subprime mortgage crisis.

Senator Charles Schumer of New York articulated his concern about Dubai's purchase of a 20 percent stake in Nasdaq: "While I am and have been a big proponent of foreign investment in the United States, we must still be careful of the kinds of investments made in our critical infrastructure, financial exchanges, utilities and other areas that are vital to the operation and security of our country." He's right about that.

Dubai has some prominent advocates in the United States. Former president Bill Clinton is a partner with Sheikh Mohammed bin Rashid al-Maktoum, the emir of Dubai, and the investor Ron Burkle of the Yucaipa Companies in a global investment fund. As the spouse of a U.S. senator and presidential candidate, should Clinton be in business with a foreign leader? Regardless of how the Clintons characterize the arrangement, it appears that Clinton is a partner in a sovereign wealth fund—a fund holding a foreign state's money.

Is this appropriate?

When Mrs. Clinton finally released her tax returns in April 2008, they showed that the former president was paid more than $15 million for his consulting with Yucaipa. The Clintons didn't disclose how much came from this highly unorthodox arrangement with the ruler of Dubai. Nor did they say what Bill Clinton did for the millions. Since Hillary can vote in the Senate on issues that affect Dubai, it's time for the Clintons to come clean.

Shouldn't we make sure that these widespread foreign investments—especially by oil-rich companies—cannot be used for political purposes or endanger our national security before we permit the massive infusion of foreign capital into our system? The question becomes even more relevant after Hillary Clinton's stunning suggestion at the Philadelphia debate that the United States should retaliate against Iran if it attacks the UAE, Saudi Arabia, or Kuwait.

Did her husband—or his partner, the Emir—suggest this crazy idea?

Dubai's lobbyists are among the most aggressive in the world. The country has hired firms close to the Clintons—such as the Glover Park Group, where Hillary Clinton's campaign spokesman, Howard Wolfson, is a partner (he is on leave during the campaign) and other former Clinton officials now work. And Burson-Marsteller, headed by Clinton's recently demoted top strategist, Mark Penn, represents both Dubai and Abu Dhabi; its sister company, Quinn Gillespie & Associates, also represents Dubai's interests. The Quinn of the firm is the former Clinton White House counsel Jack Quinn, who successfully lobbied President Clinton to pardon the fugitive financier Mark Rich. It's one big cozy circle.

In 2006, Dubai's deputy ruler, Sheikh Hamdan bin Rashid al-Maktoum, was sued in a U.S. federal district court in Miami for allegedly encouraging the enslavement of thousands of underage boys to work as jockeys in his native country. The sheikh responded by hiring a prominent D.C. lobbying/law firm to convince the Justice Department to intervene. The suit was eventually dismissed. Nice job by the lobbyists. Too bad for the kids.

This raises an important question: Why do we permit foreign agents to influence our government? Why, for example, should we permit the Venezuelan dictator Hugo Chávez and the leaders of other oppressive regimes to propagandize in the United States? They have no constitutional right to free speech in the United States.

The agendas of the lobbyists for foreign countries are often at odds with the needs of American workers and companies, and they take up valuable official government time in their efforts to convince public officials to grant their wishes. Let's keep them out of our government's business.

At least 146 foreign countries have hired lobbyists in Washington to represent their interests before Congress, the State Department, the U.S. trade representative, the foreign aid program, the Defense Department, and the White House. These countries include some of our most dubious "friends": China, Russia, Libya, and Saudi Arabia. They include some of the most egregious violators of human rights, as cited by our own State Department. Yet they've been able to hire former cabinet and subcabinet officials, as well as former senators and congressmen, to plead their case at the highest levels—levels most of us can never reach to express *our* opinions. They hear the voices of the foreign agents, not the American public—and it shows in our country's policies.

If we want to avoid being fleeced in the next administration, we need our voices to be heard in November, because one thing is certain: the next election will lead to a big difference in our national policies.

It's time to make other public officials understand that we'll no longer be fleeced.

In our last book, *Outrage,* we identified a series of policies and events that enraged Americans. Those rip-offs were bad news, to be sure—but they weren't part of a large pattern with international repercussions. In contrast, many of the shenanigans we address in this book are threatening to send the world into economic chaos—a crisis that could be as bad as the one Osama bin Laden triggered in 2001.

Consider the new paradigm that has developed in our capital markets: banks are begging sheikhs for money. Investment banking houses are failing and being bought up for peanuts with the help of foreign investors. And the real estate market is writhing in pain and dragging down the entire economy. It's a mess.

What caused this catastrophe? Not a war. Not even a terror attack. It was triggered by greed—simple, self-serving greed—which led the very, very rich to try to get even richer by manipulating the credit markets, government guarantees, and gullible consumers in the biggest mortgage scam in history.

There will always be enough gullible and foolishly optimistic borrowers who borrow money they can't afford to repay. The federal government will always subsidize bad loans, either inadvertently or because of corrupt indifference. But unless those who knowingly induce consumers to sign on the dotted line face financial and criminal penalties, they'll just keep on doing it.

We are not a nation that thrives on class warfare. Class consciousness just isn't the American way. When a rich capitalist drives his Rolls-Royce past a factory gate in Britain, the workers think, "That's not right." An American worker, on the other hand, would be more likely to think, "My boy will have a Rolls like that someday." But the obscene gluttony we've seen in CEOs' pay and bonuses could light the fires of class warfare within our borders if this kind of thing isn't stopped.

In his biography of Andrew Jackson, Sean Wilentz articulated the essence of the heritage of democracy in America. You can't make all people equal, he argued. Some will always be brighter, prettier, healthier, or more energetic than others. But you can eliminate the kinds of artificial inequality that are created by government favoritism.

It's time we got serious about that task. Hedge fund managers, for example, are among the richest people in our country. George Soros made more than $3 billion last year. The hedge fund managers defend their salaries by pointing to the risks they took, the smart investments they made, and how hard they worked. But, even so, their income is taxed at only 15 percent because they dress up their earnings as capital gains, while everyone else has to pay up to 35 percent in taxes. That's what Wilentz means by artificial inequality—and it has to end.

Why hasn't it ended already? Why didn't the Democratic Congress that swept into office in 2006 put a halt to it? Because the Democrats won't close the loophole. They say it's because hedge funds are an important New York industry. But we suspect that it's really because the party receives two-thirds of all campaign contributions that come from hedge fund managers.

John McCain is famous for attacking lobbyists and their influence peddling, yet he takes their money. Hillary Clinton greedily grabs every lobbyist campaign contribution she can. But the two candidates have something else in common: both have close advisers, at the very top of their campaigns, who are tied—directly or indirectly—to lobbying firms for EADS, the European company that owns the aviation giant Airbus. Airbus recently sought funds from the U.S. Department of Defense—yes, that's right, American tax money—to build new tanker aircraft. The contract it was after was worth at least $40 billion and potentially up to $100 billion—and the U.S. firm Boeing and the state of Washington had been counting on that contract. But the rug was pulled out from under them by the lobbying firms that helped secure the contract for Airbus—the same firms that are connected with Clinton's and McCain's campaign advisers.

And what of the young men and women who risk their lives to capture or kill terrorists before they can strike us? The heroism of these young men and women has led to the capture of 765 terrorists who have been sent to Guantánamo Naval Base to be locked up until the war on terror is over. But courts, liberal lawyers, and a cowed administration have released 425 of these anti-American militants. And now we're having to go out and recapture many of them—or kill them—because, thanks to our leniency, they're back in the field fighting us again!

So *Fleeced* is dedicated to finding the culprits, exposing their deeds, and crafting remedies. As with *Outrage,* we do so with the realization that knowledge can empower citizens to force change. When the lights come on, the cockroaches scurry for cover. Read this book and get out the roach spray!

PRESIDENT OBAMA:
What Would He Do?

This book will expose a disastrous array of fleeces that are conspiring to rob the American people of their money, their security, and their way of life. The worst among them, however, is what we'll all have to go through if Barack Obama takes office on Inauguration Day in January 2009. There's a strong chance that a Democratic winner would be accompanied by an overwhelming congressional majority, consolidating Democratic control over both houses. We believe that as many as fifty-eight Democrats will be elected to the Senate and the Democrats will extend their domination of the House. The beleaguered Senate Republicans may find it hard to summon the forty-plus votes they would need to sustain a filibuster and stop Obama from fulfilling his agenda. He would be able to do his will. But what will that be? Where would he take our country?

Obama would take the country sharply, suddenly, and dangerously to the far left. He would raise taxes immediately and substantially: increasing the top bracket to at least 40 percent, lifting the cap on Social Security taxes, and doubling capital gains taxes and taxes on dividends. He would roll back the increases in the threshold for the inheritance tax passed under Bush.

But his catastrophic intervention in our society would hardly end there.

Obama would open the door wide to illegal immigrants and make it easy for them to become citizens and voters.

- He would socialize medicine in America—through a federal insurance program that would include illegal immigrants.

- He would weaken the PATRIOT Act in important ways and would increase our vulnerability to terrorists.

- He one would weaken the standards Bush imposed for improved public education.

- He would lower penalties for some of our most dangerous drug criminals and give many a free pass to leave prison.

And, most important, Obama would pull out of Iraq unilaterally, without conditions, and leave it to its (likely bloody) fate. If it became a base for terrorists, he is likely to do little more than to wring his hands and blame President Bush. During the primary season, Obama has been relatively clear about what he would do as president. The trouble is that most voters haven't been listening to what he's been saying. Enthralled by his charisma, enraptured by the idea of electing the first black president, thrilled to have an alternative to the deadly oscillation of Clintons and Bushes in the White House, the voters have allowed the specifics of Obama's agenda to get lost along the way. They have missed the dangerously radical substance that lies behind his attractive rhetoric.

For Obama has done much more than merely promise to end the current political style in Washington and to bring the "audacity of hope" to the nation's politics. During the campaign, he explicitly outlined an ultra-liberal agenda—one that runs even further to the left than what Hillary was willing to own up to.

Whereas Hillary flip-flopped on the war in Iraq, Obama was quite clear: he wants out, regardless of the price in lost credibility or Iraqi lives.

Whereas Hillary hid her planned tax increases, Obama is quite explicit about them: he would nearly double the capital gains tax and the tax on dividends while raising Social Security and income taxes sky-high.

Hillary forced us to read between the lines to see what she would do as president. With Obama, it was all there in plain sight; we just needed to look—and pay attention.

After all, paying attention to the specifics of what Obama says he will do is vital. We must understand the policies and programs he would bring with him to the White House.

Broadly speaking, there are two kinds of presidents: ideologues and pragmatists. Ideologues have a clear agenda based on their political philosophy; they see their election as an opportunity to implement it. Pragmatists, on the other hand, take office with no clear idea of what course they will adopt until they get there. Clearly, Hillary Clinton is an ideologue—and the evidence we have so far suggests that Barack Obama is one as well.

But Bill Clinton was no ideologue. He was the ultimate pragmatist—and this is the crucial respect in which he differs from Hillary. Bill Clinton, for example, campaigned on generalities: he promised to enact a middle-class tax cut, to "end welfare as we know it," and to focus "like a laser beam" on the economy. Once he took power, however, it became clear that he had no set agenda in mind. Shortly after the election he convened an economic "summit" in Little Rock, Arkansas, with one central mission: for others to tell him what to do. For days he sat and listened as experts propounded their solutions; then, after arriving in Washington, he convened a nonstop parade of policy meetings to try to settle on a concrete agenda. What emerged was a hodgepodge. First he decided to *increase* the deficit in order to stimulate the economy. Then he decided to *cut* the deficit and raise taxes in order to bring down interest rates. But the fact is that the zigging and zagging produced a good and solid economic expansion—a stroke of very good fortune.

But the core of Bill Clinton's approach to governing was the quotation from Franklin D. Roosevelt that he often recited: a commitment to "bold, persistent experimentation," seeing what worked and discarding what did not.

But if presidents such as FDR, John F. Kennedy, George H. W. Bush, and Bill Clinton took office with only a vague sense of what they would do, many presidents were ideologues—like Ronald Reagan, Lyndon Johnson, and George W. Bush—who had clear agendas in their minds as they laid their hands on the Bible to take the oath of office.

Lyndon Johnson, empowered first by a national outpouring of grief and guilt after John F. Kennedy's murder and then by a massive electoral victory in 1964, moved quickly to pass JFK's civil rights bill and then implemented a program of domestic spending to combat poverty that he'd envisioned ever since his days as a New Deal congressman from a poor district in Texas.

Ronald Reagan had formulated his plan to increase defense spending, challenge the Soviet Union, slash personal income taxes, and cut discretionary federal spending decades before he reached the White House. When he was inaugurated, his team—led by Budget Director David Stockman— went to work to shape implementing legislation and get it passed by a compliant Republican Senate and a shell-shocked Democratic House.

Most recently, George W. Bush knew what he would do with the power of the presidency from the day he first imagined running. Bush's commitment to cutting taxes, moving the federal judiciary to the right, empowering the energy industry, and finishing his father's work in toppling Saddam Hussein predated his inauguration and likely even his declaration of candidacy. When 9/11 struck, it required little more than extending his original agenda for Bush to embark on a global moral crusade to promote democracy—an ideology that informed every aspect of his policy and program.

But what about Barack Obama, a relative newcomer to national politics. Is he a pragmatist or an ideologue? He's young enough that it's hard to know for sure. But a close examination of his record offers us some clues. He talks like a pragmatist, but would likely govern like a left-winger.

Is the real Obama the one who calls for decreasing the partisan confrontations in Washington or the one who advocates collecting hundreds of billions of dollars more in taxes—particularly on capital gains and for Social Security—than even Hillary did?

Is the Obama who calls for ending the brutality of American politics more authentic than the one who stands so fervently for immediate and unconditional withdrawal from Iraq and who backs a major weakening of the PATRIOT Act?

As he campaigns, Obama goes out of his way to reject the leftist stereotype of the angry populist and talks about embracing a politics of adjustment and compromise. But a close reading of his proposals and suggested policies leave no real doubt about his leftist mind-set. If he wins, America will experience a decisive turn to the left.

There have really been only three times in the past eighty years that American politics has lurched sharply to the left or the right. FDR's first-term legislative program of 1933–1936, which included the establishment of Social Security, securities regulation, recognition of labor unions, federal intervention in agricultural policy, and a host of other initiatives, was such a time. So was Lyndon Johnson's domestic program of 1964–1965. And, on the right, Ronald Reagan's program of 1981–1982, with its sharp tax cuts, rollback of federal regulation, reduction of domestic spending, and strengthening of national defense, was an equivalent moment.

If Barack Obama is elected, we believe that a fourth such time will be upon us. The legislative program he will pass in 2009–2010 will be a lurch to the left equal to those of the Roosevelt and Johnson administrations.

Barack Obama has always been a child of the Left. A community organizer, a civil rights lawyer, a strongly liberal state senator, and the single most liberal member of the Senate (according to the nonpartisan and respected *National Journal*), he is to the left of even Hillary on a host of issues:

- Whereas Hillary supported invading Iraq and backed the war until she started to run for president, Obama has always opposed it.

- Whereas Hillary told people—out of camera range—that she wants to raise Social Security taxes on those making more than $200,000 a year, she publicly opposed such a step. Obama, however, is quite clear that he wants the hike to apply to those earning more than $97,500.

- Whereas Hillary backed a 5 percent increase in the capital gains tax, raising it to the 20 percent level at which her husband's administration left it, Obama wants to erase Bill Clinton's capital gains tax cut and raise the rate to 28 percent.

But at the core of Obama's belief system is a commitment to income redistribution. This is one of the great debates in American politics: some political figures believe we need to raise taxes to decrease the deficit. Others, somewhat more liberal, believe we must do so to increase spending on social and security needs. Then there are those, like Obama, who believe that progressive income taxes should be raised to redistribute income from the rich to the poor and middle class.

The United States already uses its income tax to reduce the inequalities in our society. The richest 1 percent of our population earns 16 percent of our total national income but pays one third of our federal income tax. And the richest 10 percent earn one-third of the income, but pay two thirds of the tax. The poorest half of our citizens pay less than 3 percent of the total federal income tax burden.

TAX PAYMENTS BY INCOME GROUP IN THE UNITED STATES

Income Level	% of Total Income	% of Total Income Tax Payments
Top 1/10 of 1%	9%	17%
Top 1%	19%	37%
Bottom 50%	13%	3%

Obama would undoubtedly make the income tax a far more potent tool for reducing income inequality. And he would use the extra money to increase spending on health care, child care, education, Social Security, Medicare, Medicaid, and a variety of other social programs. But that would not be his main reason for the increase. His key motivation would be to redistribute income.

We all must realize one thing: if the Democrats retake the White House in November, our wallets will be considerably lighter once they're finished with us.

TAXES: GOING UP?

Obama believes deeply in higher taxation of those considered "wealthy"—a broad definition that appears to start at a household income of $100,000. Not since the income tax was originally proposed in the United States by the Populist Party, in the late nineteenth century, as a way to level incomes, have such enthusiastic proponents of taking from the rich and giving to the rest of the country come this close to the presidency.

John McCain, after initially opposing the Bush tax cuts, has repeatedly voted for making them permanent and opposes any tax increases. For those who wonder if there is any real difference between McCain and Obama, on this issue the answer is simple: ask your wallet!

Obama regularly criticizes the Bush tax cuts as benefits "for the wealthy." But he aims his tax hikes on all those who make more than $100,000.

Here's what he'd do to us.

OBAMA'S TAX PLANS

- Raise the top bracket of income taxation (on family income of $200,000 or more) to at least the 39.6 percent rate that Bill Clinton imposed in 1993 (up from the current 35 percent under the Bush tax cuts).

- Impose Social Security (FICA) tax on all income, not just earnings under $102,000 as at present.

- Raise capital gains taxes. Obama wants to almost double them from the current 15 percent to 28 percent.

- Double the tax on dividends from the current 15 percent rate to 30 percent.

- And end the planned elimination of the estate tax and, most likely, lowering the threshold of which estates can be taxed, perhaps to as low as $1 million.

Source: *New York Sun.*

Together, these proposals would be crippling to our economy. Here's how.

The Democrats' Antijob Tax Plans

Increasing the FICA tax by applying it to all of a person's income would force companies to pay a penalty for paying any employee more than $100,000 a year. With Democrats squawking about income inequality, what could be better designed to widen the gap between the rich and the middle class?

Doubling capital gains taxes would directly hit the stock market and the real estate industry precisely when they are most in danger of suffering a major depression.

Doubling the tax on dividends would make people less likely to invest in companies that create jobs.

Increasing the top bracket in personal income tax rates to almost 40 percent would mean less incentive to work and produce.

Of all the Democrats' likely tax proposals, it's the increase in the capital gains tax that would hurt the most. Obama wants nearly to double it to 28 percent, the level that prevailed before Bill Clinton signed legislation cutting it down to 20 percent. The tax now is 15 percent.

Just think of what that increase would do to our economy: it might well trigger a stock market crash and devastate the already slumping real estate industry. Obama's plans to raise capital gains taxes strike fear into the capital, real estate, and equity markets. Who would want to hold on to their stock or real estate until after Obama is elected, knowing that they'll have to pay the government 28 percent of the profits they make from selling then as opposed to only 15 percent if they sell now?

Individual stock market investors, who hold a fifth of all equity assets, face great pressure to sell before the capital gains taxes go up. Congress knows that raising capital gains tax rates is a touchy subject. In the past, it has always imposed the increases retroactively for months before the bill was finally passed. It does so to avoid spooking the markets and sending them into a collapse due to panic selling while the bill to raise taxes awaits the president's signature.

Since this tax increase would probably be retroactive, too, investors wouldn't know when to sell their stocks, so they'd probably err on the side of caution and do so as soon as it becomes clear that Obama is likely to be elected. So look for a sharp downturn as election day approaches and especially in the period between a Democratic victory and inauguration day. Obama will doubtless blame the drop on the outgoing Bush administration, but it would be his own capital gains tax plans that send the markets into a tizzy. (Institutional investors and pension funds won't be affected, since they're not subject to capital gains taxation.)

Real estate would also be hit hard by an increase in capital gains taxes under a President Barack Obama. With the market already stagnant and the inventory of unsold homes piling up, the prospect of paying more of one's dwindling profits in taxes might push many homeowners to sell their homes at bargain prices. If your home has been on the market for many months or even years, you might be tempted to unload it quickly once it becomes clear that the Democrats are about to win, so you'll have to pay only 15 percent—not 28 percent—of your profit to the government.

A selling psychology usually feeds on itself and can often induce a marketwide panic. So the nearer Obama gets to power, the faster the markets are likely to dip.

But raising the capital gains tax would not yield any revenue! In fact, there's convincing evidence that it would actually *cost* money. Whenever the capital gains tax goes up, revenue drops. And when it's cut, revenue rises.

When the capital gains tax rate was reduced in 1981, 1997, and 2003, according to Americans for Prosperity, "capital gains tax revenue increased 49 percent, 49 percent and 88 percent, respectively, over the next three years. In contrast, when the tax rate was increased from 20 percent to 28 percent in 1986, the tax's revenue dropped 44 percent over the next three years."

CAPITAL GAINS TAX:
THE TAX THAT COSTS UNCLE SAM MONEY

When capital gains taxes were cut in	Revenues rose by
1981	49%
1997	49%
2003	88%

When capital gains taxes were raised in	Revenues fell by
1986	44%

Source: Americans for Prosperity.

Why does raising the capital gains tax cause a loss of revenue? Because when the tax is cut, more people are willing to sell stock or real estate, because less of their profit will go to taxes. When the tax goes up, however, they stop selling because of the high tax rate. And even at the reduced capital gains tax rate, the more turnover there is in stocks, real estate, and other investments, the more money the government makes.

Since 52 percent of American adults own stock in some form (about 20 percent of all stock is owned directly by individuals) and 8.5 million people paid capital gains taxes in 2006, Obama's increase in the capital gains tax rate would strike many Americans very hard.

Obama revealed his real attitude toward the capital gains tax during the Democratic debate in Philadelphia on April 16, 2008. When Charles Gibson of ABC News asked him why he would raise the capital gains tax, despite the history that suggested that such an increase would not only fail to augment government revenues, but would actually depress them, he answered: "Well, Charlie, what I've said is that I would look at raising the capital gains tax for purposes of fairness."

Let's understand what Obama means by "fairness." He means that we should increase taxes on investors simply so they pay the same tax as everyone else. (Of course, this ignores the fact that those investors have already paid their full taxes when they earned the money in the first place.) This is class warfare at its most extreme: Obama wants investors to pay *more* in taxes—not to generate revenue, but to soak them so that the rest of the country can feel better about their own taxes! That's what he means by "fairness."

The capital gains tax increase will cut private investment. Capital will flow to other countries. Why invest when the tax is almost one third. Some economists feel Obama's plans would eliminate about $250 billion of private investment per year, costing 2% a year in less economic growth.

But the tax increase that would do the most damage to the most entrepreneurial and productive people in our labor force is the proposed increase in the FICA tax. Currently, the tax is imposed only on the first $97,500 of income. Self-employed people pay 12.4 percent up to that ceiling and employees pay 6.2 percent, a sum matched by their employers. (The ceiling of $97,500 is indexed to the cost of living and goes up every year.)

Obama has proposed eliminating the income cap entirely and wants to subject all income to FICA tax. That's what he means when he says he wants us to pay "a little bit" more.

As Obama says, "If we kept the payroll tax rate exactly the same but applied it to all earnings and not just the first $97,000," he says, "we could eliminate the entire Social Security shortfall."

The cost? The Cato Institute estimates that taxing all earnings at the current FICA tax rate would raise about $1.3 trillion in additional revenue over the next ten years.

Obama defends his proposal by saying that it would apply only to the rich. "Understand," he said during the Democratic debate in Las Vegas on November 15, 2007, "that only six percent of Americans make more than $97,000—so six percent is not the middle class—it's the upper class."

And those 6 percent wouldn't cost him the election either way!

So add up Obama's tax proposals (and weep):

HOW MUCH OBAMA WOULD COST YOU

Increase of income tax in the top bracket to	39.6%
Lift the income cap on the FICA tax	12.4%*
Medicare tax (no change)	2.9%
Total federal faxes	54.9%

* For the self-employed. Employees would pay 6.2 percent.

Add in state and local taxes—even after you deduct them on your federal returns—and you're still looking at paying more than 60 percent of your income in taxes if the Democrats get back into power!

Particularly unjust, of course, is the fact that Obama would lift the cap on benefits paid to people once they retire, only on the taxes they pay into the fund while they are working. Taxes wouldn't be capped, but benefits would be!

Are bosses going to be eager to pay their employees a salary of more than $100,000 a year if they have to fork over 6.2 percent of the raise to the feds in increased FICA taxes? No way! The incentive to create new jobs and to raise incomes would be vastly undermined by the Obama tax plans.

To make matters even worse, Obama would package his tax increases as a tax cut! Here's how:

When it comes to taxes, Washington doesn't live in the real world. Instead, it's legally required to look ahead five to ten years in any budget and tax program. Most of Bush's tax cuts are scheduled to expire in 2010, and the ten-year projection shows that we're in for a big tax increase when they do. But the increase will remain largely theoretical until Congress actually passes its budget for those years.

Similarly, the alternative minimum tax (AMT) is slated to ensnare more and more Americans. It was enacted in 1969 to ensure that the wealthiest people pay some taxes even if they find massive deductions and shelters behind which to hide their income, but the threshold for the tax's application has never been raised. As inflation and prosperity have pushed nominal incomes higher each year, more and more Americans are now subject to the AMT.

When it was first passed, the AMT applied to exactly 155 people who used legal means to avoid paying taxes. Now it would affect 23 million. If left on the books, it will generate $500 billion in extra tax revenues over the next five years.

This tax too remains largely theoretical because the Bush administration keeps pushing back its effective date, postponing the day of reckoning. But since each fix is only for that year, the tax remains on the books in the ten-year projection of revenues.

Here's what Obama would do to disguise his tax increases: He would sell his tax package as a "cut" by reducing these two theoretical taxes. First, he'd renew some of the Bush tax cuts on the middle class; second, he'd raise the threshold for the AMT or eliminate it entirely. But inside this beautifully wrapped Christmas present of tax cuts—on taxes that have never been actually imposed—would be very real tax increases, likely the largest in American history. The tax cuts would be just on paper. In reality, no American would experience any actual tax cut. But the tax increases would be all too real.

And, to beat all, Obama would trumpet these illusory cuts as evidence of his fiscal responsibility.

Of course, when he had the chance to repeal the AMT, Obama voted no. On March 23, 2008, Obama voted against an amendment by Senator Charles Grassley (R-Iowa) to repeal it.

Why is Obama voting against repealing the AMT even as he criticizes it publicly and each backs legislation to delay its full imposition until after the election? Because *he* wants to be the one to repeal it, so that he can announce it as a middle-class tax cut to mask his huge tax increases.

Obama would raise real taxes to the sky. Not because he has to—because he wants to.

OBAMA ON IMMIGRATION

Obama realizes that the key to a permanent Democratic majority in the United States is to court the Hispanic vote and tie it to their party with the same binding force as African-Americans have tied to it since 1964. With Latinos likely to comprise upwards of one fifth of our population by 2020, the key for Democrats is to get them legalized, made citizens, registered to vote, and loyal to their party.

Historically, the Democratic Party has survived by crowding the wharfs and docks, signing up immigrants as they stepped off the boat. Their current strategy for achieving and holding on to power is no different.

For example, Obama supported legislation to grant legal status to children under twenty-one who entered the country illegally if they have lived here for five years. He would also support granting these children access to lower in-state tuition rates at state community and four-year colleges if they are high school graduates. (These are the provisions of the Development, Relief, and Education for Alien Minors Act, called the "Dream Act" by its more enthusiastic supporters.)

And, if illegal immigrants gain legal status, Obama wants their children to receive free health insurance, courtesy of the government. In fact, Obama backs federally subsidized health insurance to all "Americans," a category in which he includes illegal immigrants.

With such a package of goodies awaiting them on the other side of the border, all the Obama approach would do is give foreigners further incentive to sneak into the United States.

If these Latino voters support the Democratic Party in the same overwhelming numbers that African Americans do, the Republican Party is doomed. With African Americans—currently 12 percent of the electorate—casting an estimated 14 percent of the ballots in 2020, the two groups combined will exceed one third of the national electorate. Can Republicans

THE LATINO VOTE: RISING AND RISING

Year	Hispanic Voters as a Percentage of Total Voters
2000	6%
2004	8%
2008	10% (est.)
2020	20% (est.)

Source: *The Hill Magazine.*

really afford to lose one third of the vote by the nine-to-one margin now common among black voters? Can any GOP contender feel confident of his or her ability to carry the white Anglo vote by two to one to offset such a handicap?

A horde of currently red states will go blue if their Hispanic population increases as fast as projected—more than enough to tip any presidential election. In fact, three quarters of all Latinos live in five states: Texas, Florida, New York, California, and Illinois. Three of these five states are solidly Democratic, each having once been largely Republican. And, if the immigration continues and Democrats win the votes of these new arrivals, Texas and Florida will soon go blue as well, making it all but impossible for a Republican ever to win.

In the past, Hispanics cast about two thirds of their votes for Democrats. Though some Latinos, notably Cuban Americans, tended to vote Republican, the vast majority sided with the Democrats. Then President George W. Bush—a former governor of Texas—decided to invest massive personal political capital in winning back Hispanics. He banished "English only" proposals from the Republican platform and opposed attempts to deny education to the children of illegal immigrants, many of whom were born in this country and are therefore U.S. citizens.

Responding to Bush's program, Hispanics, who had voted for Al Gore in 2000 by a margin of 30 points, backed Kerry over Bush in 2004 by only 10 points. The resulting shift accounted for about half of Bush's gain in the popular vote between 2000 and 2004. But in the election of 2006, Hispanics, angered by the anti-immigration policies of congressional Republicans, re-verted to type and voted Democrat by a margin of more than forty points according to most exit polls.

But Republicans may have a chance to get back in the game. John Mc-Cain was the sponsor of the immigration reform legislation Bush pushed and Hispanics overwhelmingly favored. He is as attractive a candidate to Latinos as the GOP has ever nominated.

And Obama has lost the Latino vote in state after state, because of racial tensions between the African-American and Hispanic-American communities.

In any event, McCain may break the pattern—and doom Democratic attempts at permanent domination—by actually carrying the Latino vote.

To be fair, Obama is not as far left on immigration as, for example, Hillary is. And he insists that anyone who comes to the United States must have a job waiting here. "Before any guestworker is hired," Obama says, "the job must be made available to Americans at a decent wage with benefits. Employers then need to show that there are no Americans to take these jobs. I am not willing to take it on faith that there are jobs that Americans will not take. There has to be a showing. If this guestworker program is to succeed, it must be properly calibrated to make certain that these are jobs that cannot be filled by Americans, or that the guestworkers provide particular skills we can't find in this country."

Obama offered an amendment in the Senate to the immigration reform proposals that, he said, "would strengthen the requirement that a job be of-fered at a prevailing wage to American workers before it is offered to a guestworker." Obama clearly believes that "if they are illegal, then they should not be able to work in this country."

But on the issue of whether or not illegal immigrants should be able to get driver's licenses did Hillary tack to Obama's right. In the Democratic de-bate of October 30, 2007, Obama says yes while Hillary (and McCain) say no.

Obama endorsed giving illegal immigrants licenses, saying "When I was a state senator in Illinois, I voted to require that illegal aliens get trained, get a license, get insurance to protect public safety. That was my intention. The problem we have here is not driver's licenses. Undocumented workers do not come here to drive. They're here to work. Instead of being distracted by what has now become a wedge issue, let's focus on actually solving the problem that this administration, the Bush administration, had done nothing about it."

And what of John McCain? For all his visible support for immigration reform, the only amnesty plan McCain backs would require undocumented aliens to earn legal status by learning English, working on the books, paying taxes and a special fine, and remaining arrest-free.

That's a very big difference.

HEALTH CARE

Taxes, once raised, can be lowered again. Immigration laws can be changed. Most of the damage the Democrats will inflict if they take office can be undone. But there's one part of their agenda that can never be repealed: the health care changes that a President Obama would attempt to pass once he gets into office.

If Obama wins the Democratic nomination, it's clear that a major change in our health care system is in the offing. In the endless Democratic debate over the details of health care reform, we have lost sight of the fundamentals. Right now, about 45 to 50 million United States residents don't have health insurance, including about ten million illegal immigrants; hence they usually get only emergency medical care, which is usually still provided for free.

The Democratic plans seek to extend coverage to these tens of millions of people—an approach that would dramatically increase the demand for medical services. Hospitals, nursing homes, clinics, outpatient units, emergency rooms, ambulatory care centers, and doctors' offices would be crammed to the gills with new arrivals seeking medical care under their new insurance policies.

But the supply of hospitals, clinics, doctors, nurses, and other facilities won't increase rapidly, if at all. In fact, the cost controls that Obama will impose will probably limit the income of doctors so severely that fewer and fewer young people will choose medicine as a career.

If the supply stays the same or drops while the demand rises sharply, the result is inevitable: sky-high price increases.

But the United States already spends 16 percent of its national wealth on health care. How much more can we afford? No other nation spends nearly as much as we do. While the United States spends $5,711 per capita on health care, the nearest other large country, France, spends only $3,048.

Obviously, federal health care administrators will have to find ways to cut the cost of health care. While McCain would begin with these cost-cutting measures and phase in wider coverage as cost reductions make them financially possible, Obama will likely implement them as fast as he can get them through Congress.

So what cost controls are in the offing? Obama speaks hopefully about encouraging healthy living and cutting smoking, but these steps are unlikely to produce short-term cost savings. Productivity improvements, systemic reforms, and cost reduction procedures also all take time to implement. The health care bureaucracy is more difficult to maneuver than a battleship. The more immediate answer is to ration health care.

What does rationing mean?

It means that federal bureaucrats—or private ones empowered by federal legislation—will have a veto on any medical procedure you want, even if you are prepared to pay for it yourself!

The burden would be especially heavy on the elderly, whose very life or death would be subject to a new cost-benefit analysis. Of course, every elderly person is already covered by Medicare. But the aggregate increase in demand caused by the inclusion of 50 million new people including illegal aliens, in the system would drive up costs for all—and require rationing for all. And it's easiest to ration medical care to the elderly—particularly when the question is whether to let them avail themselves of costly and risky medical procedures to stay alive for a few more months. Under Obama, our senior Americans would need the approval of some federal bureaucrat (or insurance bureaucrat empowered by Obama's law) to get a medical procedure they need. The "duty to die" ideas of former Colorado governor Richard Lamm would live to see another day.

The long-term effects of Obama's health care reforms would fundamentally change the nature of our medical system. The utilization controls and cost limits would force private health insurers into ever more draconian "health management" decisions, denying people medical care they urgently need.

Seventy-nine-year-old diabetics with high blood pressure who smoke may be told that they cannot have bypass surgery. Some cancer patients might not be able to get MRIs. Medical procedures will be increasingly doled out by bureaucrats, just as they are in Canada and most of Europe.

And why will we distort our current system? To accommodate those who are not now insured. And who are they? Mainly immigrants—legal and illegal—and those who could be covered but just don't bother.

In the interest of extending health coverage to illegal immigrants, who shouldn't be here in the first place, Obama would subject us all to health care rationing—courtesy of the government.

Obama has been very careful to mask what he really plans to do to the health care system. He pretends that he'd simply move to cover the 50 million uninsured and would leave everybody else's health care insurance intact.

But these pretensions are nonsense. The resulting increase in demand would force health care rationing.

Obama would extend the right to buy health insurance to all "Americans," a term that somehow seems to include illegal immigrants who live here. He would offer them the same gilded health care plan that members of Congress receive. Whereas he once advocated the government as the single payer, completely socializing all medicine, he has backed off that position, saying "If you're starting from scratch, then a single-payer system would probably make sense. But managing the transition would be difficult. So we may need a system that's not so disruptive."

Today, Obama proposes working through the existing insurance industry to provide coverage. He explains that he would set up a "National Health Insurance Exchange to help individuals who wish to purchase a private insurance plan. The Exchange will act as a watchdog group and help reform the private insurance market by creating rules and standards for participating insurance plans to ensure fairness and to make individual coverage more affordable and accessible. Insurers would have to issue every applicant a policy, and charge fair and stable premiums that will not depend on how healthy you are. The Exchange will require that all the plans offered are at least as generous as the new public plan and have the same standards for quality and efficiency. The Exchange would evaluate plans and make the differences among the plans, including cost of services, public."

WHO ARE THE UNINSURED?

10 million illegal immigrants

15 million people who are eligible for Medicaid but don't apply

15 million adults whose children are eligible for free insurance

And 10 million childless adults

Who are those who won't sign up for health insurance? One third of those now uninsured, as noted above, are already eligible for Medicaid but just don't bother to sign up until they're sick and need care. During the Clinton administration, the president (with little help from Hillary, despite her extravagant claims) got Congress to pass the State Children's Health Insurance Program (SCHIP), offering largely federally subsidized health coverage to all children without insurance. States generally voted to allow anyone who made two or three times the poverty level to sign up. But only about half of those eligible enrolled. A few years later, the government expanded the program and put more money into outreach—but still more than a third of the parents of those kids who were eligible never got into the program. The truth is, there are a lot of people who don't like to go to the doctor.

McCain has it right. He would give everyone a $2,500 tax credit (or a check if they are too poor to pay income taxes) for the purchase of health insurance. A family would get $5,000. He says that the problem starts with overly costly health care. He says that we need to slash these costs, to make room to cover those who have no health care. He would prioritize efforts to cut smoking and encourage healthy habits and would also focus on reducing health costs by efficiency and productivity. Then he would reinvest those savings in expanded care.

By anticipating these savings, and spending them before they are realized, Obama would drive up the cost of health care and force rationing on us for the first time.

But the differences between Barack Obama and John McCain are most profound on Iraq.

THE DEMOCRATS ON IRAQ: PULL OUT FAST?

Throughout the campaign, John McCain has been up front in his strong support for the Iraq War, its objectives, and—after his idea of a troop surge was adopted—the way it is being conducted.

Obama is just as straightforward in his opposition to the war. He didn't think we should have invaded Iraq and wants to pull our troops out as quickly and as completely as possible. He condemned the war in 2002 as "dumb," "rash," and "cynical." He called it "an attempt by Richard Perle and Paul Wolfowitz and other armchair, weekend warriors in this administration to shove their own ideological agendas down our throats, irrespective of the costs in lives lost and in hardships borne." He called the war a conflict "based not on reason but on passion." He emphasized that he saw the war as an "attempt by political hacks like Karl Rove to distract us" from pressing domestic concerns.

Throughout the campaign, Obama was quite clear that he wants to "get our troops out by the end of 2009." And he placed fewer caveats on the withdrawal than Senator Clinton did. Whereas she listed a wide variety of possible national security reasons to stay in Iraq, Obama maintained that "the only troops that would remain [in Iraq] would be those that have to protect U.S. bases and U.S. civilians, as well as to engage in counterterrorism activities in Iraq."

But Obama's intransigent position on pulling out of Iraq begs the fundamental question: What will we do if he begins to pull out and all hell breaks loose there? What if our former allies are slaughtered by the tens of thousands? What if Al Qaeda makes a comeback and establishes secure bases there? What if Iran takes over and makes Iraq a puppet state, and a base from which to launch attacks on the rest of the Middle East?

McCain says stay in Iraq and win. But Obama is silent on what he will do if his plan to pull out doesn't work.

Obama may be more dovish on Iraq, but when it comes to Pakistan and Afghanistan it's he who is hawkish. One thing many liberal Democrats may not understand is that his vehemence in opposing the war in Iraq is inspired in part by his desire to emphasize the battle against Al Qaeda in Central Asia. During the Democratic debate on August 8, 2007, he declared, "We know right now, according to the National Intelligence Estimate, that Al Qaeda is hiding in the hills between Afghanistan and Pakistan. And because we have taken our eye off the ball, they are stronger now than any time since 2001. As president, I want us to fight on the right battlefield, and what that means is getting out of Iraq and refocusing our attention on the war that can be won in Afghanistan. And that also will allow us to free up the kinds of resources that will make us safer here at home because we'll be able to invest in port security, chemical plant security, all the critical issues that have already been discussed."

Obama even said he would consider military action, without informing the Pakistani government, to hit Al Qaeda targets on the Pakistan side of the Afghan border. Asked if he stood by his comments that he would "go into western Pakistan if [we] had actionable intelligence . . . whether or not the Pakistani government agreed," he answered, "I absolutely do stand by it. We should do everything in our power to push and cooperate with the Pakistani government in taking on Al Qaida, which is now based in northwest Pakistan. . . . I said we should work with the Pakistani government . . . to do more to take on Al Qaida in their territory; and if they could not or would not do so, and we had actionable intelligence, then I would strike."

But Obama's advocacy of getting out of Iraq no matter what could backfire. It might force us to stand helplessly by if Hamas, Al Qaeda, and Iran take over. Imagine Iraq as a terrorist state! That's where Obama's ideas might lead.

OBAMA ON THE PATRIOT ACT AND WIRETAPPING OF TERRORISTS

Barack Obama would water down the PATRIOT Act dangerously, leaving Americans far more vulnerable to terrorism.

Obama speaks with passion and certitude on the dangerous changes he would demand in the PATRIOT Act. A former constitutional law professor, he displays a strong conviction on this issue—but his passion may be obscuring the impact that weakening the law would have on American security. He cites among his achievements amending the PATRIOT Act at the beginning of 2006 so that "we strengthened judicial review of both National

Security letters . . . and . . . established limits on roving wiretaps." Obama strongly opposes the warrantless wiretaps Bush has used to fight terror.

But the administration's rationale for wiretapping without warrants is that the antiterror investigators at the NSA didn't know—and, by definition couldn't know—what it was that they were after or who they wanted to tap, both necessary preconditions to getting a warrant. The whole idea of the program was to troll through billions of phone conversations between Americans and foreigners, asking the computer to spot suspicious words, phrases, or patterns that would bear further investigation. Once a target was identified, the administration was quite willing to get a warrant. But in this first, fishing phase of the investigation, it could never know who to tap or what to look for.

Curiously, one of the best examples of the need for warrantless wiretaps was the effort to save the Brooklyn Bridge from destruction at the hands of terrorists—a story we tell in depth in our chapter on terrorism (chapter two). The NSA first found out about this plot to destroy it through a warrantless wiretap—of the very sort that Obama would eliminate. If Obama should become president, we can say good-bye to this vital measure to protect our domestic security.

But Obama's opposition to the administration's efforts to protect us goes deeper than the wiretap issue. Even though he ultimately voted for the renewal of the PATRIOT Act, he sought to emasculate it at the end of 2005, when its key provisions automatically expired and required congressional reauthorization to stay on the books. Senator Obama worked closely with the Democratic minority in the Senate to weaken the bill in certain crucial respects.

Fortunately, the effort to reduce the power of the federal government to conduct antiterrorist surveillance failed, and the Republican majority renewed the act with a few modifications—but their efforts to weaken the PATRIOT Act foreshadow, chillingly, what he would do as president.

Among the controversial changes to the PATRIOT Act that Obama supported were:

• An amendment that would have required the government to "provide specific evidence to support the suspicion that an individual has links to terrorism" before seizing his business records. The PATRIOT Act itself requires only that the government show that the search would be "relevant" to a terror investigation.

But this more stringent standard would be a disaster! The government needs to be able to identify firms or people it has reason to believe are linked to terrorist organizations and then fish through their records to find specific evidence implicating a person or company. To require this evidence before they can seize the records is to put the cart before the horse. The feds would have to amass the evidence to satisfy this requirement in advance—a burden that would make the process useless.

In any event, these are business records, not personal secrets. The IRS could seize them simply to audit a tax return or to collect unpaid taxes. The DEA has the power to seize records of just this kind in a drug investigation. Why shouldn't antiterror investigators be allowed to do so as well? It's not as though there's any record of the government releasing this information to the detriment of a business or a person. Quite the contrary, the law has been on the books for six years now with no evidence of abuse. So why would Obama want to change it?

• Under the original PATRIOT Act, a company that received a National Security Letter (NSL) from the FBI demanding documents such as credit reports, financial records, or phone and Internet records could not challenge this subpoena in court, nor could it consult with an attorney. Fear that word would filter back to the terrorist organization impelled this provision, but most people agreed that it went too far.

When the PATRIOT Act was extended in early 2005, this provision was modified to allow the company to consult with an attorney. But Obama wanted to go further and eliminate the "gag order" entirely, allowing the company to tell anyone it wanted about the subpoena.

Obama said he wanted "to see stronger judicial review of National Security Letters and shorter time limits on sneak and peak searches, among other things." His proposal would obviate the purpose of the investigation, by exposing it sufficiently that word could get back to the terrorist that the government had him in its sights.

Why is Obama so eager to dilute the PATRIOT Act? Where is the evidence that the FBI has abused the NSL privilege? There are no cases to show that people have been unreasonably compromised by the provision of the PATRIOT Act.

Thankfully, neither of these proposals was accepted by the rest of the Congress. But under a Democratic president and a compliant Democratic Congress, they probably would be.

Liberals have argued long and hard against the provision allowing library records, in particular, to be examined by federal antiterror investigators. Obama told the American Library Association's annual conference that he wanted libraries to be "sanctuaries of learning where we are free to read and consider what we please without the fear that 'Big Brother' may be peering over our shoulder."

But here's an example of why these national security measures are so important: in July 2004, British authorities arrested a group of Pakistanis living in the United Kingdom on charges of planning bomb attacks in London. The key terrorist in the plot, Mohammed Junaid Babar, was caught by the British after U.S. antiterror investigators found him using computers at the New York Public Library to exchange messages with terrorists abroad.

It is vital that homeland security operatives have access to "business, library, and medical records." There is no record of them abusing this power and no indication that they have ever been leaked or even shared with other government agencies (like the IRS or DEA or INS). These agencies should not have access to them. The need to fight terror and protect our population rises far above the mandate of those seeking revenue or those who would ferret out illegal immigrants, investigate ordinary crimes, or find illegal drugs. The homeland security people should be given exceptional access to these records because of the nature of their responsibilities.

Barack Obama has criticized the search procedures, saying that we should require "federal agents to get search warrants from a real judge in a real court, just like everyone else does."

But Obama misses the point. Homeland Security doesn't want these records for criminal prosecutions. It needs them to aid their efforts to spot and stop terrorist attacks, not to put people in jail. The evidence couldn't be introduced in court. Fourth Amendment protections still stand—and should! But federal agents ought to be able to access such records to stop a terrorist plot in progress. If allowing access to business records, for example—which Obama has criticized—could have given us information about who was taking flying lessons prior to 9/11, wouldn't it have been worthwhile to know it?

Under the old PATRIOT Act, the U.S. government had the power to conduct a secret search of a terror suspect and didn't need to notify him that it has done so for 180 days. Obama wanted to collapse the notice requirement to seven days.

Again, this would be a huge—and dangerous—departure from current practice. When the government is at a relatively early stage of investigation of a terror plot, it should be able to conduct a secret search. Notifying an individual *within seven days* that we're onto him would give him plenty of time to sever contact with other terrorists, warn others in his cell, and escape. The 180-day requirement let the feds do their investigation while the suspect is unaware that he or she is being monitored—a key element in any terror investigation. Why is Obama so anxious to warn terror suspects that they are under scrutiny?

His proposal was rejected—although the final legislation modified the original PATRIOT Act to require notification of the object of the surveillance within 30 days, as opposed to the original 180. But it also allowed a longer period to elapse before notification if the government presented the FISA court with a compelling reason for the delay.

Under the PATRIOT Act, the government can wiretap a person with an order from the special court set up to issue warrants in terror cases, identifying in general terms why it wants to tap that particular phone. Obama would have required the Feds to "identify with particularity the person under scrutiny." But the FBI frequently knows only that a phone belongs to an organization possibly involved with terrorism. It may not know "with particularity" the name of the suspect it's after; indeed, the goal of the tap might be to find out who he is. But Obama's proposal would make surveillance impossible unless the feds already knew who they are after.

The liberals' irresponsible proposed changes in the PATRIOT Act were not adopted by the Republican Congress; nor were they taken up again when the Democrats took control. John McCain opposed them all. But if Obama is elected president, we can bet that they will be on the table front and center—to the lasting detriment of our war on domestic terror.

EDUCATION

On education reform, Obama, for his part, has shown an interesting independence from the teachers union. Though he criticizes the No Child Left Behind Act, he backs merit-based pay for teachers—a concept the teachers' unions and their Democratic puppets vigorously oppose.

Tying teachers' pay to seniority, without any hint of a variation based on performance, is a principle sacred to the National Education Association (NEA), the larger of the two teachers' unions—although the American Federation of Teachers (AFT), the other union, has been more open to the idea.

During the Democratic debate of June 28, 2007, Obama said, "We've got to make sure that teachers are going to the schools that need them the most. We're going to lose a million teachers over the next decade because the baby-boom generation is retiring. And so it's absolutely critical for us to give them the incentives and the tools and the training that they need not only to become excellent teachers but to become excellent teachers where they're most needed."

In the Illinois state senate, Obama was the chief sponsor of a bill to give out grants to reward high-quality teachers in low-performing schools. He now says, "If you excel at helping students achieve success, your success will be valued and rewarded as well."

Merit pay is a crucial educational reform. Without incentives and rewards, the ways we encourage performance in the private-sector economy, we will face nothing more than the deadening mediocrity we have encountered in our schools for decades. But pay good teachers well and better teachers even more, and there is a real chance of reform. In his book *The Audacity of Hope,* Obama said he would not oppose paying "an experienced, highly qualified teacher . . . $100,000 [if] in exchange for more money, teachers need to become accountable for their performances, and school districts need to have greater ability to get rid of ineffective teachers."

But Obama has not much good to say about Bush's No Child Left Behind Act.

Obama's criticism of the No Child Left Behind Act is nuanced. Speaking before the teachers' union itself, he had the guts to praise the act: "It may not be popular to say in Democratic circles, but there were good elements to this bill—its emphasis on the achievement gap, raising standards and accountability." He went on to attack the Bush administration for not coming "through with the funding," but he added that "to wage war against the entire law for that reason is not an education policy, and Democrats need to realize that."

Nevertheless, Obama agrees with the attacks on student testing as the basis for assessing achievement. "Don't tell us," Obama told his supporters, "that the only way to teach a child is to spend too much of the year preparing him to fill out bubbles in a standardized test. [Teachers] didn't devote [their] lives to testing, [they] devoted it to teaching and that is what [they] should be allowed to do."

This criticism of the No Child Left Behind Act simply echoes the teachers' unions' positions. The unions worry about testing because it shows up their failure to educate children. Instead of predicating their funding and continued employment on seniority and their performance evaluations based on the inflated grades teachers hand out to failing students, the act requires that objective testing be the basis of the system.

Unable to attack testing frontally, they speak piously of how testing is distorting education and turning teaching into a rote exercise in memorization. These attacks would be more reasonable if the tests showed that schools were getting the job done in the basic areas of reading and math. But students' test scores have been essentially flat for the past twenty years, as we reported in *Outrage*. The only logical strategy is to let teachers do their basic job before they demand that we adopt a more flexible approach to assessing students' progress.

The height of absurdity was the bill, passed by the New York state legislature in 2008, that specifically barred public schools from basing teacher pay on their students' performance on standardized tests! That's like telling a boss not to pay his workers based on how well they do the job!

The most serious threat to the reforms embodied in the act are the amendments being proposed by House Education Committee Chairman George Miller (D-Calif.). In a speech to the National Press Club on July 30, 2007, Miller presaged the changes he envisions in the program; in doing so, he was also flagging amendments a future President Obama might support.

Miller wants to water down the bill so that schools would no longer be assessed based on students' test results, which are objective; instead assessments would be based, in part, on graduation rates, which are subjective and determined by the teachers themselves. If Miller has his way, the happy delusion that we're educating our children adequately would continue. Teachers would continue to pass out good grades to undeserving students; the students would receive diplomas they can't read (even if they're not in Latin); and the schools would continue receiving funding to support the bad job they're doing. Testing, the objective measurement and the bearer of bad news, would recede into the background, and all would be well with the teachers' unions again.

Except that our kids still wouldn't be able to read.

Here's what Miller said that signals this retreat: the No Child Left Behind Act "will continue to place strong emphasis on reading and math skills, but it will also allow states to use more than their reading and math test results to determine how well schools and students are doing, in order to assess student learning and school performance more fairly, comprehensively, and accurately. For high schools, one measure will be graduation rates."

But make no mistake: this change would wreck the program. It would make for a system that relies purely on subjective grading by the teachers themselves to assess the success or failure of their own teaching. A system designed to bring higher standards to schools would bend to accommodate mediocrity—as a result of pressure from the teachers' unions.

If Barack Obama should become president, that's what we're likely to see.

SOCIAL POLICIES

Obama would do a great deal to turn the United States into two different countries: taxpayers and tax consumers. By reducing or eliminating income taxes on large numbers of Americans, on the one hand, and expanding social benefits to the middle class, on the other, both would promote the most fundamental and dangerous polarization any democracy can ever face: the givers against the takers.

Even as Obama wants those earning more than $100,000 a year to pay more in taxes, he's quite generous in distributing tax cuts to the rest of the country. CNN reports that "his plan means billions in [tax] breaks by nixing income taxes for the 7 million senior citizens making less than $50,000 a year, establishing a universal credit for the 10 million homeowners who do not itemize their deductions—most of whom make less than $50,000 annually—and providing 150 million Americans with tax cuts of up to $1,000." This plan, he says, would "effectively eliminate all income taxes for ten million working Americans." By the time Obama is finished, it's very likely that the proportion of adult Americans who pay federal income taxes at all will become a minority of our population. But he would also dramatically expand the range of social benefits government provides, particularly to middle-class families.

Obama would play Santa Claus; his proposals would reduce the number of taxpayers and expand the number of tax consumers. For families making less than $50,000 a year, for example, he has proposed to match any money they put into savings accounts, up to $2,000 per year.

President Obama would double the $2,000 tax credit President Clinton passed for college tuition. Families that don't pay that much in taxes would get the additional amount as a straight subsidy.

Obama has proposed giving more and more handouts that would decrease the tax burden on the middle class, expanding the number of those who depend on government—creating more tax consumers and fewer taxpayers.

A future President Obama would pioneer entitlements and grants for middle-class families, at once making them dependent on government aid, securing their political gratitude, and giving them a stake in benefit programs that also help the poor.

He would bring us much closer to the Swedish, French, and German model, where everybody gets a check from the government, regardless of wealth or income, making it impossible to criticize the program.

Whereas most politicians focus on aid to the poor, Obama zeroes in on funds for the middle class as the cornerstone of his strategy to grow government.

President Clinton once told me, "Democrats and Republicans don't disagree much on aid to the poor. But on middle-class entitlements, there is a big gap. Republicans oppose and fear middle-class entitlements because they know they can always cut aid to the poor. There is no constituency to defend them. But once the middle class gets a benefit, you'll never be able to take it away."

He's right. It's easy to cut food stamps, housing subsidies, or welfare benefits without provoking an electoral backlash. Few poor people vote, and most middle-class voters neither know nor care about what happens to these programs.

But try to cut Social Security or Medicare, and all hell breaks loose. Indeed, New York City is still stuck with a rent control system it passed during World War II to cope with the emergency housing shortage!

In Western Europe, nations are struggling to cut their subsidies to middle-class families. In Germany, they're trying to curb the lengthy guaranteed vacations workers take each summer. In France, President Nicolas Sarkozy is trying to increase the thirty-five-hour workweek. But middle-class voters are tenacious in clinging to their benefits—even if they rob their national economy of incentive, growth, entrepreneurial flexibility, and initiative.

You can't attack welfare spending in France, for example, because all citizens gets a check regardless of their income and they all value it highly.

So Obama's strategy for expanding government is to cover the middle class. Promoting an American equivalent of European socialism, he wants to anchor the growth of government in largesse to people who vote—so that no one will ever be able to repeal it.

ACTION AGENDA

Some people on the right are tempted to run against Obama based on the statements of his wife, his pastor, or the actions of his friends, one of whom is a former terrorist. As troubling as these facts are, they do smack of guilt by association. But those who worry about what Obama would do as president don't need to go that far. His own comments, proposals, politics, and perspectives are more than sufficient to convince reasonable Americans that he shouldn't be president.

Do we want a president who will:

• Double capital gains taxes on stock and real estate sales?

• Increase FICA taxes by 14 points on all income over $100,000?

- Double taxes on dividends?

- Expand the inheritance tax?

- Weaken the PATRIOT Act?

- Curb antiterror wiretapping?

- Extend health insurance benefits to illegal immigrants?

- Give children of illegal immigrants in-state tuition at state universities?

- Expand the number of immigrants who can enter the United States?

- Weaken education standards?

- Expand health insurance so drastically that it forces us to ration medical care, particularly to the elderly?

- Expand the welfare state, dividing America between tax-payers and tax-consumers?

Barack Obama will do all of these things—and *that's* the strongest argument against electing him president.

To win the election, John McCain's campaign must focus not on character attacks but on his opponent's stated positions. It must not become mired in arguments based on ancient history or on guilt by association. Obama can take these shots all day and not feel the pain. He can survive them all. But his future plans—his tax increases, watering down of education standards, weakness on terrorism and other positions—are his true Achilles heel.

Those who wish to see this very liberal candidate defeated in his quest for the presidency should study these positions—and walk through them with those who are considering supporting Obama. Knowledge is powerful ammunition: use it well, and it will reward you every time.

2
HOW THE LIBERAL MEDIA DOWNPLAY TERRORISM

Not all fleecing costs us money. Sometimes it can take the form of misleading us by headlining propaganda and downplaying the truth. Ever since September 11, 2001, the liberal mainstream media have been dedicated to assuaging our worries about terrorism and minimizing—and even deriding—our fears. Their motive, we suspect, is not to improve our mental health or to stimulate the economy by stoking confidence. No, their motives are much more ideological:

- **To elect Democrats.** By downplaying the threat of terrorism, they minimize our willingness to elect Republicans and conservatives who take tough stances on the issue.

- **To protect their idea of "civil rights."** They realize that a fearful nation would seek to protect itself from terror attacks by passing laws that violate its concept of civil liberties and privacy. So, to stop what they can only imagine as a constitutional catastrophe, they mislead us into thinking all is quiet on the terrorist front.

- **To tiptoe around minorities.** Ever sensitive to the plight of minority Americans—often to the detriment of the needs of the majority—

they worry that an atmosphere of tension over terrorism could lead to racism and hate crimes against Muslims. So they try to quiet the voices of vigilance against terrorist threat, lest anyone feel targeted because of his or her ethnic background.

Whatever their ideological origins, the media's efforts to minimize, mock, and mitigate the terror threat are dangerous, disingenuous, and disgusting.

Here's one manifestation of their subtle strategies. In the years since 9/11, our brave homeland security operatives have thwarted a number of serious plots to destroy some of our national landmarks and kill thousands. But each time we've triumphed against these plotters, the media have downplayed the threat, portraying the suspects as Keystone Kops who couldn't pull off a candy store robbery. Or they imply that the feds jumped too soon—that the plot was only in its embryonic stages, that it would have died on the vine if left alone. Or they delve into the investigative techniques used to unearth the conspiracy, lambasting officials for insufficient sensitivity to the rights of the suspects. Or they understate the number of likely casualties if the plot had succeeded, quoting their favorite "authorities" to reassure us that it wouldn't have been that bad.

And their efforts to distract us from the terror threat are succeeding. On May 7, 2002, a Gallup Poll asked Americans to name the major problem facing the United States today. The results were shocking. Only 2 percent cited "terrorism" as the most important problem we face.

The other 98 percent are wrong!

WHAT AMERICANS WORRY ABOUT

What is the most important problem facing this country today?

Economic problems	35%
War in Iraq	21%
Health care and costs	8%
Fuel, gas costs	8%

Immigration, illegal aliens	6%
Jobs, unemployment	5%
Government corruption, incompetence	5%
Moral decline	4%
Education	4%
Inflation, cost of living	4%
Poverty, hunger	3%
National security	3%
Terrorism	2%

Source: Gallup Poll, March 2008.

The media have effectively persuaded us that we are safe—that we can afford to disregard the terror threat that looms over us.

But are we really safe? Don't be so sure. Consider the array of terror attacks that have been thwarted since 2005 alone!

TERROR ATTACKS THWARTED SINCE 2005

(includes attacks on U.S. soil)

- Plan to attack army recruiting centers and synagogues
- Plan to travel to Iraq and kill Americans there
- Plan to attack the U.S. Capitol
- Plan to blow up the Sears Tower in Chicago
- Plan to bomb the New York City subways
- Plan to attack Fort Dix, New Jersey, to kill soldiers
- Plan to blow up fuel lines under New York's John F. Kennedy International Airport

Beyond these plots, U.S. Homeland Security operatives also worked closely with police in other countries to abort plans to blow up ten airplanes over the Atlantic Ocean.

If Americans have forgotten about the terrorist threat, then, it's not for want of terrorists' trying. They have done their best to keep us, well, terrorized. But the news media have been incredibly effective in lulling us to sleep.

THREAT? WHAT THREAT?

What the Mainstream Media Said About Terror Plots

What the Plot Was	What the Media Said About It
Destroy the Brooklyn Bridge	"pathetically amateurish and unthreatening . . . highly improbable"—*The New York Times*
Blow up Kennedy Airport	"lameness of the plot . . . [a] less-than-mature terror plan . . . longer on evil intent than on operational capability" —*The New York Times*
Invade Fort Dix to kill troops	"would-be terrorists . . . leaderless . . . [with] no rigorous military training"—*The Washington Post*
Explode a dirty bomb in the United States	"an unlikely attacker, a small-time crook with grand plans" —*Time*

At its National Convention in Seattle, on October 6, 2007, the Society of Professional Journalists took a massive step toward what some call political correctness—and we call media bias—by proposing "diversity guidelines" that journalists are supposed to use in covering terrorism.

One of their recommendations, for example, is that writers should "avoid using word combinations such as 'Islamic terrorist' or 'Muslim extremist' that are misleading because they link whole religions to criminal activity. Be specific: Alternate choices, depending on context, include 'Al

Qaeda terrorists' or, to describe the broad range of groups involved in Islamic politics, 'political Islamists.' Do not use religious characterizations as shorthand when geographic, political, socioeconomic, or other distinctions might be more accurate."

One wonders how "political Islamists" can be construed to refer to those who blow up school buses and kill little children!

P.C. SPEECH: THE DIVERSITY GUIDELINES ISSUED TO JOURNALISTS

- Use language that is informative and not inflammatory.
- Portray Muslims, Arabs, and Middle Eastern and South Asian Americans in the richness of their diverse experiences.
- Seek truth through a variety of voices and perspectives that help audiences understand the complexities of the events in Pennsylvania, New York City, and Washington, D.C.
- Seek out people from a variety of ethnic and religious backgrounds when photographing Americans mourning those lost in New York, Washington, and Pennsylvania.
- Seek out people from a variety of ethnic and religious backgrounds when photographing rescue and other public service workers and military personnel.
- Do not represent Arab Americans and Muslims as monolithic groups. Avoid conveying the impression that all Arab Americans and Muslims wear traditional clothing.
- Use photos and features to demystify veils, turbans, and other cultural articles and customs.
- Seek out and include Arabs and Arab Americans, Muslims, South Asians, and men and women of Middle Eastern descent in all stories about the war, not just those about Arab and Muslim communities or racial profiling.
- Cover the victims of harassment, murder, and other hate crimes as thoroughly as you cover the victims of overt terrorist attacks.
- Make an extra effort to include olive-complexioned and darker men and women, Sikhs, Muslims, and devout religious people of all types in arts,

(continued)

business, society columns, and all other news and feature coverage, not just stories about the crisis.

- Seek out experts on military strategies, public safety, diplomacy, economics, and other pertinent topics who run the spectrum of race, class, gender, and geography.

- When writing about terrorism, remember to include white supremacist, radical antiabortionists, and other groups with a history of such activity.

- Do not imply that kneeling on the floor praying, listening to Arabic music, or reciting from the Quran are peculiar activities.

- When describing Islam, keep in mind there are large populations of Muslims around the world, including in Africa, Asia, Canada, Europe, India, and the United States. Distinguish between various Muslim states; do not lump them together as in constructions such as "the fury of the Muslim world."

- Avoid using word combinations such as "Islamic terrorist" or "Muslim extremist" that are misleading because they link whole religions to criminal activity. Be specific: Alternate choices, depending on context, include "Al Qaeda terrorists" or, to describe the broad range of groups involved in Islamic politics, "political Islamists." Do not use religious characterizations as shorthand when geographic, political, socioeconomic, or other distinctions might be more accurate.

- Avoid using terms such as "jihad" unless you are certain of their precise meaning and include the context when they are used in quotations. The basic meaning of "jihad" is to exert oneself for the good of Islam and to better oneself.

- Consult the Library of Congress guide for transliteration of Arabic names and Muslim or Arab words to the Roman alphabet. Use spellings preferred by the American Muslim Council, including "Muhammad," "Quran," and "Makkah," not "Mecca."

- Regularly seek out a variety of perspectives for your opinion pieces. Check your coverage against the five Maynard Institute for Journalism Education fault lines of race and ethnicity, class, geography, gender, and generation.

- Ask men and women from within targeted communities to review your coverage and make suggestions.

Source: Society of Professional Journalists.

No wonder that a March 2008 We Media/Zogby Poll reported that "nearly 70 percent of Americans believe traditional journalism is out of touch, and nearly half are turning to the Internet to get their news."

The poll found that "half of the 1,979 people who responded to the survey said their primary source of news and information is the Internet, up from 40 percent just a year ago. Less than one third use television to get their news, while 11 percent turn to radio and 10 percent to newspapers."

Shortly after 9/11, federal investigators, using the very tools liberals object to—wiretapping without warrants, interrogations without attorneys, and the PATRIOT Act—managed to foil an attempt to bring down the Brooklyn Bridge in the heart of New York City. From the day the plot was uncovered and announced to the media, the nation's news organs did all they could to minimize the threat it represented.

THE BROOKLYN BRIDGE PLOT

In 2002, the National Security Agency (NSA), through its as yet unrevealed wiretaps-without-warrants intercepts, heard repeated mentions of the words "Brooklyn Bridge." (Apparently that's one phrase that's hard to translate into Arabic.) Under the provisions of the PATRIOT Act, the NSA was required to advise the New York Police Department of the intercepts; accordingly, it passed the information on to Commissioner Raymond W. Kelly.

As soon as he was alerted, Kelly flooded the bridge with cops and commissioned an engineering study to determine how the span could be destroyed. The study indicated that a simple blowtorch could send it crashing into New York's East River by severing its cables. Further investigation indicated that a saboteur pursuing this plan could work on the cables in seclusion in a hidden area beneath the bridge.

Alarmed, Kelly stationed special patrols at the vulnerable location. A few weeks later, NSA intercepted a conversation saying "it is too hot" on the Brooklyn Bridge, presumably terminating the operation.

When the feds captured Khalid Sheikh Mohammed, the mastermind of 9/11, and interrogated him, he gave up the name of the man tasked with destroying the bridge: Lyman Faris, aka Mohammad Rauf—a thirty-four-year-old naturalized U.S. citizen who had immigrated from Pakistan fourteen years before and lived in Columbus, Ohio. A truck driver with a license to carry hazardous materials, according to the Justice Department he used his job and quiet suburban lifestyle as a cover for his efforts to plan attacks on U.S. targets. Besides the plot to destroy the Brooklyn Bridge, he was assigned to derail a passenger train in the Washington, D.C., area at the same time.

There's no doubt that Faris was the real deal. According to media reports, "prosecutors said Mr. Faris traveled in Afghanistan and Pakistan beginning in 2000, meeting with Osama bin Laden and working with one of his top lieutenants, Khalid Sheikh Mohammed, to help organize and finance jihad causes. After returning to the United States in late 2002, officials said, he began casing the Brooklyn Bridge and discussing via coded messages with Qaeda leaders ways of using blowtorches to sever the suspension cables."

Faris was involved with Al Qaeda up to his neck:

FARIS AND AL QAEDA: PERFECT TOGETHER

- In late 2000, Faris traveled to Afghanistan and met with bin Laden.

- He ordered 2,000 lightweight sleeping bags to be shipped to Afghanistan for Al Qaeda's use.

- Dressed in disguise, he bought airline tickets that allowed Al Qaeda operatives to travel to Yemen.

- In 2002, he met Khalid Sheikh Mohammed in Afghanistan and agreed to deliver money and cell phones to him.

The fact that Faris had several of these conversations *before* 9/11—before bin Laden became a globally known figure—underscores the intimacy of his connection to Al Qaeda. Clearly, this was no disgruntled Muslim with a grudge: Faris was a young, trained, professional terrorist seeking to mount a sequel to the 9/11 attacks with the full backing of bin Laden and Khalid Sheikh Mohammed. That his target was a bridge frequented by more than 140,000 people each day makes the story even more chilling.

Acting on the tip from the Khalid Sheikh Mohammed investigation, the New York Police Department raided Faris's Brooklyn apartment and took him into custody. A search of his residence found equipment that would have been able to cut the cables on the bridge and a diagram specifying where on the structure he could work without being discovered—the very spot Kelly had already identified.

Yet, even as *The New York Times* covered the arrest of Faris, it did everything it could to minimize the seriousness of the plot. The paper editorialized that the terror plot "seemed pathetically amateurish and unthreatening" and that "the alleged plan—to use blowtorches to cut the suspension cables of the bridge—seems highly improbable, given both the structure of the 120-year-old span and the police scrutiny it has received since Sept. 11, 2001."

It was not the "police scrutiny [the bridge] has received since Sept. 11, 2001" that saved it from Faris's blowtorch. It was the feds' focus on the bridge, triggered by the NSA wiretap intercepts, that specifically revealed it as an ongoing target. But neither the NSA nor the New York Police Department could reveal the existence of the intercepts or even note that the bridge had been receiving special police protection since then. To have done so would have compromised the entire program. (Which is exactly what happened years later, when *The New York Times* broke the story.)

So, lacking the information about the massive police presence on the bridge and the NSA intercepts that had caused it, the news media—led by the *Times*—perpetrated the illusion that the plot was not feasible.

The *Times* was right about one thing: the plot to bring down the bridge wouldn't have worked—not because it wasn't technically feasible but because the NSA intercepts had led the police to mount a massive surveillance campaign.

When the NSA intercepts were revealed to the public years later and the Bush administration cited their role in protecting the bridge, the media had already created the totally mistaken impression that the plot was hopeless because the bridge couldn't be brought down with a blowtorch. The *Times* heaped scorn on the plot, quoting a "Brooklyn resident [who] said, 'I'm more concerned about getting mugged.' " The onlooker dismissed the police presence at the bridge as "window dressing. If somebody really wants to do something, they'll do it."

As the leading newspaper in the city where the bridge is located, of course, *The New York Times* had a special responsibility to explain the nature and seriousness of the plot. Its decision to belittle the enterprise sent a signal to media outlets nationwide to downplay the threat.

The *Times* even hinted at political motivations in the timing of the plot's exposure. The press conference announcing the arrest of Faris several months earlier was held in June 2003, as the 2004 elections were looming on the horizon. The *Times* wrote that "Justice Department officials decided to announce the case at a time when [Attorney General John] Ashcroft has been put on the defensive by charges from his own inspector general this month that the department mistreated many illegal immigrants after the Sept. 11, 2001 attacks in its aggressive pursuit of terrorist suspects. The Faris case allowed Mr. Ashcroft to claim another high-profile victory in the campaign against terrorism. . . . Although he declined to discuss details, he said the timing in making the case public was driven solely by law enforcement concerns."

In the same article, the *Times* also found an FBI official who was willing to say—anonymously—that he didn't know whether Faris could really have pulled off the attack. "[A]n F.B.I. official said investigators were still seeking to determine just how far the plot proceeded and how serious a threat Mr. Faris posed. 'Obviously he had contacts with people at Al Qaeda so he has to be considered somewhat important, but to say whether he really could have accomplished this or not, we're still not sure,' the official said."

But the plot to bring down the bridge was all too real and could well have succeeded. Even as it editorialized about the seeming implausibility of the plot, the *Times* ran a news story reporting that "a senior law enforcement official in New York said . . . that the possibility [of destroying the bridge] was never taken lightly. 'Apparently, there are ways that obviously we don't want to go into,' the official said, 'that make that easier than you might think, sort of along the lines of a domino effect in how they would attack that cabling.' "

The paper went on to note that "another senior law enforcement official pointed out that the main suspension cables on the Brooklyn Bridge, as on many suspension bridges, are made up of many individual cables bound together and anchored at individual points on each side of the bridge. You are vulnerable at one of those locations because first of all it's enclosed—you may not see the activity."

Yet elsewhere in the same article the *Times* stressed how difficult it would have been to sever the cables that hold the bridge aloft. "Several engineers interviewed yesterday," the newspaper wrote, "said they believed that even for someone with unfettered access to the bridge, a substantial amount of time and a lot of hard work would be required to do serious damage with acetylene torches." The story reported that "each of the four main suspension cables is more than 15 inches in diameter, containing 19 individual strands within it. Each of these strands contains 280 separate wires, all of which would have to be cut."

The paper quoted Matthys Levy, a structural engineer at Weidlinger Associates in New York and an author of the appropriately titled book *Why Buildings Fall Down: How Structures Fail,* as saying "think of the time it would take to cut through [the cables]. . . . if he had all the time in the world, sure. If nobody is watching him, he can cut the cable in half in a day or so."

Did Faris have "all the time in the world?" No—but only because police officers "now patrol the bridge's sensitive locations, and alarms and sensors have been placed at those points," as the *Times* reported. " 'If someone gets into proximity,' one police official noted, 'it sets off a camera.' "

Without those security measures and the NSA intercepts that inspired them, Faris would have had all the time and privacy he needed to sever the cables and bring the bridge down.

A quote from New York's mayor, Michael Bloomberg, closes the *Times* story: "The thought of losing the Brooklyn Bridge is just something that you can't contemplate. It would be a disaster. But it's not going to happen."

Once the NSA wiretap operation was exposed, the Bush administration argued that its role in uncovering and preventing the destruction of the bridge helped to justify the program. That set off liberal alarms throughout the country—and triggered a new campaign to dismiss the idea of a credible plot to destroy the Brooklyn Bridge. Suddenly liberals had an investment in minimizing the possibility that its span could be sent crashing into the East River. In their mockery, they disregarded the basic fact that it was not the technical difficulties Faris would have faced that had kept him from carrying out his plan but the police surveillance—scrutiny that had been prompted by the same NSA wiretap information the Left derided.

The liberals even tried using humor to win the debate—trying to discredit the horrific story of the plot by making fun of it. Left-wing commentators couldn't resist sniping at the very idea that the Brooklyn Bridge could be taken down with a handheld welding tool. *The New Yorker*'s Lawrence Wright told the *Huffington Post,* "We captured Khalid Shaikh Mohammed and tortured him. Only one person has been arrested because of that capture . . . and that is a guy named Lyman Faris, the guy that was going to take down the Brooklyn Bridge with a blowtorch. . . . So under torture, Khalid Shaikh Mohammed gave up a guy who was going to bring down the Brooklyn Bridge with a blowtorch, if that's conceivably possible."

Kelli Arena, a CNN justice correspondent, even implied that Faris was insane: "Prosecutors say the Ohio truck driver [Faris] was an al Qaeda foot soldier, travelling to Afghanistan and Pakistan to carry out errands. Back in the United States, he scouted potential sites for terror attacks, including the Brooklyn Bridge. Faris pled guilty to all of that in May, before undergoing a psychiatric evaluation. And now, the only confessed sleeper agent caught on U.S. soil wants to withdraw that plea for reasons even his lawyers cannot yet explain."

Another liberal voice in the *Huffington Post,* Larry C. Johnson, called Faris "a man of wild dreams with no competence to harm the bridge. He was the type of guy who could be conned into buying it, but he had trouble blowing up balloons."

Very funny. But the cold fact is that it *would have been* possible to bring down the bridge with a blowtorch—if you had a confined, private space in which to work long hours without danger of detection. Still, liberals disregard the facts and persist in describing the plot as fanciful. Well, it's no less fanciful than hijacking airplanes and using them to bring down the World Trade Center.

Even a U.S. senator, the chairman of the Intelligence Committee, has joined in the ill-informed mockery. When the government announced that four Southeast Asian terrorists had been arrested for a plot to steer a plane into the tallest building on the West Coast—the seventy-two-story Library Tower in Los Angeles, now called the U.S. Bank Tower—Senator Jay Rockefeller of West Virginia commented sarcastically, "Maybe they're tired of talking about [the] Brooklyn Bridge and they're trying to find a different edifice of some sort."

Rockefeller's scorn reflects the received wisdom of the Left: that the Brooklyn Bridge was never in serious jeopardy.

The New York Times' columnist Paul Krugman piled on in his November

6, 2006, column. If you're gullible, he jibed, "I have a plot to blow up the Brooklyn Bridge to sell you."

Part of the Left's argument is that terror cases that are presented as mortal dangers to the public in press conferences often end up in convictions for more minor offenses. Faris, for example, was convicted only of providing material support to terrorists. He was sentenced to twenty years in prison. Why "material support" and not a more serious charge? Faris originally faced thirty years to life for his crimes. But he evidently earned a reduced sentence by cooperating with federal prosecutors, laying out a virtual road map of Al Qaeda operations in the United States.

Often, however, terrorists are convicted on lesser charges because federal officials, anxious to nip such operations in the bud, arrest the terrorists so early in the process that only lesser charges are viable.

Still, liberals point out that Faris did not pull off any terror plot in the United States—that the only crime he actually managed to commit was to supply aid to other terrorists who might or might not have used the aid in attacks on the United States. This was, of course, exactly the crime for which he was convicted.

But his twenty-year sentence, and the publicity surrounding the arrest and conviction, all suggested that Faris was actually prosecuted only because he had attempted to develop a way to blow up the Brooklyn Bridge. But aren't the FBI, federal prosecutors, and the courts justified in arresting people who are *planning* terrorist attacks? Lyman Faris was no hapless simpleton. He was obviously well connected with Al Qaeda—and he was fully capable of attempting whatever attack it wanted, as long as it was technically feasible.

Faced with the prospect of an Al Qaeda operative whose mission was to blow up one of America's greatest monuments, we believe the federal Homeland Security operatives had no choice but to arrest the man. In doing so, they may have saved thousands of lives—including those of liberal voices who mocked the arrest after the fact.

THE JFK BOMB PLOT

The single most graphic example of the media's tendency to tamp down coverage of terrorism occurred on June 3, 2007, when *The New York*

Times—again, not just a national newspaper but the most important source of local news for millions of city residents—buried its story chronicling the arrest of three men plotting to blow up John F. Kennedy International Airport—and much of Queens—on page A-30, deep inside its pages.

After the story ran, the paper received a flurry of angry letters demanding to know why a newspaper that covers Queens would so downplay our success in frustrating such a major terror attack. In response, the *Times'* national editor, Suzanne Daley, offered this explanation:

> In the years since 9/11, there have been quite a few interrupted terrorist plots. It now seems possible to exercise some judgment about their gravity. Not all plots are the same. In this case, law enforcement officials said that J.F.K. was never in immediate danger. The plotters had yet to lay out plans. They had no financing. Nor did they have any explosives. It is with all that in mind, that the editors in charge this weekend did not put this story on the front page.
>
> In truth, the decision was widely debated even within this newsroom. At the front page meeting this morning, we took an informal poll and a few editors thought the story should have been more prominently played. Some argued it should have been fronted, regardless of the lameness of the plot, simply because it was what everyone was talking about.

Lameness of the plot? There they go again!

This plot was anything but lame: in fact, it was audacious. As the *Times* itself described it, the plot involved "detonating fuel storage tanks and pipelines and setting fire to Kennedy International Airport, not to mention a substantial swath of Queens." According to Roslynn R. Mauskopf, the U.S. attorney for Brooklyn: "had the plot been carried out, it could have resulted in unfathomable damage, deaths and destruction. The devastation that would be caused had this plot succeeded is just unthinkable."

Apparently, though, *The New York Times* hardly gave the threat a second thought. Instead it belittled the plot, noting that the evidence "suggests a less than mature terror plan, a proposed effort longer on evil intent than on operational capability."

In other words, the plot was smashed in its relatively early stages. The *Times* quoted Ms. Mauskopf as saying that "the public was never at risk" and that law enforcement "had stopped this plot long before it ever had a chance to be carried out." But anyone who read the newspaper's coverage would assume that it had never had a chance of coming to fruition—that the plan was nothing more than the half-baked dream of some demented men with no capacity to translate them into action.

Not so.

Consider how serious this plot really was:

THE PLOT TO BLOW UP KENNEDY AIRPORT

- The lead suspect, Russell M. Defreitas, was a sixty-three-year-old retired airport cargo worker who was planning to use his inside knowledge of Kennedy Airport to pull off the attack.

- One of the coconspirators had significant financial resources—enough to pay for Defreitas's extensive travel expenses as he concocted the plot.

- Defreitas had already traveled to his native Guyana and Trinidad in South America—an epicenter of drug kingpins and crime—to find further financial backing for his plot.

- Defreitas had actively sought the financial aid of a sophisticated terror group that had once attempted a deadly coup in Trinidad and Tobago.

- Defreitas made it clear that he wanted to pull off an attack that would dwarf the 9/11 assaults.

- The FBI had infiltrated the plotters' cell using an informant who accompanied Defreitas on a drive out to the Kennedy fuel tanks at night and also joined him in conducting surveillance and making videos of JFK and the surrounding area.

- Defreitas had located satellite photographs of JFK to assist in his plotting.

- One of the plotters discussed disabling the airport control tower to provide cover for the planned destruction of the fuel tanks.

This plot was obviously much more serious than the barroom boasting the *Times* seemed to describe.

Nevertheless, the paper worked hard to discredit the federal authorities' portrait of the danger the plot represented. The *Times* described Defreitas as a "home-grown Islamic terrorist" who could never have pulled it off. While Defreitas "talked of his dreams of inflicting massive harm," it continued, he "appeared to possess little money, uncertain training and no known background in planning a terror attack."

After diligent reportorial work, the newspaper even managed to find "some law enforcement officials and engineers [who] also dismissed the notion that the planned attack could have resulted in a catastrophic chain reaction; system safeguards, they said, would have stopped explosions from spreading."

All these aspersions on the ability of the terrorists to bring mayhem to Kennedy Airport were reported under the headline "Papers Portray Plot as More Talk than Action." (The term "papers" referred to the criminal filing against the plotters, although it described the *Times* and its coverage better than the feds' complaint.)

To read the *Times'* account of the JFK plot, you might think 9/11 had never happened. One of the most profound lessons of that attack was the importance of stopping such terror plots in their "less than mature" phase—when the plans are still "longer on evil intent than on operational capacity." If we fail to do so, before we know it we may be picking up body parts in the rubble of the next terrorist attack.

Rather than praise federal investigators for being so skilled at infiltration and so attuned to terror plots that they can catch them in their incipient stages, the *Times* dismissed the efforts of these Islamic terrorists, calling their deadly plans—which were already deep in formulation—nothing but "dreams."

Particularly absurd were the newspaper's accounts of the judgment of "some law enforcement officials and engineers" that the explosions that the terrorists might have ignited could have been "stopped from spreading." How could they know? Are these the same engineers who assured us that the towers of the World Trade Center would never collapse? Could they truly be certain that a former JFK worker would not know how to get around the safeguards in which these unnamed experts placed such hope?

Like a good defense lawyer, the *Times* worked hard to discredit the man who—at the risk of his own life—infiltrated the terrorist group and reported on their activities to the feds. They tarred this hero, who might have saved the lives of thousands, as "a convicted drug trafficker [whose] sentence is pending as part of his cooperation agreement with the federal government."

As one conservative blogger noted, however, the background of the man who stopped the plot is far less important than the ease with which it might have been triggered. After all, "one man with a Ryder truck destroyed the Alfred P. Murrah Federal Building in [Oklahoma City in] 1995. The federal government was not there to stop it and 168 died. It does not take much to create death and destruction in America."

Why would *The New York Times* want to minimize a threat to the city it covers? After all, don't newspapers usually do the opposite—blow stories out of proportion to sell newspapers?

Well, in the case of the *Times'* coverage of the JFK plot, the answer was buried at the end of one of its stories, in a comment by Neal R. Sonnett, a defense lawyer who is a past president of the National Association of Criminal Defense Lawyers. The *Times* gave the final word in its piece to Sonnett, reporting that he saw "a broader risk in overstating the sophistication of a terror plot. At a time when many Americans live in justified fear of an attack, the risk is that drumbeating creates a climate of fear and drives public policy." Sonnett complained that "there unfortunately has been a tendency to shout too loudly about such cases" and mocked the plotters as "the gang that couldn't shoot straight."

What Sonnett calls a "climate of fear" we think is a proper appreciation of the dangers we face.

Liberals have said that the JFK plot was not serious because "its ring leader made a living exporting broken air-conditioner parts to Guyana," and thus presumably wasn't a fully qualified terrorist. They have also claimed that the plotters had "no set plan. There was no financing. They didn't have any explosives."

What of these liberal objections?

That the "ring leader made a living exporting broken air-conditioner parts to Guyana"? Most of the 9/11 terrorists didn't even have that much of a job—they were *unemployed*.

That "there was no financing"? They had sufficient money for repeated foreign travel and were actively peddling their ideas in terrorist circles to line up the funding they needed.

That "they didn't have any explosives"? As any liberal gun control advocate will surely agree, it's not hard to get explosives in the United States.

Nora Ephron, the witty liberal commentator, was particularly vicious in her sarcastic mockery of the federal informant who brought down the plot. In an article for *The Huffington Post* headlined "How to Foil a Terrorist Plot in Seven Simple Steps," she derided the informant's courage and implied that the entire plot and its denouement had been a setup.

Ephron is not exactly an established political commentator or student of terrorism. Many of her articles on *The Huffington Post* are of a very different genre: She likes to write about food. In October 2007, she waxed eloquent on pancakes. On November 18, she entreated readers, "Tell Us What You're Cooking for Thanksgiving This Year That You Didn't Cook Last Year." In the column she praised an apricot Jell-O mold that had survived fourteen of her family holidays and shared her newest recipe for succotash. She has shared her love of butter on steak, bread pudding, and various products from Zabar's. Even when her books aren't about food, they often include recipes.

Strange credits for someone who wants to educate us about politics— and about terrorism. Ephron may be a great screenwriter, a very funny light columnist, and even a good food writer. But she knows nothing about the criminal justice system—and less about how terrorists work. And her column showed it.

True to form, Ephron rendered her commentary on terrorism in the form of—what else?—a recipe. "In order to foil a terrorist plot," Ephron clucked, "you must first find a terrorist plot." Since "this is not easy," she went on, it helps to have an "incentive." The best, she said, "is to be an accused felon, looking at a long prison term." So far, she wasn't wrong: there's no question that plea bargaining is a proven tool for law enforcement to use in stymieing terror threats. There's nothing wrong with that—it's a basic tool of our criminal justice system.

But then Ephron went off the deep end. If you're a felon searching for a terror plot to expose, she said, the best way is to find "a sad, sick, lonely, drunk, deranged, disgruntled or just plain anti-American Muslim" and "make [him] your very own terrorist." (She doesn't seem to realize that it's pretty hard to find a drunk devout Muslim. The religion bans alcohol consumption.)

Ephron went on to imply that the informant wanted to live in luxury while exposing the plot. "Now the good part begins," she wrote. "Money! The FBI will give you lots of money to take your very own terrorist out to lots of dinners" and "more money . . . to travel to foreign countries." She said that for "months and even years" you can "get the FBI to pay for everything you do." This is sniping, but it's more or less harmless.

But then she warned that "at a certain point, something will go wrong": it will become evident that there is no plot, "just a case of entrapment." Never fear, she said. "The FBI has as much at stake as you do. So before it can be obvious to the world that there's no case, the FBI will arrest your very own terrorist. . . . [s]o congratulations, you have foiled a terrorist plot. Way to go."

It's hard to tell where to start in critiquing Ephron's column. She seemed to ignore the plain fact that the armed terrorists the FBI informant was following could easily have killed him—that he was putting his life on the line in going undercover.

But to suggest that the JFK terror plot was not real—worse, that it was a case of "entrapment"—is absurd in light of the evidence. Even if the FBI would ever lend itself to the kinds of shenanigans Ephron fears—which we doubt—U.S. attorneys aren't likely to let such measures stand; neither are U.S. district court judges or their appellate courts. But then these are things Ephron knows nothing about.

The more serious question raised by the arrests in the JFK plot is whether the FBI is at risk of criminalizing people who merely talk about committing terror plots.

The New York Times wrote that the arrests in the JFK plot are "inspiring a new round of skepticism from some lawyers who are openly questioning whether the government, in its zeal to stop terrorism, is forgetting an element central to any case: the actual intent to commit a crime. 'Talk without any kind of an action means nothing,' said Martin R. Stolar, a New York defense lawyer. 'You start to criminalize people who are not really criminals.' "

On the other hand, Homeland Security Secretary Michael Chertoff had a good point when he explained, "We don't wait until someone has lit the fuse to step in." Chertoff pointed out that "the government could not waste time trying to determine whether the suspects were smart enough or serious enough to turn their threats into destructive action." He added, "it is a mistake to assume that the only terrorist that's a serious terrorist is the kind of guy you see on television, that's a kind of James Bond type. The fact of the matter is mixing a bomb in a bathtub does not take rocket science."

But the suspicions of the Left are not easily assuaged. Carl W. Tobias, a law professor at the University of Richmond, is among those characterizing such prosecutions as feel-good projects: "There is some kind of public relations gained by making Americans on the one hand feel concerned that the Sears Tower in Chicago or some tunnel in Manhattan is targeted yet on the other hand feel comforted that the government is on top of it."

But Mark J. Mershon, an FBI assistant director, said of the JFK conspiracy: "Plotting for this attack had matured to a point where it appeared that the individuals were about to move forward. They were about to go to a phase where they would attempt to surveil targets, establish a regimen of attack and acquire the resources necessary to effectuate the attacks." As Pasquale J. D'Amuro, former assistant director in charge of the FBI's New York office, has pointed out, by the time such a terror plot has matured it's often too late to stop it. "When they go operational, they run silent [and] it becomes very difficult to follow them and try to trail them."

Chertoff acknowledged the critics' charges that "the people you are arresting are not really serious or they don't really have the capacity of actually carrying something out." But he warns that we need to act swiftly to counter such threats. "We are dangerously putting people at risk if somehow we believe that only criminal masterminds or terrorist masterminds are a threat," he said.

The liberal media should take Chertoff's warning to heart. Their efforts to downplay serious threats like the JFK terror plot not only carry partisanship too far—they encourage Americans to lower their guard just when we may be at our most vulnerable, adding to a general sense of complacence about terrorism that can only weaken our country's defenses.

DEFENDING FORT DIX

Low-tech terror plots pose a special threat: they're relatively easy to plan and pull off and require less preparation time than sophisticated conspiracies. It would be far simpler to enter a facility such as Fort Dix, the 14,000-soldier New Jersey army base, and use automatic weapons to mount a killing spree, than to bring down the Brooklyn Bridge. And the simpler a plot is, the less time the FBI has to infiltrate it and stop it before it can reach fruition.

In 2007, however, federal agents were able to stop six men from entering Fort Dix on exactly such a mission. An alert citizen and a responsive federal investigative bureaucracy, working just as they're supposed to, stopped the conspiracy before it could become operational. Yet once again they have been mocked for their diligence and subjected to the usual dose of liberal skepticism about the plot they broke up.

The terrorists chose Fort Dix, the news media reported, because "one defendant . . . had delivered pizzas to the base from his family's nearby restaurant . . . and knew the area 'like the palm of his hand.' "

The FBI was tipped off to the plot when the terrorists asked a clerk at a video store to transfer a video of "men firing assault weapons, calling for jihad and yelling 'God is great' in Arabic' " onto a DVD. For fifteen months, two brave federal agents infiltrated the group, intimating that they could help supply weapons for the attack.

The group was already well armed. Journalists noted that "they had substantial firepower, including handguns, an assault rifle and a semi-automatic assault weapon." They were arrested "as they tried to buy, from the F.B.I. informer, four AK-47s and M-16s." As U.S. Attorney Christopher J. Christie said, "they were at the point where they wanted the final piece of their plan, to obtain the final weaponry."

The group had scouted several other possible targets, including Fort Monmouth in New Jersey, Dover Air Force Base in Delaware, the U.S. Coast Guard Building in Philadelphia, and a number of warships docked in that city; they even considered attacking the annual Army-Navy football game. But they settled on Fort Dix because of their knowledge of the base.

Newspapers reported that "one of the terrorists was a former sniper in Kosovo and they all had trained with automatic weapons at a shooting range in Gouldsboro, Pa."

According to *The Washington Post,* shortly before the arrests "the women and children of the large clan moved away, leaving only the men [the terrorist suspects] and the mother."

Prosecutors left little doubt that the plot was real. J. P. Weiss, head of the Philadelphia FBI office, said that "Today we dodged a bullet. . . . In fact, when you look at the type of weapons that this group was trying to purchase, we may have dodged a lot of bullets. We had a group that was forming a platoon to take on an army. They identified their target, they did their reconnaissance. They had maps. And they were in the process of buying weapons. Luckily, we were able to stop that."

Yet despite the apparent severity of this easily executed plot, the mainstream media seeded its initial stories with doubts and cautions not to take the story at face value. *The Washington Post* called the gang "would-be terrorists," noting that they were "leaderless." Despite the presence of a military sniper from Kosovo in the group—and the fact that they had all trained with automatic weapons—the newspaper claimed that "the group had no rigorous military training." Despite evidence that they were on the verge of purchasing highly sophisticated weaponry and that they had sent their families home, the newspaper reassured its readers that the group "did not appear close to being able to pull off an attack."

The *Post* story went on to quote an unidentified "law enforcement source close to the investigation" as saying it was "hard to say" whether the group could have managed to mount an attack. "It's not like they were going to be able to get rocket-propelled grenades and blow things up," the official contended. But of course the plot was exposed precisely *because* the group was trying to buy such weapons. The fact that the sellers were undercover federal agents hardly means that the terrorists couldn't have secured the weapons they wanted elsewhere. After all, they had already collected handguns, an assault rifle, and a semiautomatic assault weapon on their own.

The New York Times also downplayed the story of the plotters' arrest, writing that "prosecutors described a complicated operation that was at once ambitious and meandering, marked by deadly weapons and a certain lack of sophistication." Again, though, sophistication was hardly the issue: as Chertoff has said, it wouldn't be "rocket science" to mount a blitz attack on Fort Dix.

As if on cue, the liberal bloggers went to work disparaging the plot. In *The Huffington Post*, Anthony Kaufman mocked the "Fort Dix Six" for going to "Circuit City where all new jihadists take their holy war recruitment tapes to be burned onto a DVD." Making a more serious charge, he asked, "Is it a coincidence that the alleged plots to attack Fort Dix and JFK [airport] come at a time when this U.S. Administration's support is flagging, and Americans are increasingly doubtful of its ability to effectively fight terrorism? While we'll never know for sure . . . the media needs to do a better job of cutting through the propaganda."

Other liberals have echoed Kaufman's critique, wondering aloud whether the plotters were simply "boobs" who got caught because of an amateur mistake—or, perhaps, "low-level criminals with delusions of grandeur, goaded into grander fantasies and bigger targets by informants who are getting paid or getting their sentences reduced by the FBI if they deliver."

We disagree. These plotters look no more or less sophisticated than the guys who got caught because they wanted a refund of the money they paid to rent the van they had used in attacking the World Trade Center in 1993, or than Timothy McVeigh, a misfit former infantryman who filled a truck with fertilizer and exploded it outside the federal building in Oklahoma City. And the officials who tracked them down and prosecuted them look to us like brave Americans heading off potential threats before they can endanger the lives of our fellow citizens.

JOSE PADILLA: THE DIRTY BOMBER

The media have worked overtime to portray Jose Padilla as a misunderstood youth whose crimes were overblown by an administration anxious to keep the public on edge. Taxpayer-funded lawyers have appealed his case all the way up to the U.S. Supreme Court. But at bottom Padilla was a convicted killer who was trying to pull off a massive terrorist plot, and his conviction was an appropriate measure to prevent that threat from execution.

Padilla's story is simple. After a lifetime of crime in the United States— including knifing and killing a man when Padilla was just fourteen—he converted to Islam in 1994 and became increasingly enmeshed in the world of radicals and terrorists.

Padilla's moment in the sun came in the spring of 2002, when he visited Pakistan and met with Abu Zubaydah, Osama bin Laden's operations chief, to present a plan to build a nuclear bomb and detonate it in an American city. As *Time* magazine noted, this first "plan" that Padilla presented was ridiculous: he had simply downloaded instructions for making a bomb from the Internet and hoped to follow them. One top official called the instructions "laughably inaccurate—more a parody than a plan." But Padilla didn't know that when he proudly presented his proposal to Abu Zubaydah.

As *Time* described it, "In response, Abu Zubaydah apparently cautioned his eager job applicant to think smaller—to get some training and attack America with a so-called 'dirty bomb,' a conventional explosive packed with radioactive waste that would spew out when the bomb blew up. 'They sent him to the U.S. to see what he could do—plan and execute,' [a senior U.S.] official says."

But shortly after his meeting with Padilla, Abu Zubaydah was captured in Pakistan. *Time* cited a U.S. official who said that Padilla "hinted to his FBI and CIA interrogators that he had talked to people who wanted to put together a dirty bomb. . . . He provided no details, but agents started comparing intelligence as well as materials from safe houses they had raided. Out popped Padilla's name, the official says. They then matched the name to a passport photo of Padilla and checked the identification with Abu Zubaydah, who confirmed it."

The CIA located Padilla in Cairo in early May and trailed him as he boarded his connecting flight back to the United States in Zurich. When he arrived in Chicago, they arrested him. In 2007, he was convicted of conspiring to aid terrorists in plots against the United States.

In the past few years, controversy has swirled around Padilla because the FBI arrested him quickly, before he had the chance to do anything or even to mature his plans. *Time* reported that "FBI officials, including Director Robert Mueller, had debated whether to continue following Padilla in hopes of turning up accomplices. But they could not risk losing him, sources tell *Time*, as they had a couple of times during his far-flung journey, so they took the more cautious approach" and arrested him right away.

In covering the story, however, *Time* proved just as susceptible to spinning the story as other mainstream media. Its report called him "an unlikely attacker, a small-time crook with grand plans." What's so small-time about knifing a man in the stomach, kicking him in the head, emptying his pockets, and leaving him in an alley to die? Or firing a .38-caliber revolver at another driver during a road rage incident in Sunrise, Florida? Padilla was no angel; he was a hardened criminal who had morphed into a terrorist.

In announcing Padilla's arrest, Attorney General John Ashcroft called him a "known terrorist" and said he was pursuing an "unfolding terrorist plot." *Time* accused Ashcroft of creating an erroneous impression that there were other plotters involved who were still at large. *Time* also criticized Ashcroft for saying that a dirty bomb could "cause mass death and injury."

But the Nuclear Regulatory Commission (NRC) explained that the effects of a dirty bomb can, indeed, be felt for *up to several miles* from the blast site, depending on the amount of radiation released, the power of the explosive, and where the bomb is exploded. Casualties can range from a few people to a few hundred or more. But *Time* said flatly that Ashcroft had made his statement about "mass death or injury . . . wrongly."

Padilla's legal odyssey through the U.S. court system has become a focus of civil libertarian criticism. After his arrest, federal authorities tried to develop a criminal case against him over the dirty bomb plot. When the feds failed to craft one that would stand up in court, President George W. Bush reclassified him as an "enemy combatant" on the last day before "he could have been released under laws protecting U.S. citizens from indefinite incarceration."

Padilla's lawyers appealed his detention on the grounds that, as a U.S. citizen, he had the right to be released in a timely fashion if the feds were not ready to charge him. The Supreme Court rejected the appeal, 5 to 4, on a technicality. When Padilla's attorneys refiled the appeal, correcting the error, the administration announced, shortly before the Supreme Court argument was to begin, that it was going to indict Padilla on charges that had nothing to do with the dirty bomb plot. Those are the charges on which he was subsequently tried and convicted by a jury.

Critics such as those at the *Los Angeles Times* say that convicting Padilla—without a ruling on whether his detention was legal—ensured that "the fundamental question of whether the government has the legal authority to detain U.S. citizens arrested within the United States without charges would be left unanswered, perhaps for all time." The newspaper is right. But the government was right to prosecute Padilla on any charges it could make stick and lock him up for as long as it could.

In Padilla's trial, *USA Today* reported, "the key piece of physical evidence [was] a 'Mujahideen Data Form,' which the indictment describes as an application form for a terrorism training camp." The prosecution brought in a CIA agent, who testified—in disguise—that the form bore Padilla's fingerprints. "Wiretaps in the case contain snippets of coded conversations between the alleged co-conspirators. Padilla is heard to say they planned to send $3,500 to Lebanon for 'zucchini.' The men also discussed going on picnics so they could 'smell fresh air and eat cheese' and training for 'football matches.' "

Defense attorneys for Padilla said that he went to Pakistan to study to become an imam. Though the wiretaps don't refer specifically to any acts of violence by Padilla, the jury was evidently satisfied that he had been to the training camp during his visit to Pakistan and rejected the defense's contention that he was merely in the country to attend classes.

The dirty bomb charges, which lay at the base of Padilla's initial arrest, played no part in his trial or conviction. Instead, *The New York Times* explained, "Mr. Padilla was added to the case against two men of Middle Eastern descent, one of whom Mr. Padilla, a former gang member with a criminal record, had met at a mosque in Broward County. The three were charged with belonging to a North American terrorism support cell that provided money, recruits and supplies to Islamic extremists around the world. Like Mr. Padilla, the co-defendants, Adham Hassoun and Kifah Jayyousi, were convicted."

Liberals have cast aspersion on Padilla's arrest, arguing that the government acted in haste, picking him up before he had committed any crime and only later realizing it didn't have enough evidence to convict him of the offense for which he was arrested. So the central question hangs over the Padilla trial and verdict: Why wasn't he indicted, tried, or convicted on the dirty bomb charges?

Appearing on PBS before Padilla's conviction, David Cole of the Georgetown University Law Center argued that "the government knew about Mr. Padilla before it arrested him. It followed him for a period of time. If it followed him until he engaged in conduct that was criminal, it could have then charged him with that crime. What it did, apparently, was arrest him before he engaged in any kind of criminal conduct. And they don't [even] have to wait until the bomb is detonated. They have to simply wait until he takes an overt act in furtherance of a conspiracy. They arrested him before that. And now they want to hold him despite the fact they have no evidence that they can produce that he's guilty of anything."

But the problem the government faced was not that it lacked evidence of

Padilla's involvement in the dirty bomb plot but that they *couldn't admit the evidence it had* in a U.S. court.

Ruth Wedgwood of Yale Law School and Johns Hopkins University, who appeared with Cole on PBS, explained the situation:

> The government's dilemma is that . . . much of the evidence [on] which . . . they are basing the conclusion that [Padilla is an enemy] combatant may well be classified extremely sensitive. Abu Zubaida, for example, the source in Afghanistan who is the number three in al Qaeda, is the source of much of the information against Mr. Padilla, and he would simply not be available as a witness. The intelligence that the government has gotten against Padilla has been gotten through a very difficult interrogation, which apparently requires that one not let the interlocutor know what the purpose is of various statements solicited from him. If you brought Abu Zubaida to a courtroom to testify, he'd refuse. So your dilemma is, do you want to let folks go when you have good intelligence that they are involved in such things as terrible as a dirty bomb that would really destroy city blocks and thousands of people's health, or do you want to simply treat this in a . . . treat it in a criminal justice paradigm alone? You have to make a choice, really, between evils, here I think.

Wedgwood demolished Cole's breezy assumption that the government could have waited to arrest Padilla until it came up with more evidence. "The problem here," Wedgwood says, "[is that] I wish that law enforcement ever could be as efficient as my friend David Cole wants it to be. There's no such thing as a close surveillance where you don't take a significant chance of losing the person. And if Padilla goes off on his merry own and slips the traces and hooks up with an al-Qaeda cell elsewhere in the U.S., I wouldn't want to follow the consequences. So the problem is you really can't afford to let the string play out as you might if it were just a bank robbery or even a murder. In this kind of case where it's catastrophic harm, the government's put to a very hard choice of having to act to prevent the harm."

As *The New York Times* noted, part of the problem the government faced was that "elaborating on the original allegations [of the dirty bomb plot] would compromise intelligence 'sources or methods.' " The government's brief to the U.S. Supreme Court in the Padilla case said that that "there is nothing remotely sinister about the government's effort to pursue criminal charges that minimize evidentiary complications. There is no basis for questioning the good faith of the government in moving forward with the indictment."

THE SEARS TOWER

But on at least one of the potential terror attacks cited by the government, the critics may have a point. In 2007, seven men were arrested for planning to blow up the Sears Tower in Chicago. But were they just indulging in idle boasting and verbal fantasies? The case against them ended in one acquittal and a mistrial for the six other defendants, suggesting that this time the government may have gone too far.

The men were charged with "conspiracy to levy war against the United States and to provide material support to Al Qaeda." The plot was uncovered by two men who approached the FBI with evidence of the group's malignant intentions. Paid more than $100,000 by the feds to investigate the group, they came up with tapes on which the men spoke of wanting to "kill all the devils we can" in terrorist attacks that would be "just as good or greater than 9/11."

Assistant U.S. Attorney Richard Gregorie said that "these defendants came together with the sole purpose of creating a holy war against the United States . . . [and their plot involved] things as small as poisoning salt shakers in restaurants and as big as blowing up the Sears Tower in Chicago and killing any survivors."

But Deputy FBI Director John S. Pistole said the plot was "more aspirational than operational," and then–Attorney General Alberto R. Gonzales said that the plot was in the discussion stage and posed "no immediate threat."

The ringleader of the plotters was Narseal Batiste, whom the *Los Angeles Times* described as "a construction odd-jobs worker and self-styled religious figure who paraded around Liberty City in flowing robes and a head wrap, carrying a shepherd's staff. He called himself a sheik, preached against drugs and domestic violence at a corner park on Sundays and, with the other six defendants, formed a Miami chapter of the Moorish Science Temple, a sect that blends Christianity, Islam and Judaism and claims autonomy from the U.S. government akin to that of Native American tribes."

Their defense attorneys, according to the *Los Angeles Times,* "painted a picture of ignorance and ineptitude among the seven men who were homeless but for the Embassy, a windowless cinder block storage room that lacked running water. They had only two rundown cars, no steady income and a single weapon among them—a handgun legally registered to defendant Lyglenson Lemorin, who had left it behind when he moved to Atlanta two months before the alleged terrorist cell was busted."

Unlike the Brooklyn Bridge plot and the dirty bomb attempt, however, the group had no actual terrorist training or links with Al Qaeda. While the JFK group had obtained financing, these plotters had none. And they were arrested before they seriously attempted to buy weapons—as distinguished from the Fort Dix plotters, who arrived at the scene of their arrest expecting to harvest a haul of lethal firepower.

All they got from the government's two operatives who had infiltrated their group was a pair of boots for each of the seven men. *The New York Times* reported that "the conspirators gave the [FBI] informer their shoe sizes so he could buy them military boots. Later . . . Mr. Batiste gave the informer lists of other items needed for the proposed war like uniforms, binoculars, radios, vehicles, bulletproof vests, machine guns and $50,000 in cash." But all he got was the boots.

Was it true, as the defense attorneys argued, that these men were merely homeless losers with "delusions of grandeur"? Or were they truly plotters in the early stages of a terrorist attack? Did the government incite them to talk of a conspiracy and then arrest them only for their dreamy conversation, or did it simply move early because, as Jeffrey F. Addicott, director of the Center for Terrorism Law at St. Mary's University in San Antonio, has noted, it couldn't "wait to see if these guys back up that rhetoric with real action."

The failure of a jury to convict any of the seven defendants indicates that perhaps, in this case, the liberal critics have a point.

ACTION AGENDA

As long as the Republican Party controls the White House or one or both houses of Congress, we can be reasonably secure that the PATRIOT Act and the NSA wiretapping will remain in force and that the Department of Justice will take terrorist investigations seriously and pursue them aggressively.

But if the Democrats should keep control of Congress and take over the White House in the 2008 elections, we can't be so sure.

Pivotal among the questions for any new administration will be how far law enforcement and Homeland Security agents can go in wiretapping conversations without warrants.

On *The New York Times'* op-ed page, Philip Bobbitt, a professor of law and the director of the Center for National Security at Columbia University—and a National Security Council senior director from 1998 to 1999 under the Clinton administration—recently offered a helpful clarification of the issue.

Bobbitt distinguished between surveillance aimed at prosecution and that which seeks to "learn the identity of people who may be planning atrocities." He says that for information gathering "warrants are utterly beside the point." He quotes Judge Richard Posner as saying "once you grant the legitimacy of surveillance aimed at detection rather than at gathering evidence of guilt, requiring a warrant to conduct it would be like requiring a warrant to ask people questions or to install surveillance cameras on city streets."

Bobbitt also dismisses the debate over whether the location of one of the parties being tapped is in the United States. He notes that some time ago, for technological reasons, "it became difficult to determine the true origin of any communication that was routed through the United States. If a terrorism suspect in Pakistan is having conversations with someone on a computer with a New York Internet protocol address via a chat room run by an Internet service provider in London, where exactly is the intelligence being collected? If the answer is the United States simply because the servers are here, of what possible relevance could that be to the protection of the rights of Americans?" He says that we must focus on "protecting American people" from civil liberties intrusions, "rather than an American address."

The fact is that the National Security Agency cannot hope to know what it is looking for when it conducts electronic surveillance. It typically has neither a name nor a location nor even a subject. The surveillance is conducted not by some balding man with sweaty palms listening on earphones but by a computer intercepting millions of conversations and looking for anomalous patterns.

For example, the computer likely picked up the phrase "Brooklyn

Bridge" in the days before the feds alerted the NYPD to the potential threat to the structure. How could the NSA have asked the court for a warrant to pick up mentions of the bridge when it had no idea what the computer would turn up?

And why couldn't they go to the FISA (Foreign Intelligence Surveillance Act) court set up to issue warrants after it found out about mentions of the bridge? (The law allows the NSA a grace period to seek a warrant retroactively for surveillance already conducted.) The simple answer is that the NSA had no idea after it turned up the mentions of the bridge whether this was a terror plot of some kids discussing their toys or tourists planning a visit to the Big Apple. If it had to report every coincidence and each possible pattern that emerged from surveillance, it would have no time for anything else.

It became clear that a probable terror plot had been uncovered only when the NSA intercepted Faris saying that it was "too hot" on the bridge. And that comment was made, by definition, *after* Commissioner Kelly had been tipped off by the earlier taps and acted accordingly. Not until Khalid Sheikh Mohammed coughed up the information during interrogation in Pakistan was it confirmed that we had intercepted an Al Qaeda plot.

Wiretaps have proved their importance in breaking up terror plots around the world. On September 20, 2007, Mike McConnell, the director of national intelligence, told a Senate committee that wiretap surveillance had helped German officials arrest three Islamic militants charged with plotting to bomb targets in Germany. The media reported that "German officials have said that American intercepts of e-mail messages and telephone calls between Germany and Pakistan and Turkey tipped them off to the plot last year."

McConnell told the committee that if the wiretapping rules were tightened, as liberals are suggesting they be, the United States would lose "50 percent of our ability to track, understand and know about these terrorists, what they're doing to train, what they're doing to recruit and what they're doing to try to get into this country."

But the chilling stories of the Brooklyn Bridge and the German plot make it clear how badly we need the wiretapping to continue, unfettered by the need to obtain warrants.

Indeed, it might be wise to look across the ocean at the United Kingdom to find additional safeguards that we may profitably use to stop terrorism from hitting new targets in the United States. Shortly after taking office, the new British prime minister, Gordon Brown, announced a series of new steps to battle terror, which he said would help Britain "confront a generation-long challenge to defeat Al Qaeda–inspired terror violence."

The measures make sense on both sides of the Atlantic. Brown proposed that Britain require all visa applicants to have "biometric" screening after March 2008, a system that "would enable border officials to check passports of people entering and leaving Britain in real time against a database."

In our most recent book, *Outrage*, we criticized federal officials for keeping careful tabs on everyone entering the United States legally with a visa but making no effort at all to figure out who has left the country and who is still here overstaying their visas. Since nine of the nineteen 9/11 hijackers fell into the latter category, we stressed the urgency of such a step. Even with all the furor over border illegal immigration issues, however, this gaping loophole remains wide open: millions of foreigners still enter our country legally each year, and we have no idea what becomes of them.

The only resource available to U.S. officials is a tiny Visa Fraud Detection Division—which, according to one newspaper report, is "staffed by 375 lonely souls, scattered in more than 70 offices around the country." Unarmed and unable to make raids, they sift through a workload of 6 million visa applications each year. "On a recent visit behind the unmarked steel doors of the fraud unit's [New York City] office at 26 Federal Plaza, one wall was stacked high with suspect files. . . . The unit supervisor, Joseph T. Knipper, cast a quizzical look from the stacked files to his investigators—all six of them." The New York office, and its six staffers, are responsible for monitoring 150,000 visa applications each year.

The visa fraud unit is a step in the right direction—but only a baby step. If we want to be serious about combating terrorism within our borders, we would do well to start by taking a page from Gordon Brown's playbook and institute a national system that will enable us to screen visas—and track those who enter our country carrying them.

THE LIBERALS' SECRET PLAN TO MUZZLE TALK RADIO

In the past year, conservatives have been on the alert to block efforts by the Left to force right-leaning talk radio hosts off the air. They worry that the Federal Communications Commission (FCC) will reimpose the "Fairness Doctrine," which it instituted in 1949 but repealed in 1987. The regulation required that broadcasters provide a "reasonable opportunity for ample play for the free and fair competition of opposing views . . . [for all] issues of importance to the public." In practice, as the Pew Foundation explains, the doctrine meant that "stations . . . had to carry contrasting opinions on the important issues of the day."

But liberals are planning a far more insidious and destructive attack on conservative talk radio—one that would go much further than the Fairness Doctrine, not just regulating the content of talk radio programming but also forcing basic changes in management and ownership.

For decades, broadcast television and radio have been dominated by the Left. Anyone who followed the 2004 election could plainly see how thoroughly CBS News, for example, was dedicated to John Kerry's election, even going to the length of airing forged documents—and swearing they were accurate—to besmirch President Bush's military service record.

But cable news and talk radio, both largely conservative, have evened the playing field. While ABC, NBC, CBS, National Public Radio, PBS, MSNBC, and CNN all skew left, Fox News and talk radio attempt to redress the imbalance.

Recent polling suggests that this division is pretty equitable. One recent national survey indicated that while 54 percent of Americans get their television news from local channels and 28 percent from network broadcast newscasts, 34 percent regularly watch cable news channels for their news reporting. Since Fox News' audience typically exceeds that of CNN and MSNBC combined, the balance seems increasingly equitable.

But the Left is not content with balance. It wants to restore its historical domination of the airwaves—and its drive to do so is a form of intellectual fleecing that qualifies it for inclusion in this book.

The idea that we should regulate broadcast media is based on the premise that the airwaves are public and that government confers a benefit on private broadcasters by giving them a monopoly over a particular frequency. Unlike newspapers or cable television, which use no public airwaves but buy their own paper or cable position, government (so the theory goes) has an implicit responsibility to ensure that the public airwaves are being used fairly and not skewed to any particular political point of view.

The Pew Foundation points out that the Fairness Doctrine was originally "based on the idea that the airwaves were in scarce supply and were owned by the public, with TV and radio stations functioning as 'public trustees.'"

The Supreme Court affirmed the constitutionality of the Fairness Doctrine in 1969, but during the Reagan administration, the Pew report notes, "the FCC revisited the subject. The agency concluded that the rise of cable television had eased some of the scarcity issues and that the Fairness Doctrine might be chilling speech by keeping broadcasters from addressing important issues out of a reluctance to represent both sides. In August 1987, the FCC repealed the Fairness Doctrine."

The fact is that today the so-called Fairness Doctrine is totally unnecessary—and unfair. Anyone can hear and study—or proclaim—any shade of opinion he wants on the Internet. The geographic monopolies once enjoyed by newspapers or broadcast media no longer matter very much. All media have become national, indeed international.

Even within the medium of radio, often dismissed as monolithically conservative, there is ideological balance. National Public Radio, which has a decidedly liberal tilt, has a huge national audience and offers a distinct alternative to conservative talk shows. And, of course, the combined ratings of the three broadcast TV networks plus CNN, MSNBC, and PBS far outnumber those of Fox News.

But the effectiveness of conservative talk radio has goaded liberals into demanding a restoration of the Fairness Doctrine. If they have their way, this measure will kill talk radio. Suddenly, any radio station that wished to broadcast three hours of Rush Limbaugh or Sean Hannity every day would have to find time for three hours of a left-leaning commentator to offset the time Rush and Sean have on the right. The Fairness Doctrine—we call it the Alan Colmes full employment project—would force stations to hire liberals even where they might not draw an economically viable audience.

It's a simple economic fact that liberal talkers have decidedly lower ratings than conservatives do. When a group of liberals, led by the comedian Al Franken, launched the Air America Radio network as a liberal counterpoint to the conservative talk shows, it flopped so badly that it had to be "bailed out of bankruptcy," as *The Washington Times* reported, "by real estate tycoon Stephen L. Green."

If stations were forced to give liberal talk show hosts equal time, they would lose money—and before long you can bet that most of them would abandon talk radio altogether in favor of top forty music.

In the absence of the Fairness Doctrine, talk radio has thrived. There were only 360 news/talk radio stations in 1990; today there are more than 1,300.

As Pew explains, the repeal of the Fairness Doctrine was only one reason for the growth of talk radio. "The major reason for the rise of national talk personalities like Limbaugh . . . was a change in the cost of national satellite distribution. Syndicated programming meant that stations no longer had to develop their own local talent. Instead, they could simply bring in national voices that had already proven themselves in other markets for less money. Those national voices belonged to the most successful talk hosts, many of whom were conservatives."

The domination of the talk radio circuit by conservatives was highlighted on June 20, 2007, in a report by the Center for American Progress, a liberal think tank. The report concluded that conservatives outnumbered liberals on talk radio by 9 to 1—a statistic that helped ignite the Fairness Doctrine debate.

Why can't liberals make it on talk radio? There is no clear-cut answer, but we have a theory: although there is about an equal number of self-described liberals as conservatives in the United States, a disproportionate percentage of liberals are Latinos, African Americans, or young people who tend to prefer radio that's aimed at their particular audience over main-stream national radio shows. Moreover, National Public Radio skims off many of the liberal listeners who might otherwise sustain leftist commercial talk radio.

For more than a year, speculation has been mounting that liberals—either now or after the 2008 election—might try to rein in talk radio.

The Washington Times reports that "days after the release of the Center for American Progress report, Sen. James M. Inhofe, Oklahoma Republican, shared a conversation he said he overheard three years earlier between Democratic Sens. Hillary Rodham Clinton of New York and Barbara Boxer of California, in which the women called for a 'legislative fix' to counter the influence of 'extremist' talk-radio hosts. Mrs. Clinton and Mrs. Boxer denied the conversation took place."

The current law permits the FCC to reimpose the Fairness Doctrine whenever it wishes. By statute, the five-person board consists of two Democrats and two Republicans, along with a chairman who is appointed by the president and serves at his or her pleasure. Undoubtedly, as *The Washington Times* observed, "the current Republican-led FCC poses no threat of reinstating the Fairness Doctrine." Of course, if a Democrat is elected in 2008, the doctrine could make a swift comeback. It could be passed with the stroke of a pen by the new FCC chairman.

To try to forestall that possibility, Republicans introduced legislation to bar the use of federal funding to implement any reinstatement of the Fairness Doctrine. On June 28, 2007, the bill passed the House by an overwhelming margin of 309 to 115, surprising many observers.

But a tougher bill, introduced by Norm Coleman (R-Minn.), was killed in the Senate a month later by 49 to 48. (The bill would have required sixty votes to be considered.) Coleman's bill would have prevented the FCC from imposing the doctrine. As he noted, "we live in an age of satellite radio, of broadband, of blogs, of Internet, of cable TV, of broadcast TV. There is no limitation on the ability of anyone from any political persuasion to get their ideas set forth. The public in the end will choose what to listen to." Even had the Coleman bill passed, the next such bill could just as easily have been overturned—which might not be hard to do with a Democratic president and Congress.

Liberals clearly want the Fairness Doctrine to be revived. Senate Majority Whip Richard Durbin (D-Ill.) has said, "It's time to reinstitute the Fairness Doctrine. I have this old-fashioned attitude that when Americans hear both sides of the story, they're in a better position to make a decision." And a recent victim of talk radio, Senator John Kerry (D-Mass.), has also said that the Fairness Doctrine should return.

Steve Rendell, a senior analyst with Fairness and Accuracy in Reporting, a liberal group, said: "For citizens who value media democracy and the public interest, broadcast regulation of our publicly owned airwaves has reached a low-water mark. . . . What has not changed since 1987 is that over-the-air broadcasting remains the most powerful force affecting public opinion, especially on local issues; as public trustees, broadcasters ought to be insuring that they inform the public, not inflame them. . . . That's why we need a Fairness Doctrine. It's not a universal solution. It's not a substitute for reform or for diversity of ownership. It's simply a mechanism to address the most extreme kinds of broadcast abuse."

But there may be a more devilish and fiendish plot afoot to cripple talk radio than the simple reinstatement of the Fairness Doctrine. A clue to what might be up came in an article by Mark Lloyd in the online publication of the Center for American Progress, the liberal group that objected to the right-wing bias of talk radio. He outlines a far more extensive effort to rein in talk radio than merely reimposing the Fairness Doctrine.

He argues that the FCC should adopt "ownership rules [for radio stations] that . . . will create greater local diversity of programming, news, and commentary. And we call for more localism by putting teeth into the licensing rules. *But we do not call for a return to the Fairness Doctrine*" (emphasis added).

Did you catch that? Even though it would likely destroy conservative talk radio as we know it, it seems that the Fairness Doctrine doesn't go far enough for these liberal advocacy groups! The Center for American Progress contends that the Fairness Doctrine itself wouldn't be sufficient to end the domination of talk radio by conservatives. Rather, the Center argues, the Left needs to deal with the "underlying elements" of local accountability and input. In other words, it isn't enough for liberals to insist on elbowing their way in front of the microphone—they want to own the station!

The Left says that the conservative bias of talk radio is merely a symptom of the "underlying market control" of conservative owners on radio. Ironically, the liberals complain that these owners aren't just in it for the money—that their motive is to push an ideological line. Only in America would being motivated by idealism, not by money, be considered a negative!

The liberals' agenda is to go back beyond the Fairness Doctrine to the provisions of the Federal Communications Act, which the courts have held requires that stations' licensing—the very core of their existence—depends on their willingness to "afford reasonable opportunity for the discussion of conflicting views of issues of public importance."

Not only do they want to impose an arbitrary restriction requiring equal time for liberal viewpoints—even if the stations' listeners don't want to hear them—they want to condition stations' licenses on their willingness to dilute the control management and owners have over station content.

The Left believes that, in exchange for broadcast licenses, radio stations must accept that "the public" must be "involved in telling them whether they are actually serving the public interest. . . . [In] providing a reasonable opportunity for the diverse expression of issues of local importance." (Translation: liberals should be in on all the key ownership and management decisions to ensure that their ideology is being represented and served.)

The *National Review*, which has been attuned to the need to protect talk radio, says that the liberal agenda includes:

- "Strengthened limits on how many radio stations one firm can own, locally and nationally"

- "Shortening broadcast license terms"

- "Requiring radio broadcasters to regularly show they are operating in the 'public interest.' "

- "Imposing a fee on broadcasters who fail to meet these 'public interest obligations' with the funding to go to the Corporation for Public Broadcasting"

The magazine notes that "the goal of the reforms is the same as the Fairness Doctrine: to reduce the influence of conservative talk radio. Limiting ownership, the authors believe, will eliminate many of the owners who favor conservative causes." After all, "public interest requirements can be defined almost any way a regulator wants—up to and perhaps even beyond that required by the old Fairness Doctrine. And the proposed fee provides regulators with a quite effective stick to compel compliance—as well as to direct funds to more ideologically compatible public broadcasters."

So whereas the Fairness Doctrine focuses on *what* a station says, the liberals would zero in on *who* is making the decisions, using the local input requirements of the FCC to put liberals on the boards of directors of radio stations—a far more insidious, and probably far more effective, strategy for seizing the upper hand on the talk radio airwaves. Their offensive is aimed not just at content, programming, or politics but at the ownership and management of the radio stations themselves—a matter nearer and dearer to the heart of any owner. If it works, it will change the radio landscape. Worse yet, even the threat of such an insurgency might lead station owners to trim their sails in a prudent effort to fend off the newly constituted Talk Radio Police.

Just as the Fairness Doctrine debate was brewing, talk radio shock jock Don Imus found himself enmeshed in controversy for calling the African-American players on the Rutgers women's basketball team, who came so close to winning the national championship, "nappy-headed hos." After years of insulting blacks, Hispanics, Jews, and women, Imus's daily fare of racial and religious humor had finally caught up with him and he was forced off the air.

Imus is now back. But his forced leave of absence still worried liberals and black political leaders, concerned that the same standards that had been applied to the white male talker might also be used against rappers, whose lyrics routinely use the N-word—and who, like Imus, frequently refer to black women as "hos." The lyrics of many of their songs are so gross, they might make even the I-man blush. The spectacle of African-American entertainers demeaning black women as blatantly as they do may even have contributed to Imus's feeling that he could get away with saying the same kinds of things. Certainly CBS turned a blind eye on the filth he was broadcasting, figuring that if it was acceptable for black rappers to use these words, there'd be no reason to object when Imus followed suit.

The conservative columnist Michelle Malkin has made a point of highlighting the racist and sexist lyrics of rappers, emphasizing how they demean women and minorities. Her work, and that of others, has turned on the rappers the same spotlight that was shined on Imus—and the result was that there appeared to be little difference whether or not racist or sexist remarks are set to music or rhyme.

But liberals and African-American political leaders needed the rappers to raise money and energize the black political base. Singers like Ginuwine, Kenneth "Babyface" Edmonds, Q-Tip, and Outkast frequently appear at Democratic events and are closely linked to the African-American political establishment. So when the storm began to build around Imus, and civil rights leaders such as the Reverend Al Sharpton joined the attack, liberal politicians and black elected officials shifted uneasily in their seats.

The liberals organized a concerted offensive against conservative talk radio, hoping to use the controversy over Imus's sexual, racial, and sexist remarks to shift the public agenda to critiquing political opinions they considered offensive to blacks, Hispanics, or women. This transition from dirty words to controversial ideas was a crucial pivot for the liberals, one that served two purposes: the offensive maneuver of disciplining their conservative talk radio tormentors and the defensive tactic of steering controversy away from their beloved and useful allies in the hip-hop world.

But this shift of focus could be deadly to free speech. It's one thing to use the N-word on radio or to call women "hos" just because they're young, black, and female. Neither of these is acceptable.

It is quite another to speak out against affirmative action, school busing, or hiring preferences. We need to be free to speak over the radio about public policy positions as long as we do so in a civil tone that does not invoke racial or sexist epithets. That's what the First Amendment is all about. When Bill O'Reilly singles out a judge for letting child abusers go free or Sean Hannity laces into Barack Obama for his dalliances with former terrorist William Ayers, they are engaging in political speech and must be permitted to speak without inhibition.

As Congressman Mike Pence (R-Ind.), himself a former talk show host, has noted, "If anyone ever doubted that there is enmity between Democrats and American talk radio, they need look no further than the personal attacks leveled on Rush Limbaugh on the floor of the Senate. I thought it astonishing that members of the U.S. Senate would engage in repeated and distorted personal attacks on a private citizen. It gives evidence of a level of frustration with conservative talk radio that is very troubling to anyone who cherishes the medium."

Pence isn't the first to notice that animosity. Late one night in late 1995, after one in the morning, my phone rang. It was President Clinton. "We are getting hammered over the radio," he reported.

"Your ratings are still sky high," I replied groggily.

"But you wouldn't believe what they're saying," the president persisted.

"Did you hear something specific?" I asked, probing for the source of this new discovery.

"Hillary's mother was driving in from Pennsylvania and she listened to Rush Limbaugh on the radio. You wouldn't believe the stuff he was saying," Clinton replied.

The Clinton campaign soon set up a response team to answer these radio attacks, handing out talking points to liberal hosts such as Alan Colmes, who's doubtless still on their mailing list.

In the years since, however, they've taken their ambitions to Washington—attempting to quash the source of the criticism by muzzling talk radio through the Fairness Doctrine and taking management away from radio station owners under the Federal Communications Act. We must not let them succeed!

ACTION AGENDA

If the Democrats win the White House in 2008, the harassment of talk radio won't just continue—it will expand. The new Democratic majority on the FCC will likely seek to reimpose the Fairness Doctrine and to dilute the ownership and management of conservative-leaning radio stations.

Conservatives must be vigilant, watching for attempts to undermine free speech and to impose a doctrinal uniformity on news/talk stations under the guise of equal time for competing viewpoints. Free speech has never been easy to maintain—and nowhere will the battle lines be more clearly drawn than over the coming assault on talk radio.

4

THE DO-NOTHING CONGRESS IS STILL DOING NOTHING!

House Democrats Scale Back the Congressional Workweek— It's Too Burdensome!

When the Democrats took over the House of Representatives in 2007, Nancy Pelosi immediately pledged to bring about one big reform: a five-day workweek.

Imagine!

Well, even that was a bit of an exaggeration. It wasn't really *five days* she was promising—not five days as we know it. If you thought she meant five days spent working, you'd be wrong. Even if you thought she meant five days of just *showing up for work,* you'd still be wrong.

In the House of Representatives, five days doesn't really mean anything.

At the beginning of last year, House Majority Leader Steny Hoyer (D-Md.) announced that House members would be expected to be available to vote from about 6:00 P.M. on Mondays through 2:00 P.M. on Fridays—not exactly a five-day workweek, but a start. But even that mediocre goal was apparently too much for our elected representatives.

In the entire year 2007, the House of Representatives worked only *three* five-day workweeks.

Since apparently even that was *way* too burdensome, the majority leader rescinded that reformed schedule and announced that in 2008 there would be no more "five-day workweek" for the House.

And Congressman Hoyer has religiously stuck to his commitment. If there's one time you can truly trust the word of a member of Congress, it's when they tell you how much time he's going to spend not working.

In January 2008, the House had roll-call votes on only six days, including one day when there was a three-minute session to call a quorum. That's considered a workday!

In February, they scheduled roll-call votes on nine days, and in March on eight days. So for the ninety-day period from the beginning of the year through the end of March, they held roll-call votes on only twenty-three days. That's an average of a little less than one and a half days each week.

The rest of the workforce put in about sixty days.

And the Senate is just as bad. They've had roll-call votes on only twenty days from January through March. And not a single five day workweek. The rest of the workforce put in more than sixty days during that same time period.

We send them there to vote for us, don't we? To be our voice in Washington?

While more and more people are looking to Congress to deal with the economy, to address the growing number of home foreclosures, credit card abuses, rising oil prices, predatory telemarketers, and many other crucial issues, our elected representatives are, unfortunately, AWOL.

DON'T BOTHER ME, I'M RUNNING FOR PRESIDENT

All of the senators who were candidates for president stopped going to their day job in the United States Senate a long time ago. They've all been all over the country campaigning. When the field dwindled down to Senators McCain, Obama, and Clinton, the presidential candidates rarely showed up. Each of them was present for roll-call votes on only five days in the first three months of 2008. They're not doing their job. But they're all still getting paid—$165,000 a year!—for doing nothing.

Would you still get paid if you took a year or two off to compete for another job? Of course not. And neither should the presidential candidates. If they want to take almost two years away from their responsibilities as elected officials, they should resign from the Senate.

They're fleecing us.

And it's not as if their absences never made a difference. This year, the Senate defeated a bill that would have increased the amount of the capital gains exemption for primary residences based on inflation. Currently, there is a $250,000 exemption for individuals and $500,000 per couple. The bill was defeated 44 to 41. So the three votes of the missing presidential candidates might have made a difference.

The problem with Congress isn't just its light schedule. There's more to it. There's also an issue about what they do when they actually are there. When you look at their actual accomplishments, you have to wonder why we're paying these folks $165,000 a year.

Here's a sample of what the House of Representatives has done so far in 2008. (All of the following came from the website of the Clerk of the House: http://clerk.house.gov/legislative/index.html?curr_month=1&curr_year= 2008.)

Take a look:

January 3
- House convened at 12:00 P.M. and adjourned at 12:02 P.M.

January 11
- Mourning the passing of President Gerald Rudolph Ford and celebrating his leadership and service to the people of the United States

January 15
- Quorum Call at 7:31 P.M.; business completed at 7:53 P.M., except for members' Special Order Speeches, which are given after the finish of House business for the benefit of constituents and C-SPAN

January 16

- Commending the University of Florida Gators for their victory in the 2006 Bowl Championship Series and for winning the national college football championship

- Observing the birthday of Martin Luther King, Jr., and encouraging the people of the United States to observe the birthday of Martin Luther King, Jr., and the life and legacy of Dr. Martin Luther King, Jr., and for other purposes

- Commending the Boise State University Broncos football team for winning the 2007 Fiesta Bowl and completing an undefeated season

January 17

- Honoring the Mare Island Original 21ers for their efforts to remedy racial discrimination in employment at Mare Island Naval Shipyard.

- Honoring Muhammad Ali, global humanitarian, on the occasion of his 65th birthday and extending best wishes to him and his family

January 18

- Congratulating the Grand Valley State University Lakers for winning the 2006 NCAA Division II Football National Championship

January 22

- Designating a post office in Roanoke, Virginia, as the Judge Richard B. Allsbrook Post Office

January 23

- Raising awareness and encouraging prevention of stalking by establishing January 2008 as "National Stalking Awareness Month"

January 28

- Designating the facility of the United States Postal Service located at 427 North Street in Taft, California, as the Larry S. Pierce Post Office

- Designating the Port Angeles Federal Building in Port Angeles, Washington, as the Richard B. Anderson Federal Building

- Commending the West Virginia University Mountaineer football team for exemplifying the pride, determination, and spirit of the Mountain State and overcoming adversity with skill, commitment, and teamwork to win the 2008 Tostitos Fiesta Bowl

- Honoring the Texas Water Development Board on its selection as a recipient of the Environmental Protection Agency's 2007 Clean Water State Revolving Fund Performance and Innovation Award

- Designating the facility of the United States Postal Service located at 10799 West Alameda Avenue in Lakewood, Colorado, as the Felix Sparks Post Office Building

January 29

- Commending the Louisiana State University Tigers football team for winning the 2007 Bowl Championship Series national championship game

- Passing the New England National Scenic Trail Designation Act

- Designating the facility of the United States Postal Service located at 2633 11th Street in Rock Island, Illinois, as the Lane Evans Post Office Building

- Designating the facility of the United States Postal Service located at 1300 North Frontage Road West in Vail, Colorado, as the Gerald R. Ford, Jr. Post Office Building

- Commending the University of Louisville Cardinals football team for their victory in the 2007 Orange Bowl

January 30

- Calling on the United Kingdom to establish a full, independent, and public judicial inquiry into the murder of Northern Ireland defense attorney Patrick Finucane

- Honoring the life of Percy Lavon Julian

February 6

- Commending the Houston Dynamo soccer team for winning the 2007 Major League Soccer Cup

- Recognizing the significance of Black History Month

- Remembering the Space Shuttle Challenger disaster and honoring its crew members, who lost their lives on January 28, 1986

February 7

- Calling for a peaceful resolution to the current electoral crisis in Kenya

- Congratulating Lee Myung-Bak on his election to the presidency of the Republic of Korea and wishing him well during his time of transition and his inauguration on February 25, 2008

February 12

- Honoring the life of senior Border Patrol agent Luis A. Aguilar, who lost his life in the line of duty near Yuma, Arizona, on January 19, 2008

- Commemorating the courage of the Haitian soldiers who fought for American independence in the Siege of Savannah and for Haiti's independence and renunciation of slavery

- Celebrating the birth of Abraham Lincoln and recognizing the prominence the Declaration of Independence played in the development of Abraham Lincoln's beliefs

February 13

- Supporting the goals and ideals of National Engineers Week

- Congratulating the National Football League champion New York Giants for winning Super Bowl XLII and completing one of the most remarkable postseason runs in professional sports history

February 14

- Passing the American Braille Flag Memorial Act

- Commending the people of the State of Washington for showing their support for the needs of the State of Washingtons veterans and encouraging residents of the other states to pursue creative ways to show their own support for veterans

- Honoring African-American inventors, past and present, for their leadership, courage, and significant contributions to our national competitiveness

- Supporting the goals and ideals of National Salute to Hospitalized Veterans Week

- Supporting the goals and ideals of American Heart Month and National Wear Red Day

- Making technical corrections to the Federal Insecticide, Fungicide, and Rodenticide Act

February 25

- Expressing support for the designation of the week of March 3–7, 2008, as School Social Work Week to promote awareness of the vital role of school social workers in schools, and in the community as a whole, in helping students prepare for their future as productive citizens

- Supporting the goals and ideals of Career and Technical Education Month

- Honoring the service and accomplishments of Lieutenant General Russel L. Honoré, United States Army, for his thirty-seven years of service on behalf of the United States

February 28

- Designating the facility of the United States Postal Service known as the Southpark Station in Alexandria, Louisiana, as the John "Marty" Thiels Southpark Station

- Designating the facility of the United States Postal Service located at 116 Helen Highway in Cleveland, Georgia, as the Sgt. Jason Harkins Post Office Building

- Designating the facility of the United States Postal Service located at 3050 Hunsinger Lane in Louisville, Kentucky, as the "Iraq and Afghanistan Fallen Military Heroes of Louisville Memorial Post Office Building," in honor of the servicemen and women from Louisville, Kentucky, who died in service during Operation Enduring Freedom and Operation Iraqi Freedom

- Designating the facility of the United States Postal Service located at 3100 Cashwell Drive in Goldsboro, North Carolina, as the John Henry Wooten, Sr. Post Office Building

March 4

- Recognizing the 60th anniversary of Everglades National Park

- Honoring the life of Marjory Stoneman Douglas, champion of the Florida Everglades and founder of Florida's environmental movement

- Redesignating Dayton Aviation Heritage National Historic Park in the State of Ohio as Wright Brothers–Dunbar National Historical Park, and for other purposes

- Supporting Taiwan's fourth direct and democratic presidential elections in March 2008

- Condemning the ongoing Palestinian rocket attacks on Israeli civilians, and for other purposes

- Designating the facility of the United States Postal Service located at 10250 John Saunders Road in San Antonio, Texas, as the Cyndi Taylor Krier Post Office Building

- Expressing the sense of Congress that Earl Lloyd should be recognized and honored for breaking the color barrier and becoming the first African-American to play in the National Basketball Association League fifty-eight years ago

- Designating the facility of the United States Postal Service located at 160 East Washington Street in Chagrin Falls, Ohio, as the Sgt. Michael M. Kashkoush Post Office Building

March 10

- Endorsing the establishment of April as National 9–1–1 Education Month

- Designating the facility of the United States Postal Service located at 22 Sussex Street in Port Jervis, New York, as the E. Arthur Gray Post Office Building

- Designating the facility of the United States Postal Service located at 701 East Copeland Drive in Lebanon, Missouri, as the Steve W. Allee Carrier Annex Post Office Building

March 11

- Congratulating Iowa State University of Science and Technology for 150 years of leadership and service

- Congratulating the University of Kansas football team for winning the 2008 FedEx Orange Bowl and having the most successful year in program history

- Congratulating the women's water polo team of the University of California, Los Angeles, for winning the 2007 NCAA Division I Women's Water Polo National Championship, and congratulating UCLA on its 100th NCAA sports national title, making it the most accomplished athletic program in NCAA history

March 12

- Honoring the 200th anniversary of the Gallatin Report on Roads and Canals, celebrating the national unity the Gallatin Report engendered, and recognizing the vast contributions that national planning efforts have provided to the United States

March 13

- Recognizing the exceptional sacrifice of the 69th Infantry Regiment, known as the Fighting 69th, in support of the Global War on Terror

March 31

- Supporting the observance of Colorectal Cancer Awareness Month

April 1

- Expressing the sense of Congress that the fatal radiation poisoning of Russian dissident and writer Alexander Litvinenko raises significant concerns about the potential involvement of elements of the Russian government in Mr. Litvinenko's death and about the security and proliferation of radioactive materials

- Expressing support for a national day of remembrance for Harriet Ross Tubman

- Supporting the goals and ideals of Borderline Personality Awareness Month

- Supporting the goals, ideals, and history of National Women's History Month

- Designating the facility of the United States Postal Service located at 19101 Cortez Boulevard in Brooksville, Florida, as the Cody Grater Post Office Building

- To require the Secretary of the Treasury to mint coins in commemoration of the semicentennial of the enactment of the Civil Rights Act of 1964

- Expressing the sense of the House of Representatives regarding the creation of refugee populations in the Middle East, North Africa, and the Persian Gulf region as a result of human rights violations

April 8
- Congratulating the Army Reserve on its centennial

April 9
- Designating the facility of the United States Postal Service located at 6892 Main Street in Gloucester, Virginia, as the Congresswoman Jo Anne S. Davis Post Office

- Designating the facility of the United States Postal Service located at 2650 Dr. Martin Luther King Jr. Street in Indianapolis, Indiana, as the Julia M. Carson Post Office Building

- Designating the facility of the United States Postal Service located at 11001 Dunklin Drive in St. Louis, Missouri, as the William "Bill" Clay Post Office Building

- Welcoming His Holiness Pope Benedict XVI on his first apostolic visit to the United States

- Recognizing the plumbing industry and supporting the goals and ideals of National Plumbing Industry Week

- Calling on the government of the People's Republic of China to end its crackdown in Tibet and enter into a substantive dialogue with His

Holiness the Dalai Lama to find a negotiated solution that respects
the distinctive language, culture, religious identity, and fundamental
freedoms of all Tibetans, and for other purposes

April 14

- Expressing sympathy to the victims and families of the tragic acts of
violence in Colorado Springs, Colorado, and Arvada, Colorado

- Supporting the goals and ideals of National Glanzmann's Thrombas-
thenia Awareness Day

April 15

- Designating the facility of the United States Postal Service located at
7231 FM 1960 in Humble, Texas, as the Texas Military Veterans Post
Office

- Recognizing and honoring the 40th anniversary of congressional
passage of title VIII of the Civil Rights Act of 1968 (the Fair Housing
Act) and the 20th anniversary of the Fair Housing Amendments Act
of 1988

- Supporting the mission and goals of National Crime Victims' Rights
week in order to increase public awareness of the rights, needs, and
concerns of victims and survivors of crime in the United States

- Permitting active-duty members of the Armed Forces who are assigned to a congressional liaison office of the Department of Defense
at the House of Representatives to obtain membership in the exercise
facility established for employees of the House of Representatives

Get the picture? With so many resolutions to consider, there's little time left
for serious matters.

There are times when Congress does spend time on a substantive vote
that really shouldn't take up their time. When the House was considering a
bill to require the cancellation of U.S., IMF, and World Bank debt, Representative Dana Rohrabacher (R-Calif.) introduced an amendment that
would limit the debt cancellation to countries that hold free elections. This

makes a lot of sense. Are we really willing to cancel debt to oppressive dictatorships? Well, some members of Congress opposed the provision. See the chart below.

MEMBERS VOTING AGAINST AMENDMENT TO REQUIRE THAT POOR COUNTRIES RECEIVING DEBT CANCELLATION FROM U.S., WORLD BANK, AND IMF MUST HOLD FREE ELECTIONS

Baldwin	Kucinich	Payne
Blumenauer	Lee	Price (NC)
Butterfield	Lewis (GA)	Rahall
Capuano	McDermott	Richardson
Cleaver	McGovern	Scott (GA)
Cohen	McNulty	Serrano
Gutierrez	Miller, George	Snyder
Hinchey	Mollohan	Towns
Honda	Moore (WI)	Tsongas
Jackson (IL)	Moran (VA)	Waters
Jackson-Lee (TX)	Nadler	Watt
Johnson, E. B.	Obey	Woolsey
Jones (OH)	Olver	Wynn
Kilpatrick	Ortiz	

Representatives Clarke and Ellison voted "present."
Source: *Congressional Record,* Roll Call votes.

THE SENATE

It's not just the House that spends its time on lots of unproductive and unnecessary resolutions. The Senate considers its share, too. Here's a list of some they've passed this year: according to the senate records, which can be found at http://www.senate.gov/pagelayout/legislative/a_three_sections _with_teasers/votes.htm.

- National Funeral Director and Mortician Recognition Day

- Tribute to Dr. Michael Debakey

- Tribute to Louisiana World War II veterans

- Small Business Week

- Commending Morrison Chevrolet dealership in Maine

- Recognizing the Greater Philadelphia Association of Realtors

- National Adopt a Library Day

- Designating a post office in Port Jervis, New York as the Arthur Gray Post Office Building (and many other namings of post offices that are too numerous to mention)

- Honoring the life and extraordinary contributions of Diane Wolf

- Congratulating Iowa State University of Science and Technology on its 150 years of leadership and service to the United States and the world as Iowa's land-grant university

The list goes on. Both the House and Senate spend an enormous amount of time on sometimes senseless resolutions and ignore the important issues that truly need their attention.

It's time for major reform. We need to start keeping track of our elected leaders' votes and their attendance—and to let them know we're watching.

And maybe it's time for term limits.

WE'VE BEEN FLEECED!

ACTION AGENDA

When the Republicans ran Capitol Hill, they were just as bad as the Democrats. In fact, they worked even less! But the Democrats swept into office in

2006 pledging to reform the way Congress conducted its business—and they made a special point of promising to put in all the hard work it would take to get the country back on the right track.

Well, they've broken that promise—and for nearly two years they've been getting away with it. We need to stop thinking of ourselves as helpless when it comes to this kind of behavior and start remembering that *these people work for us.* We need to start holding our elected leaders accountable for their actions (or lack of action), even if it means throwing them out of office. Why should we sit back and let them take a paid vacation for two years at our expense, wasting their time on ceremonial nonsense when we sent them to Congress to fix what's wrong with this country?

We thought changing parties might help, but it hasn't. Only by toppling the comfortable, self-indulgent establishments in both parties—and replacing them with people who are actually interested in working for our interests—do we stand a chance of creating a Congress that works for us.

If we can't muster up a little anger over this, they'll just keep fleecing us.

5

FOREIGN COMPANIES AND AMERICAN PENSION FUNDS THAT HELP IRAN BUILD THE BOMB

One of our national nightmares is that Iran, in the grip of the ayatollah and his religious fanatics, will develop nuclear weapons. Iranian President Mahmoud Ahmadinejad has boasted publicly and frequently of his plan to wipe Israel off the map. And once he acquires delivery systems to go with his bombs, he will undoubtedly come gunning for us.

After the debacle in Iraq, Americans are rightfully skittish about getting into a war with Iran. And the most recent National Intelligence Estimate, published in November 2007, indicates that although Iran continues to enrich uranium—the necessary precursor to both building a bomb and supplying a nuclear power plant—in 2003 its leaders decided not to proceed with construction of a bomb.

This good news was greeted with skepticism by conservatives. Whether the Estimate was right or wrong, however, one thing is clear: by continuing to enrich uranium, Iran is developing the *capability* to build a bomb, whether its current *intentions* are to do so or not.

Do you trust Iran?

If you don't— as we don't—the key is to deny it the capability to build a bomb by stopping it from enriching uranium. If Iran wants fuel for nuclear power plants, Russia is quite willing to provide it under U.N. inspection. (As of this writing, Iran doesn't even have a completed nuclear power plant to receive the fuel, or to generate electricity.)

So the real question is: How can we stop Iran from enriching uranium?

Most people realize that the sanctions imposed by the United Nations are only slaps on the wrist, unlikely to deter the fanatics in Tehran. But today some of the most prestigious publicly traded companies in the world are supplying the Iranian regime with the resources it needs to stay in power—and, in some cases, even directly subsidizing its efforts to acquire nuclear weapons! And we are enabling these companies to subsidize Iran by buying their stock through our mutual funds, 401(k)s, and individual portfolios, even our state pension funds.

Of course, few people in the United States realize that investing in these companies means being complicit in the aid they give Iran. These companies put on a benign front—and Americans are none the wiser.

So here is a list of the "dirty dozen"—the twelve worst offenders when it comes to trading with Iran—all of them publicly traded companies that do business with Iran—as identified by an important group called Divest terror.org, headed by Frank Gaffney, Jr., formerly an official in Ronald Reagan's Pentagon. www.divestterror.org is devoted to exposing investments of foreign owned companies in nations that sponsor terrorism. These investments are lawful for foreign companies—although not for American firms—but they do much to help prop up these terror-sponsoring governments. The group that sponsors www.divestterror.org hopes that by publicizing the names of foreign companies that they maintain make these investments, as they do on their site, they can persuade individuals and institutions to divest themselves of their holdings in these companies.

THE DIRTY DOZEN

Companies that Do Business with Iran

Alcatel-Lucent

BNP Paribas

ENI

Hyundai

Lundin Petroleum

Oil & Natural Gas Corporation

Royal Dutch Shell

Siemens

Sinopec

Statoil

Stolt Nielsen

Source: www.divestterror.org.

Some of these companies invest overtly in elements of the Iranian military. Others simply help the nation's energy economy or infrastructure. Both policies contribute to the potential threat that Iran poses to our national security.

The only way to stop Iran from developing the bomb is to squeeze it economically. Iran is very vulnerable to economic pressure: its government derives 85 percent of its revenues from the energy sector, but the country's oil exports have dropped year after year as domestic demand has risen by 10 percent annually and production has lagged. Current estimates are that the nation's oil exports will be cut in half by 2011 and eliminated entirely three years later, even though it has the world's second largest oil reserves.

The problem is that Iran can't get at the reserves and bring them to the surface without foreign investment. And that's where the activities of these companies are hurting our national interest.

The ayatollah's regime desperately needs these export revenues to pacify its population. Only 40 percent of Iran's population is Farsi, and the country is torn by a severe lack of ethnic cohesion. Most Iranians are under the age of thirty and restless under the constraints of theocratic rule. The government is hanging on by the skin of its teeth by subsidizing prices to stop discontent from boiling over—holding the cost of gasoline down to a mere thirty cents a gallon, for example. But can the government continue these steep subsidies while oil production continues to drop? Without energy revenues, the regime cannot afford subsidies to keep its population pacified.

Dennis Ross, Bill Clinton's Middle East negotiator, is just one of those who believe that disinvestment "could be important in bringing about a change in Iranian policy on nuclear weapons." After all, let's remember that it was the international disinvestment movement that forced South Africa to alter its centuries-old policy of apartheid. An equivalent pressure on Iran could be incredibly effective.

If we all sell our stock in companies that do business with terror-sponsoring nations, the CEOs and boards of directors of these companies will see the value of their portfolios crash—and, most likely, their own pay envelopes, since the personal compensation and bonus provisions these CEOs enjoy are usually based on stock prices.

On a personal level, this kind of disinvestment means combing your personal portfolio and checking out your mutual fund to make sure the companies you invest in aren't helping Iran—or other terrorist-sponsoring countries such as Syria, North Korea, and Sudan.

How can you find out which companies to avoid?

As Frank Gaffney explains, the FTSE Group, a leading global investment index, is now providing "the world's first series of terror-free screened indexes." Now it will be possible for investors, sophisticated and novice alike, to put their money into profitable companies ensuring a good rate of return that do *not* invest in companies that help Iran and the other terror-sponsoring nations. The information available to the FTSE Group about the activities of various companies in Iran, he says, will be "the gold standard" in measuring their "global security risk."

"Thanks to the FTSE index," Gaffney says, "it will be possible for every investor in America to ensure that their portfolios, be they in the public or private sector, become a part of the effort to defeat our enemies on the financial front of this War for the Free World—rather than serve, however unintentionally, as resources for those who help them."

Here are the details about how these companies are keeping Iran afloat, quoted with permission from www.disinvestterror.org:

HOW THE DIRTY DOZEN KEEP IRAN AFLOAT
Alcatel-Lucent

- An $11.8 billion 2006 merger of Alcatel SA and Lucent Technologies, this company now operates a multi-million-dollar contract with Iran to provide a fully integrated communication system at the South Paris gas fields.

- Iran's Asre Danesh Afzar signed a deal with Alcatel for the installation of high-speed internet connectivity in Iran.

- In March 2007, the East Africa Submarine Cable System consortium awarded Alcatel-Lucent a U.S. $240 million turnkey project to lay an optical submarine cable network landing.

BNP Paribas

- In March 2005, Iran Petrochemical Commercial Company signed a five-year U.S. $1 billion secured loan through a consortium of mandated lead arrangers, including BNP Paribas. The loan was the largest pre-export financing loan to date.

- In July 2002, BNP Paribas, along with Commerzbank AG, launched the first Iranian Eurobond since the beginning of the Islamic Revolution in 1979. Despite U.S. sanctions, the $497.1 million offering was oversubscribed by at least 20 percent.

ENI SPA

- ENI SPA is working on a number of different oil and gas development projects. The company's website reports that ENI's quota of the production of oil and condensates in Iran was 35,000 barrels per day in 2005.

- ENI operates out of three offices in Tehran: Saipem SpA Iran, Snamprogetti, and ENI Iran BV. The latter handles exploration and production while the first two manage all oilfield services, construction, and engineering projects.

- ENI and its subsidiaries have interests in the Darkhovin and Balal oil fields, and in 2007, submitted a bid for Phases 19 through 21 of the South Pars gas field. Also, a Saipem-led consortium entered into talks with the National Iranian Oil Refining & Distribution Company to build a refinery at Bandar Abbas. In addition, ENI is reportedly a "term lifter" of oil from Syria.

Hyundai

- The Hyundai Group has Iran contracts including shipbuilding, machinery, steel, chemicals, and home appliances for some U.S. $1.9 billion.

- Another entity, Hyundai Engineering and Construction (HEC), completed Phases 4 and 5 of the South Pars Development project, having completed Phases 2 and 3 in February 2003. HEC is also part of the Rotem consortium that won a U.S. $140 million contract to export 120 diesel-powered rail cars and related technology to the Iran Khodro Rail Transport Industries Co. in 2004.

- Hyundai Heavy Industries (HHI) will deliver 39 ships, worth a total of U.S. $1.7 billion, to the Islamic Republic of Iran Shipping Lines in the second half of 2008.

- Hyundai Motor Corp. won a U.S. $227 million order from Iran to supply completed vehicles to the country's government agencies and taxi operators.

Lundin Petroleum

- Lundin Munir Ltd. has a 30 percent nonoperating interest in the Munir Block in Iran's Khuzestan province. Edison International owns 40 percent and is the contract operator, and Petronas owns the remaining 30 percent.

Oil & Natural Gas Corp.

- ONGC Videsh has a 100 percent participating interest in the Jufeyr project and a 10 percent interest in the Yadavaran field.

- In November of 2006 ONGC Videsh found oil in Iran's Farsi exploration block and continues to test the discovery.

- The ONGC Group includes Himalya Energy (Syria) B.V. ONGC Videsh holds a U.S. $2.7 billion stake in Syria's Sakhalin-I oil field. It is officially producing crude oil as of January 2007.

Royal Dutch Shell

- Shell's Tehran offices arranged a tentative liquefied natural gas (LNG) plant deal worth U.S. $10 billion. The deal, which will not come into effect until the final investment decision is made in 2008, was signed along with Spain's Repsol. In October 2007, Shell CFO Peter Voser attributed delays in the project to "technical and economic aspects," but also stated that the company would have to consider political issues in continuing to pursue this South Pars LNG deal.

- Shell is also in partnership with Iran's Oil Industries Engineering Company and Japan's JJI, which jointly finished developing the Soroush and Nowruz fields in Iran, totaling U.S. $1.45 billion.

- Syria Shell Petroleum Development BV is headquartered in Damascus, and represents Shell as the majority owner of Al Furat Production Company, Syria's largest oil company.

Siemens AG

- Siemens AG has a number of Iranian subsidiaries: Demag Delaval Desoil Services Qeshm; Sherkate Tarhaye Siemens, Tehran; Siemens Sherkate Sahami (Kass), Tehran; Iranian Lamps Ltd., Tehran; Iranian

Telecommunications Manufacturing Co., Shiraz; ITS Tehran; OSRAM Iran Ltd., Tehran.

• Siemens also has offices in Damascus, Syria. The company is under investigation for a series of suspicious transactions in which the group's general manager in Damascus allegedly received 72 million euros between 1999 and 2006. Siemens has a global purchasing contract with Egypt's Orascom Telecom for construction of GSM (Global System for Mobile Communication) wireless systems. Orascom has a license to provide wireless telecom to 750,000 subscribers in Syria.

Sinopec

• China Petroleum & Chemical Corporation (Sinopec) operates in all stages of the crude oil discovery, extraction and refining process.

• Sinopec will pay Iran some U.S. $100 billion during 25 years for oil and gas supplies and for a 51 percent stake in the Yadavaran oil project.

• Royal Dutch Shell received compensation for preparing this deal in the form of an option to take a stake in this oilfield. Yadavaran is expected to eventually produce 300,000 barrels of oil per day.

Statoil ASA

• Statoil's Tehran office facilitates business development activities such as a technical training agreement with the Islamic Republic of Iran Shipping Lines (IRISL), signed in August 2006. Under the agreement, the companies will jointly invest U.S. $200,000 to plan and hold training courses for Iranian personnel in firefighting, rescue boat management, and maritime environment safety and security.

Stolt Nielsen

- The U.S. Treasury's Office of Foreign Assets Control issued a cease and desist order in April 2002 after investigating bank transactions initiated by U.S. based employees of Stolt-Nielsen Transportation, Stolt-Nielsen SA's U.S. unit, and shipping agents in Iran.

Total SA

- BEH TOTAL Co., and subsidiaries TOTAL SIRRI and Elf Petroleum Iran continue operations at Sirri and South Pars 2–3, and are currently pursuing development on Balal and Dorood.

- TOTAL's chairman, Thierry Desmarest, has acknowledged the potential effects of an IAEA ban on business with Iran but stated that as long as an international ban is not implemented, business would continue. The primary obstacle to a final agreement at South Pars remains the price to be charged for gas.

- The original 1997 development contract with Gazprom and Petronas was then the largest ever made with the Iranian government.

- In 2005 the Jafra and Qahar fields on the Deir Ez Zor project accounted for the majority of TOTAL's oil production in Syria. TOTAL also operated a condensate and reprocessing plant at Deir Ez Zor, of which TOTAL owned 50 percent. That contract, however, expired at the end of 2005. The facilities have now been transferred to the state-owned company SGC.

In addition to these interests, many of these companies have stakes in other terror-sponsoring states. Lundin Petroleum, Oil & Natural Gas Corporation, Royal Dutch/Shell, Siemens, Stolt Nielsen, and TOTAL all do business in Sudan, thereby aiding the genocide now in progress. And Hyundai does extensive business in North Korea.

These companies are hardly the only ones that help terror-sponsoring countries. Divestterror.org has identified 485 such companies but lists only these twelve publicly.

Think you don't own stock in any of these companies? Think again. Your pension fund might.

A report by the Conflict Securities Advisory Group (CSAG) found that, on average, between 15 and 23 percent of the assets of state pension funds in the United States "involved companies doing business with countries on the State Department's list of state sponsors of terror. Then, the value of these holdings was estimated to be roughly $188 billion, with more than $70 billion actually associated with activities in Iran, Syria, North Korea, and other safe-havens for terror."

Fortunately, a number of states are taking action to stop their pension funds from subsidizing terrorism. The pioneer in this initiative has been Missouri State Treasurer Sarah Steelman, who exercised her power to ban state pension investments in companies that sponsor terrorism. Since she acted, a number of other states have followed suit either by executive action or by legislative fiat.

These include:

• **California:** Governor Arnold Schwarzenegger signed into law a bill initiated by freshman Republican Assemblyman Joel Anderson ordering CALPERS and CALSTERS, two of the nation's largest pension funds, to divest tens of billions of dollars' worth of investments in companies doing business in Iran.

The Governator said, "I couldn't be more proud to sign this bill. Last year I signed legislation to show our defiance against the inhumane murder and genocide in Sudan. This year I am pleased to support additional efforts to further prevent terrorism by doing what's right with our investment portfolio and signing this legislation to divest from Iran."

• **Florida:** Republican Governor Charlie Crist signed legislation forcing disinvestment.

• **New Jersey:** Passed legislation to require disinvestment.

• **Louisiana:** Has not only disinvested but authorized its state treasurer to develop a terror-free investment vehicle that individuals around the country can use for their own portfolios.

• **New York City:** City Comptroller William Thompson used his power over pension fund investments to press companies to disinvest in Iran. He reports, "My office has forced a number of U.S. companies to cease doing business, through their foreign subsidiaries, in Iran . . . [we have] prompted Halliburton, the Aon Corporation, Cooper Cameron, ConocoPhilips, Foster Wheeler, and General Electric to not only assess their financial and reputational risks posed by their business ties to Iran, but to commit to ceasing those activities."

If your city or state isn't on this list, it's time it was!

Some pension bureaucrats have argued that they have a "fiduciary duty" to their retirees to make investments without regard to social or political circumstances. A spokesman for New York State Comptroller Thomas P. DiNapoli, for instance, gave us that line when we interviewed him for this book.

But this argument ignores the fact that each of these pension funds participated in the boycott of companies that invested in South Africa during apartheid—and that states such as California, Florida, Missouri, and Louisiana have been able to disinvest without triggering litigation from pension funds or retirees. There's no evidence that one must compromise even a point of interest income by abstaining from investments in companies that do business in Iran, Syria, North Korea, or Sudan.

Quite the contrary: the risk of such investments in these countries is enormous. As huge state pension funds like New York, California, and Florida stop investing in these companies, their stock prices and values are likely to come crashing down, making them very bad bets indeed. And as the public becomes aware of their activities, their reputations could be massively sullied, making ownership of their stock even iffier.

At the diplomatic level, Secretary of State Condoleezza Rice has done a terrific job of building pressure on companies that do business with terrorist countries. American companies are already prohibited from making such investments by U.S. law, and she has used that high ground to inform companies such as Repsol (a Spanish firm) and Royal Dutch/Shell that they may be endangering their U.S. business by continuing to invest in Iran. Her warnings have sent chills through boardrooms across Europe.

But pension funds are not the only source of pressure. The World Bank also needs to get its act together in isolating Iran economically. Incredibly enough, the bank—headed by a former Bush administration official—is planning to proceed with almost $900 million in loans to Iran. These loans were approved several years ago in the wake of the devastating earthquake that rocked Iran. But most of the loans—which can still be stopped—have nothing at all to do with the earthquake.

WORLD BANK LOANS TO IRAN

- "A project to improve access to health care for rural Iranians"
- "Improvements to Teheran's sewage system"
- "An air and water quality monitoring project"
- Total cost: $870 million

Source: *New York Sun.*

Only part of this huge cash infusion would go for relief for earthquake victims. The rest would find its way into Iran's deeply corrupt economic bloodstream.

Though these may be worthy projects in another country, to give the money to Iran at the same time that the United Nations is voting sanctions to force it to comply with its resolutions on the development of nuclear weapons is a travesty.

Congressman Mark Kirk (R-Ill.) has been working to induce Robert Zoellick, the president of the World Bank, to cancel the loans. Zoellick was appointed head of the bank by President Bush (the United States, as the largest lender, usually gets to name the head of the bank), having previously served as the U.S. trade representative in the Bush cabinet.

The results of Kirk's overtures to Zoellick have not been encouraging. "When I initially talked to him," Congressman Kirk reports, "he said they [the World Bank] are not approving any new loans [to Iran]." When Kirk pressed Zoellick about the $870 million of earthquake loans scheduled to be sent to Iran over the next three years, however, the World Bank president responded, "Oh, that."

"He said, 'I don't know if I can stop that.'" Kirk says he told Zoellick, "Think of the embarrassment if the UN Security Council approves three separate sanctions, and the United States imposes its own unilateral sanctions and three blocks away the World Bank cuts a check to the Ahmadinejad government."

So far, the World Bank has spewed administrative gobbledygook about the Iranian loans. The *New York Sun,* the new city paper that has been both intrepid and creative in exposing issues like this one, quotes a spokesman for the World Bank defending its conduct: "The bank adheres to the requirements of UN Sanctions frameworks. In relation to Iran, the Security Council resolutions exempt activities by international financial institutions for humanitarian and development purposes. The bank has been in touch with the Security Council sanctions committee on Iran to insure the bank acts consistently with the sanctions framework, which prohibits dealings with designated individuals and entities."

Okay, but has President Zoellick or this spokesman ever heard of the spirit of the laws, not just the letter of the law? The whole point of the U.N. sanctions is to deny Iran funds and legitimacy and keep it isolated. Pumping $870 million into Iran over the next three years hardly qualifies.

ACTION AGENDA

There is much we can all do to help isolate Iran, cut off its funding, starve its economy, and force it to abandon the pursuit of nuclear weapons. Here are some ideas to start with:

- Write your state governor, treasurer, or comptroller and your local state legislator, urging them to take administrative or legislative action to stop your state's pension fund from investing in companies that do business with Iran or other terrorist nations. They should sell their stocks in these companies and channel all their future investments only to firms that are listed on the new FTSE Index. Urge them to go to www.divestterror.org for more information.

- Contact your individual broker and ask him to shift your personal portfolio away from companies that invest in terrorist countries. Again, the FTSE index can provide him or her with a guide.

- If you are a retiree, write your pension fund and ask it to desist from investments in companies that invest in Iran and other terrorist nations.

Write to World Bank President Robert Zoellick to express your anger that an American is allowing the World Bank to lend money put up by U.S. taxpayers to Iran. His e-mail address is rzoellick@ustr.gov.

He'd love to hear from you!

6

THE NEW LOBBYISTS:
Peddling the Agendas of Foreign Governments, Oppressive Dictators, and Foreign Corporations to the U.S. Government and the American Public

Saudi Arabia*†

Libya*

Iraq*

Iran*

Dubai†

Qatar

Abu Dhabi

Venezuela*

Sudan*

China

Azerbaijan

Taiwan

United Arab Emirates

Pakistan*

Israel

Turkey

Palestine*

* Countries on the U.S. State Department Travel Warning List.
† Countries identified by the U.S. State Department as human rights violators.

Has it ever seemed to you that America's political leaders are sometimes ignoring our national interests? If so, here's one possible reason for it: there are thousands of lobbyists, lawyers, PR firms, and political consultants in Washington, D.C., who are getting paid fat sums to push the agendas of foreign governments—often in direct opposition to what is best for the United States and the American people. Under such pressure, our politicians too often march to the beat of a different drummer—and it's foreign governments, through their lobbyists, who are calling the tune.

Lobbying for foreign entities has become a huge business for lobbying firms in Washington—there's now a growing and lucrative niche peddling the agendas of foreign countries, private foreign corporations, and even exiled former foreign leaders seeking to return to power. More and more, these wealthy foreign interests are trying to influence our federal laws, policies, and budgetary choices to serve their interests. And the lobbyists are collecting millions in fees each year to do their bidding.

In 2006 and 2007, more than 146 foreign entities retained Americans to act as their agents in Washington—including some nations that are overtly hostile to the United States and have been cited for human rights violations by the State Department. In these past two years, for example, Iran, Libya, Sudan, Côte d'Ivoire, the Palestinian Authority, and Hugo Chávez's Venezuela—human rights violators all—have hired Americans to deliver their propaganda.

The State Department Travel Advisory list warns Americans against traveling in some of these very same countries. In Sudan and Pakistan, for instance, it warns that terrorism is a serious threat to Americans traveling there. In Libya, terrorist attacks threaten American interests. In Iran, tourists should watch out for unwarranted anti-American detentions and arrests. Political unrest and violence toward foreigners are a fact of life in the Ivory Coast; in Venezuela, the same goes for kidnappings, violent crimes, and violent political rallies. State cites Saudi Arabia for the continued presence of terrorist groups—some affiliated with Al Qaeda—that may target Western interests.

Yet these same regimes march arrogantly onto our soil and try to bend U.S. foreign policy toward their own ends by dealing outside of official diplomatic channels. Even when the United States has no diplomatic relationship with a particular country, that doesn't stop any foreign government from bypassing the State Department and taking its case right to our lawmakers to get what it wants.

Countries such as Saudi Arabia and Dubai—two more nations cited as human rights violators by the State Department—maintain an army of lobbyists to plead their cases and improve their images in Washington. Pakistan, Turkey, China, Abu Dhabi, Qatar, Azerbaijan, Taiwan, the United Arab Emirates, and hundreds of other countries hire lobbyists to try to influence U.S. government policies to benefit them. (For a complete list of all foreign agents, go to www.usdoj.gov/criminal/fara.)

These alien entities pay big bucks to well-heeled Washington insiders— officially known as "foreign agents"—to propagandize the American government, the American public, the elite press, and respected opinion leaders to gain support for their self-serving objectives, many of which are directly at odds with American workers, businesses, foreign policy, and core values.

It's done all the time. And, regrettably, it's perfectly legal.

Here's how they do it: foreign countries and corporations routinely hire former high-level government officials, politically well-connected lawyers, and public relations flacks to plead their case in Congress, at the White House, within the State Department, throughout the executive branch bureaucracy, and in the press. For these seasoned lobbyists, it's easy work: not only is it their business to maintain friendly relationships with these players, but in many cases, they are actually former coworkers, bosses, mentors, protégés, and employees. And they have no shame about using their intimate relationships to open the door to foreign nationals and their sometimes dubious causes . . .

Former members of Congress are especially sought after as lobbyists. Several years ago, Public Citizen issued a report that described this new revolving door between Congress and the lobbying industry. According to the report, 43 percent of the 198 members of Congress who retired between 1998 and 2005—including half the senators—became lobbyists, a practice virtually unheard of in previous years. During that period, a total of 2,200 former federal employees and 250 members of Congress and former heads of executive branch agencies turned to lobbying. And that number continues to grow. Experienced insiders know how to get things done and the foreign clients appreciate that. Most lobbyists show little, if any, concern about whether the foreign government is a democracy or a dictatorship. They all pay the same.

The bottom line is that these lobbyists are helping to empower foreign governments—regardless of a country's history and record, and often at the expense of the U.S. interests we once elected them to serve.

Ken Silverstein, a critic of the growing influence of lobbyists for foreign entities, summed up the problem:

> How is it that regimes widely acknowledged to be the world's most oppressive nevertheless continually win favors in Washington? In part, it is because they often have something highly desired by the United States that can be leveraged to their advantage. . . . But even the best-endowed regimes need help navigating the shoals of Washington, and it is their great fortune that, for the right price, countless lobbyists are willing to steer even the foulest of ships.

Our nation's capital has become an inviting harbor for these rich special interests from foreign shores.

HOW A $40 BILLION U.S. DEFENSE CONTRACT WAS AWARDED TO—THE FRENCH

The ultimate example of the widespread—and highly successful—use of Washington lobbyists by a foreign company was demonstrated in the Pentagon's recent decision to award a $40 billion contract for aerial refueling tankers to a partnership between Northrop Grumman and EADS (European Aeronautics Defense and Space), the European parent of the Airbus aircraft manufacturer, instead of the American defense contractor Boeing.

The New York Times called the decision a "stunning upset" that placed "a critical military contract partly into the hands of a foreign company."

This is no small matter. The amount of money involved alone is staggering: over time, the contract is expected to grow to about $100 billion. Of greater concern, however, is the basic decision to turn to foreign suppliers for U.S. defense equipment—a move that is virtually without precedent. Not surprisingly, the unexpected decision was viewed as "a sign of the growing influence of foreign suppliers within the Pentagon." Translation:

Airbus won by hiring well-connected American lobbyists. As the *Times* noted, the Airbus contract "breaks a relationship that has lasted decades with Boeing, which had built the bulk of the existing tanker fleet and had fought hard to land the new contract."

Among the casualties of the decision are American jobs. Boeing estimates that it would have used the money to hire 44,000 Americans if it had secured the contract. But Airbus reports that the new contract will initially create only a meager 1,300 new jobs at a plant in Mobile, Alabama. Eventually, it suggests, that number could grow as high as 25,000, but that remains to be seen. Even if the projection is correct, why did the U.S. government direct this American investment to a foreign company—denying jobs to at least 19,000 of our countrymen and possibly compromising American national security?

There is one place where the Airbus contract will create lots of jobs: in Europe. A company spokesman stated that the contact would "sustain employment in Europe for decades." Though the final assembly of the tankers would take place at an Airbus plant in Alabama, the parts would be made outside the United States, resulting in additional jobs for "production of the wings, fuselage, and tail sections for the planes."

This is not good news for the American economy.

Amazingly, the air force seemed oblivious to the economic impact, claiming that "the creation of domestic jobs was not a factor in the decision." Not a factor? With a recession looming, did the Pentagon actually believe that giving away up to $100 billion of our money to a foreign company and spurning an American alternative should be done without factoring in the potential loss of American jobs?

Something is very wrong here.

How did it happen?

Ask the lobbyists! One of the biggest reasons for Airbus's success in winning the contract was the help it received from sophisticated American lobbyists, who convinced the Pentagon of the firm's superior product while garnering congressional and public support for the deal.

Who were these lobbyists?

Surprise: some of the top campaign aides to Hillary Clinton—and John McCain—were paid huge fees to help close the deal.

McCain has been a longtime, legitimate critic of Boeing for waste and corruption. But he injected himself into the Boeing-Airbus competition by writing letters asking the Defense Department to ignore the issue of a U.S.-Airbus trade dispute—letters that appear to have been helpful to Airbus's case. He also asked for a change in the criteria for evaluating bidders. Now Boeing is appealing the decision, based in part on McCain's intervention. And closer scrutiny of the role of his advisers may cause problems for McCain: though he has a reputation for fighting lobbyists and special interests, his campaign aides were front and center on the Airbus issue.

For her part, Hillary Clinton spent much of the 2008 campaign decrying the export of American jobs—especially in the Ohio primary. But even as she excoriated the effect of NAFTA in displacing American workers, some of her closest advisers and supporters were working to shift defense jobs to Europe. She's been silent on that.

Airbus had a large team of expensive lobbyists, as the following chart of last year's lobbying fees illustrates.

EADS/AIRBUS LOBBYING EXPENDITURES, 2007

Firms Hired	Contract Income	Subsidiary (Lobbied For)
EADS North America	$1,300,000	EADS North America
Airbus North America	$440,000	Airbus North America
Quinn Gillespie & Associates*	$360,000	EADS North America
Fierce, Isakowitz & Blalock	$320,000	EADS North America
Rhoads Group	$280,000	EADS North America
Ogilvy Government Relations*	$240,000	EADS North America
Loeffler Group	$220,000	EADS North America
Stonebridge International	$180,000	Airbus North America
Spectrum Group	$160,000	—
Glover Park Group	$120,000	Airbus North America
TOTAL	$3,670,000	

* Both Quinn Gillespie and Ogilvy Government Relations are owned by the British company WPP and are sister companies to Burson-Marsteller, where Hillary Clinton's recently fired chief strategist, Mark Penn, is the worldwide CEO.
Source: www.opensecrets.org.

In addition to the company's own employees at EADS and Airbus, eight other lobbying firms were retained by Airbus/EADS in 2007. Three of the eight have extremely close ties to Hillary and Bill Clinton; three others have close ties to John McCain.

AIRBUS LOBBYING FIRMS CLOSE TO HILLARY CLINTON

- Quinn Gillespie & Associates, headed by Jack Quinn, the former White House counsel to President Clinton. Quinn Gillespie lists a team of nineteen lobbyists, including Quinn, former RNC chairman Ed Gillespie, and many former top executive branch and congressional staffers.

- Glover Park Group, frequently referred to as "The Clinton White House in Exile." Clinton confidant and former White House press secretary Joe Lockhart is a partner, as is the Hillary Clinton campaign communications director, Howard Wolfson (who took a leave of absence to campaign with Hillary). The firm lists four lobbyists, including two former Clinton White House legislative aides. Hillary Clinton's former campaign manager, Patti Solis Doyle, is another Glover alum.

- Stonebridge International, headed by disgraced former National Security Council head Sandy Berger, who was convicted of stealing classified documents from the National Archives in 2005 by shoving them down his socks and pants. Berger remains one of Hillary's top foreign policy advisers.

AIRBUS LOBBYING FIRMS CLOSE TO JOHN McCAIN

- Fierce, Isakowitz & Blalock, where Kirk Blalock, a national chairman of Young Professionals for McCain, is a registered lobbyist.

- Loeffler Group, headed by Thomas Loeffler, the cochairman of the McCain campaign. In addition to Loeffler, former Navy secretary William L. Ball III was a lobbyist for Airbus at the firm until he resigned to work for the McCain campaign. Another Airbus lobbyist for the firm, Susan Nelson, has also resigned to work for the campaign.

- Ogilvy Government Relations, where Wayne Berman is a partner and lobbyist for Airbus. Berman is also a fund-raiser and vice chairman of the McCain campaign.

The nexus between the McCain campaign and the lobbyists who convinced the Pentagon to sell out American jobs is extensive, and it raises legitimate questions about McCain's intercessions. There's one more factor to note: EADS/Airbus employees gave more than three times the amount of campaign contributions to congressional candidates this year than in the past—and McCain was the single biggest recipient of their largesse.

Both sides spent a lot of money on lobbyists' fees and campaign contributions to key members of Congress, but Airbus spent significantly more. Airbus/EADS contributed a total of $75,600 toward congressional reelection efforts, while Northrop Grumman's PAC gave $669,000 for the 2008 election cycle, for a total of $744,600. Federal Election Commission (FEC) reports show that the Boeing PAC contributed $525,500.

The McCain campaign calls its ties with these high-priced Airbus lobbyists "coincidental." But there's also some important history to note here. McCain himself has been after Boeing for years and played an upfront and courageous role in outing its efforts to bribe Pentagon officials to win contracts. McCain insists that "I had nothing to do with the [tanker] contract except to insist in writing on several occasions as this process went forward that it be fair and open and transparent."

What, then, is McCain doing with advisers who collected a combined total of more than a million dollars to advance the interests of a foreign company over those of an American firm, costing the United States tens of thousands of jobs? At the very least, it doesn't look good.

But what's best for America is of no concern to the well-paid lobbyists: whatever the foreign government wants, they'll fight for.

Hillary Clinton's close associates were also big players in the deal, as the chart above shows. The firm founded by Sandy Berger, Bill Clinton's national security adviser, represented Airbus for years, as did Quinn Gillespie and Glover Park. They've raked in millions on this project.

In courting the lobbyists who are close to the major presidential candidates, EADS/Airbus is apparently looking to the future. And there's more to come: Boeing's decision to challenge the Airbus contract will be another bonanza for the lobbyists.

Northrup Grumman, EADS/Airbus's American partner, isn't taking any chances. It has already added the formidable lobbying firm of former senators Trent Lott and John Breaux to its team.

This proliferation of lobbyists for foreign countries and companies raises a serious public policy question: Why do we permit *any* foreign governments to lobby our own government? Why do we permit our bureaucracy and Congress to spend their valuable time catering to the whims of foreign interests?

Especially when the figure hiring U.S. lobbyists is someone like Venezuela President Hugo Chávez—an avowed foe of the United States.

HUGO CHÁVEZ HIRES D.C. LOBBYISTS

In recent years, Hugo Chávez has made something of a spectacle of himself, declaiming his hatred and contempt for the United States to anyone who will listen. After the State Department labeled him as a threat to stability in South America, Chávez retorted, "The planet's most serious danger is the government of the United States." He has called the U.S. government the "first enemy" of the Venezuelan people. Our government has publicly criticized Chávez, but that hasn't stopped him from trying to influence what we do. Even as Chávez employs numerous foreign agents on our soil, our State Department has suspended the sale of arms to Venezuela because of what it terms as his "nearly total lack of cooperation with the United States anti-terror activities."

Chávez apparently believes that the United States wants to invade his country, recently claiming that our government was planning to attack Venezuela by using Colombia as a proxy.

Yet he and his flunkies continue trying to influence our public policy. A friend and ally of Iran, North Korea, Cuba, and Russia, Chávez has hired lobbyists and created a propaganda organization in Washington to try to influence our government, media, and citizens. Last year, Chávez spent more than a million dollars trying to spread his anti-American message right in our own backyard.

As the advance guard in his campaign to counteract Chávez's rather negative image in the United States, the Venezuelan Embassy has created and funded the Venezuelan Information Organization (VIO). A filing with the Justice Department describes the organization's mission:

> [T]o prevent U.S. intervention in Venezuela, using tools of media outreach, grassroots public education and Congressional advocacy, the VIO seeks to

present a more moderate view of the current process in Venezuela for the U.S. public, build strategic alliances for the Venezuelan people, and prevent the U.S. government from intervening in the democratic process in Venezuela.

Translation: Chávez wants to try to convince the U.S. Congress and the media—and ultimately all of us—that his maniacal government is a legitimate democracy and that his oil companies, which are unquestionably political tools of his government, should be left alone.

Let's tell him to go away.

Chávez is sparing no expense in his attempt to turn public opinion in his favor. The VIO received $755,000 during the six-month period ending on August 31, 2007, and engaged in extensive activities to try to stop a congressional resolution—House Resolution 77 and Senate Resolution 211—that criticized Chávez for closing down Radio Caracas Television (RCTV), his country's most popular television station, after he decided that it had backed a short-lived anti-Chávez coup in 2002. Chávez didn't want any opposing points of view being broadcast to his people. So he simply shut it down.

Note to Chávez: if you want to convince people you're running a democracy, you might start by remembering that you're not supposed to stop the media from criticizing the political system and it leaders.

In response to Chavez's crackdown, a U.S. congressional resolution called on Venezuela to end all censorship and permit a free and open press in the country.

That was apparently a huge insult to Chávez—a slap in the face so serious that he decided to launch his own charm offensive, aiming it at the American media and Congress. According to filings with the U.S. Department of Justice, VIO met with numerous members of Congress and contacted news organizations, student groups, liberal organizations, labor unions, academics, and others, purportedly trying to "balance" the conventional negative image of Venezuela. In other words, VIO was assigned to get Chávez's wacky point of view into every story written about Venezuela and its screwball president. During that same period, the organization hired two consultants, Segundo Mercado Llorens and Leila McDowell, at about $30,000 each to perform lobbying and public relations services in the United States.

VIO widely distributed propaganda materials describing the great works of Chávez and the charitable largesse of his state-owned oil company, Petróleos of Venezuela—including developing extensive voter registration projects and increasing the democratization of the press.

It also distributed reprints of Chávez's tirades against the injustice of the American government for instituting the 2006 arms embargo against his country because of his failure to cooperate in the war on terrorism. Mr. Chávez seems obsessed with that policy; he uses VIO to complain relentlessly about what he perceives as its injustice.

But VIO is not Chávez's only advocate in Washington. This is a long-term project for Chávez. In 2007, he also retained high-powered lobbyists to watch out for the interests of Citgo, the Venezuelan state-owned oil company based in Houston, and its parent company, Petróleos, and almost $500,000 in 2006. Many commentators have described Citgo as a new political tool of Chávez. For their work, the international lobbying firm Dutko Worldwide was paid $220,000 in 2005, almost more than $400,000 for this work in 2006, and took in $355,000 from Citgo in 2007. Since Chávez was elected in 1998, Dutko has been paid more than $3 million by Citgo. Another lobbying firm, Kelley, Drye, was paid $280,000 to advocate for Petróleos in 2006 and $280,000 in 2007. Lobbying filings indicate that the issues addressed are "fuel supply, foreign oil supply and legislation affecting crude oil and production imports into the United States."

Chávez doesn't mind spending a buck to protect his interests.

WHAT HUGO CHÁVEZ SPENDS ON LOBBYING IN THE UNITED STATES

Firm	2006	2007
VIO	$135,000	$755,000
Dutko	$483,993	$355,000
Kelley, Drye	$280,000	$280,000
Bracewell & Giuliani	$150,000	$100,000*
TOTAL:	**$2,538,993**	

* State of Texas lobbying only.
Sources: www.politicalmoneyline.com; www.opensecrets.org.

There's no question that Chávez hired some powerful lobbyists. And some observers say he's getting his money's worth. Here's a good example: When the renewable energy bill passed the House in early 2008, it allowed Citgo to retain an important tax benefit that would no longer be available to American companies. Whereas U.S. companies Chevron, BP, ExxonMobil, Shell, and ConocoPhillips would lose a lucrative subsidy for domestic manufacturing, Citgo would maintain the 6 percent deduction because it does not actually drill for oil and gas in the United States.

Some members of Congress weren't happy with the continued handout to Chávez. "This bill raises taxes for U.S. oil and gas production . . . while giving more American dollars to a dictator that has threatened to take away U.S. energy supplies," said Republican Phil English of Pennsylvania.

The bill has not passed the Senate.

The lobbyists that Chávez chose are no political neophytes. Dutko is active in Republican politics and recently held a fund-raiser for former presidential candidate Mitt Romney. The company's president, Craig Pattlee, was one of the national cochairmen of the aborted Romney campaign, and its employees have contributed more than $15,000 to Romney. The chairman of Dutko is Ron Kaufman, a former political director for President George H. W. Bush. Kaufman was also an adviser to Romney. After years on the White House staff, Kaufman knows how to get things done in Washington.

But Chávez didn't limit his lobbying to Capitol Hill. He watched out for his interests in Texas, too. Even failed presidential candidate Rudy Giuliani was drawn into the Chávez lobbying efforts. His law firm, Bracewell & Giuliani, was paid $150,000 to represent Citgo in Texas in 2005–2006 and expects another $100,000 in 2007. (In fairness, although Giuliani's firm represented Chávez, Rudy Giuliani appears to have had no personal involvement in the Citgo lobbying efforts. But presumably his name didn't hurt.)

Petróleos of Venezuela is wholly owned by the Venezuelan government. This is no secret: Citgo's own Web site confirms that Petróleos is the "state oil company of the Bolivarian Republic of Venezuela" and that "the Venezuelan State is sole stockholder under the provisions of the Constitution of the Bolivarian Republic of Venezuela." Peculiarly, though, when Kelley, Drye submitted its Lobbying Registration Form for Petrólcos, it claimed that no foreign entity held "at least 20% equitable ownership in the client."

Isn't the government of Venezuela a foreign entity?

Unfortunately, Kelley, Drye isn't the only lobbying firm that provides incomplete information on the lobbying registration forms. Other firms have done the same thing: When the Glover Park Group registered to lobby for Airbus, the French-based company, it listed its client as "Airbus Industrie and Airbus Industry North American Holdings, Inc." and provided an address in Biagnac Cedax, France, as well as one in Virginia. Yet Glover Park then denied that there was any substantial foreign interest in the client. When Sandy Berger's company registered its lobbying activities for Airbus, it too claimed that no foreign entity held more than a 20 percent interest in the company. The same held true for Glover Park when it registered to lobby for the British-based Standard Chartered Bank: its registration cited the company's London address but it also denied any major foreign interest. (Does the name Standard Chartered Bank sound familiar? It became well known in 2001 because its Dubai branch was the bank that wired money to and from the 9/11 terrorists.)

Cassidy & Associates is registered to lobby for RAO UES, the Russian power company. According to the company's Web site, "Unified Energy System of Russia was established in 1992 pursuant to Decrees of the President of the Russian Federation. . . . As of 31 December 2006, the state owned 52.68 percent of shares in RAO UES of Russia which account for 54.99 percent of issued ordinary shares." Yet, once again, the lobbying firm indicated that no foreign entity owns 20 percent or more of its client.

The purpose of the lobbying disclosure requirement is to identify any party that is trying to influence Congress and to alert the public about the issues it intends to lobby for. But the law was also designed to provide information about who owns the lobbying clients and exactly how much they're paying for the lobbying services. Special attention is given to identifying foreign entities, but lobbyists routinely provide inaccurate information, and nothing whatsoever is done to enforce the requirement. Because of that, it's often impossible to figure out who the client really is.

That's why Senators Barack Obama and John McCain introduced ethical reform legislation that would have created a Senate Office of Public Integrity to regulate and police lobbyists. With the help of Hillary Clinton—

one of only a few Democrats to oppose the sorely needed legislation—the bill was defeated in the Senate. After the lobbying scandals of last year, it seems obvious that serious reform is needed. But not according to Hillary Clinton, whose campaign is run by a team of lobbyists.

So, what's wrong with this picture? Why are we letting anti-American forces become a part of the political process?

Is it simply because we always have permitted it?

Well, then, it's time to change.

These countries obviously have no legal or constitutional right to petition our government—and they shouldn't. Many of them are oppressive regimes that don't even deserve a hearing—not to mention the advocacy of respected American lawmakers—until they change their ways.

So why do we allow them to influence the direction of our executive and legislative branch decisions? It makes no sense—particularly in the case of countries such as Venezuela, which is both hostile to the United States and recognized as a serious violator of human rights.

But it's big business all the same.

THE HUNGER FOR FOREIGN LOBBYING BUSINESS

To demonstrate the blind fervor on K Street for any new foreign lobbying business—even from the most oppressive regimes—the journalist Ken Silverstein, writing for *The Atlantic,* posed as an intermediary for a group of investors who were close to the repressive and corrupt government of the former Soviet satellite of Turkmenistan, where the former Communist Party remains the only sanctioned political party. Human rights violations are commonplace there; the State Department reports that "security officials [have] tortured, routinely beat, and used excessive force against criminal suspects, prisoners, and individuals critical of the government, particularly in detention while seeking a confession." Silverstein set out to learn whether lobbyists would decline to represent such a tyrannical country and whether they would check into his own background before discussing a lucrative partnership. To test this, he deliberately chose to pose as an agent for a country with a poor record in human rights and democratic procedures.

In his brilliant exposé, published in *Harper's,* Silverstein describes contacting two of the most powerful lobbying firms in Washington, APCO Worldwide and Cassidy & Associates. Both firms immediately responded and arranged meetings with him to discuss a possible business relationship. Their representation of prior dictators made them likely targets for the exercise: APCO had represented a former Nigerian dictator, while Cassidy had represented Equatorial Guinea, which urgently needed public relations and other representation after a Senate committee accused the Riggs Bank of money laundering for failing to report the withdrawal of $35 million by the country's longtime dictator and his family. For its services, Cassidy was initially paid $120,000 per month.

Both firms were very familiar with Turkmenistan's negative image and its history of human rights violations, but both were nevertheless eager to do business. And neither firm said it would have any problem with working for such a client.

Both firms offered the traditional services of foreign lobbyists: setting up meetings with members of Congress; arranging for a visit to the United States by government officials from Turkmenistan; creating a media campaign to change the country's image; generating op-ed pieces to highlight the importance of Turkmenistan to the United States because of its energy resources; working with think tanks to organize a conference on the energy issue; and creating an alliance with other American businesses in the region. Both firms emphasized their ability to work with both parties and their special relationships with people in Congress and federal agencies and the White House. And both bragged about their high-level former government officials, who would lend invaluable help.

APCO assembled a much more dazzling array of experts for its meeting than Cassidy did. APCO offered a former assistant secretary of state for Europe and Eurasia and a former ambassador to Kazakhstan, a former flack for the CIA and Dick Cheney, and a past staffer to Bob Dole. Cassidy offered a former public relations consultant for the John Kerry campaign and a woman who had formerly worked for Saudi Arabia. Yet Cassidy wanted twice as much money for the job as APCO did: Cassidy asked for $1.2 million a year for three years, while APCO asked for only $600,000 a year.

Neither firm raised any question about the client or the reputation of the totalitarian regime. At APCO, someone actually said, "No one is looking for perfection on democracy and human rights reforms." Really? At Cassidy, one participant even bragged about how its dictator client in Equatorial Guinea had once been named the sixth worst dictator by *Parade* magazine but had recently dropped below the top ten.

Now, that's a PR coup to be proud of!

There seems to be little, if any, objection to these foreign manipulators. And now a new breed of Washington advocates has appeared to join the lobbyists in serving the interests of foreign governments: political consultants.

SPIN DOCTORS FIND A NEW FIELD

Political consultants—with all the varied tools of their trade—are falling over themselves to claim this new niche in the Washington lobbying sphere. From their comfortable perches on K Street, these masters of spin now subtly and masterfully manipulate U.S. foreign policy by influencing not only Congress and the executive branch but the American public as well.

Suddenly in demand to orchestrate well-funded public relations campaigns on behalf of these foreign entities, this emerging breed of special-interest lobbyist use polling, media, (often phony) grassroots organizing, and carefully coordinated targeting of elite opinion leaders in their efforts to influence American foreign policy and convince the American public to support their parochial positions. Their tactics are similar to those employed in a hotly contested election campaign.

Their patrons are a new genre of profitable lobbying clients: foreign countries, foreign corporations, and even exiled foreign leaders who want to shape American public opinion in support of their sometimes questionable goals.

As the 2008 presidential election approached, many foreign interests began showing a special interest in lobbying firms close to Hillary Clinton. In fact, the line of foreign countries and corporations waiting to hire lobbyists with close ties to Hillary and Bill Clinton winds around the block on K Street, where D.C.'s top influence peddlers hold court. Many of Bill's key operatives, Hillary's closest advisers, and former Clinton administration officials are making millions signing up clients eager to buy future interests in an anticipated Hillary Clinton presidency—sometimes in direct response to a hint or two by the former president himself.

At the center of the web of companies currently in demand by foreign interests are several firms with close ties to Mark Penn, Hillary's longtime chief strategist who was forced to resign his position in early April after he was caught advising the Colombian government about how to get Congress to pass a free trade treaty that Hillary Clinton (and her labor supporters) fiercely opposed. Penn is the CEO of the British lobbying/PR giant Burson-Marsteller—a firm that is owned by WPP, another British conglomerate that has been gobbling up American lobbying firms. Last year, WPP raked in close to $70 million in U.S. lobbying fees alone, up from about $55 million in 2006. That figure, of course, does not count the enormous fees generated by Burson-Marsteller for public relations and crisis management for clients that don't have to be disclosed.

Lobbying firms in the United States might seem like an odd niche for a foreign company, but it certainly has been good business for WPP. And it must be helpful for WPP and Burson-Marsteller to tell their corporate clients—in the United States and throughout the world—of their close relationships with lawmakers and presidential candidates. Who knows when one might need a favor in the future?

In addition to Burson-Marsteller, WPP owns numerous U.S. lobbying firms, as well as the polling firm Penn, Schoen & Berland.

U.S. LOBBYING FIRMS OWNED BY BRITISH WPP

Burson-Marsteller

BKSH

Quinn Gillespie & Associates

Ogilvy Government Relations

Wexler & Walker

Public Strategies

Dewey Square

Hill & Knowlton

360 Advantage

Through its various subsidiaries, WPP is extremely well connected to the U.S. presidential campaigns and has almost all bases covered:

- Mark Penn works for Hillary Clinton.

- Howard Paster, executive vice president of WPP, joined the Clinton campaign.

- Charles Black, who headed BKSH until late March, is a senior strategist and spokesman for the McCain campaign.

- John Green of Ogilvy is an adviser to the McCain campaign.

- Howard Wolfson is a partner at Glover Park and the communications director for Hillary Clinton's campaign. (He is on a leave of absence.)

- Ken Reitz, a former CEO of Burson-Marsteller who is also associated with 360 Advantage, was a senior strategist for Fred Thompson's doomed presidential campaign.

Only Barack Obama has escaped an alliance with one of the ubiquitous WPP affiliates. And it's probably not a coincidence that he's the only presidential candidate who has refused to accept campaign contributions from lobbyists.

In the past few years, several of the related companies have signed lucrative contracts with foreign entities. It's been a lobbying gold rush. But that doesn't mean there aren't some serious potential problems.

From the start of the Clinton campaign, Mark Penn steadfastly refused to separate from his lobbying firm while working in the Clinton campaign. That's what finally got him into trouble. He was never personally paid by Hillary's campaign, but his salary at Burson-Marsteller is based on the company's performance. That's worked out fine for him. As Penn wrote in his corporate blog, "I have found that the mixture of corporate and political work is good for business."

Given the breadth of his company's representation of special interests, that might be the understatement of the year. The number of Burson-

Marsteller clients—both corporations and foreign governments—that have an interest in the next administration is staggering.

So is the potential for a serious conflict of interest. As a campaign strategist, Penn met and spoke constantly with both Clintons and with other key policy advisers. He's been in a unique position to influence what the candidate supports or opposes—not only during the campaign, but also in the Senate. And he has had ample opportunity to weigh in on issues that are vital to Burson-Marsteller's clients.

And while Hillary ultimately professed to be furious at Penn's overt lobbying while he worked for her, it could not have been a surprise. Her campaign is up to its eyeballs in lobbyists.

Take the case of the Colombian Free Trade Agreement, which triggered Penn's ouster. In late March 2007, Bill Clinton traveled to Cartagena for an eightieth-birthday tribute to the Nobel Prize winner Gabriel García Márquez. While there, he spoke to Colombian President Álvaro Uribe about the difficulties in passing the agreement. According to one high-level Colombian official who was privy to Bill Clinton's private conversations at the time, the former president urged Colombia to shift its focus from GOP legislators to Democrats (who'd taken control of Congress). Eager to help, Bill picked up the phone and called several Democratic congressmen.

Ten days later, on April 5, 2007, ColombiaProExport signed a $40,000 a month contract with the Glover Park Group. And a few weeks later, Penn's firm, Burson-Marsteller, also signed a $300,000 contract on the Colombia trade deal. Bill himself made $800,000 in speeches that he gave to pro-trade groups in Colombia.

How did the Colombians end up hiring lobbying firms with close ties to the Clintons' political operations? It's doubtful that they simply picked up the yellow pages.

Colombia wasn't the only country to hire Clinton-linked lobbyists right after a visit from the former president. On February 27, 2005, Bill Clinton gave a speech in Taiwan and had dinner with the country's president. On April 15, Glover Park was hired to lobby for the Taiwan cultural and economic minister at $25,000 a month. Before then, Taiwan had relied on Republican Bob Dole.

Others sought Clintonian heft, too. In 2007, the Pakistani government hired the Quinn Gillespie firm for a two-year stint for $1.2 million. In addition, Hill & Knowlton, yet another WPP subsidiary, was retained by the Pakistanis. Also in 2007, Burson-Marsteller, Penn, Schoen, and BKSH received a total of $250,000 for polling, lobbying, and developing a strategy for the return to power by the late former prime minister Benazir Bhutto's People's Party of Pakistan, which opposed the Musharraf government. Their mission was to influence the Bush State Department—and U.S. opinion leaders—to support Bhutto's return to power. After a year, she returned to Pakistan as a credible challenger to Musharraf. A short time after she returned, she was assassinated.

Several other countries have joined the bandwagon, ostensibly to gain access to the Clintons. The government of Turkey entered a new contract with Glover Park for $300,000, the French food services company, Sodexho, hired it for $40,000 a month, and Jordan hired it for $20,000 a month. Serbia hired Quinn Gillespie for $106,000 per month, Macedonia hired them for $30,000 a month, and the Albanian Foundation for Democracy paid $80,000 a month.

In the past few years, Penn's Burson-Marsteller lobbying affiliate, BKSH, was retained by the Dominican Republic for $25,000 a month, by Maldives for $20,000 a month, Greece and Cyprus for $15,000 each, Haiti for $100,000, and China's CNOOC Ltd. for $60,000 for a two-month contract, according to Justice Department filings.

In June 2007, Burson-Marsteller signed on with the Abu Dhabi Investment Authority, the world's largest sovereign wealth fund, for $802,250—in Bill Clinton's favorite Arab country, the UAE.

Armenia was another big contract for Burson's BKSH. According to Justice Department filings, BKSH signed a contract with one Stepan Martirosyan, a member of the Armenian community in Glendale, California, to "share information with the U.S. government, regarding the policies and actions of the government of Armenia as well as facilitate meetings for [Prime] Minister Sarkisian."

At the same time that Burson-Marsteller was lobbying for the Armenians and Mark Penn was actively involved in her presidential campaign, Hillary Clinton became one of the thirty-two Senate cosponsors of the controversial congressional resolution to declare that the Turkish killings of hundreds of thousands of Armenians from 1915 to 1923—at the end of the Ottoman Empire—was genocide.

Without a doubt, the key policy priority of the Armenian government is to get the genocide resolution passed. Although there was strong support for the Armenian resolution, it suddenly ran into tough opposition from the Turkish government, one of our most important allies in the Iraq War. (Turkey permits the United States to use its airfields, which are critical to the operation.)

Eight former secretaries of state—Democrats and Republicans—wrote to Congress urging defeat of the resolution because it would "endanger our national security interests." And three former secretaries of defense have warned that Turkey might decide that the United States can no longer use its air bases. But Hillary is still sponsoring the resolution. Wonder why?

Here's one thing to consider: the Armenia contracts paid Burson-Marsteller's subsidiary close to a half million dollars.

The money keeps flowing. What's interesting is how many times these firms—related to Mark Penn and the Clintons—have been hired by the same mix of companies. Do you see a pattern here?

While this unique mixture of lobbying and campaigning may be personally profitable for Hillary and Bill's friends, it spells increasing trouble for Hillary as her rivals attack her for accepting lobbyists' contributions—and could continue to dog her, whatever her political future.

Until the Colombia uproar, neither Hillary nor Penn seemed at all concerned about his dual roles—even though Penn had already shown questionable judgment on another trade issue.

During Bill Clinton's second term, while Penn was the president's chief political strategist—with unfettered access to the president, first lady and high-level officials—his polling firm, Penn, Schoen & Berland, contracted to lobby the Clinton administration on behalf of the Central American Bank for Economic Integration, a group operated and controlled by Guatemala, Honduras, El Salvador, Costa Rica, and Nicaragua, with Mexico, Taiwan, Argentina, and Colombia as additional shareholders. The fee was half a million dollars. Penn was the designated foreign agent listed in the handwritten Justice Department filings. (The polling firm had never before registered as either a lobbyist or a foreign agent.)

According to Penn's handwritten filings with the Justice Department, he was the only partner working on the contract that required his firm to "lobby the [Clinton] Administration" and "encourage" it to adopt a NAFTA-like trade bill for Central America as "a primary legislative priority." It's not clear whether anyone in the White House ever knew that Penn was being paid by a special interest to work on an issue that was clearly outside his polling and strategy portfolio.

Yes, you read that right: a group of foreign governments, seeking to persuade the president of the United States to adopt legislation in their economic interest, paid the president's trusted adviser to make their case in the White House.

Not surprisingly, once Clinton was gone, Penn's lobbying skills were no longer needed in the White House. Penn's handwriting indicates that his contract expired on January 1, 2001—days before Clinton left office. Burson-Marsteller ultimately bought Penn's firm, and Penn became Burson's head honcho. Now Penn oversees a vast lobbying empire.

The firm's publicly known clients are a veritable Who's Who of corporations in crisis, as well as companies and foreign governments looking for favors from Congress and the White House. The firm and its subsidiary BKSH's recent foreign clients have included:

- SpinMaster Toys, the Canadian distributor of the Chinese-manufactured toys that were coated with a chemical that disintegrated into the date rape drug GHB (the toys have since been recalled by the U.S. Product Safety Commission)

- CNOOC, the Chinese national oil company that was unsuccessful in its bid to buy the American corporation Unocal, the ninth-largest oil company in the world

- Iraq

- Greece

- Cyprus

- Liberia

- The Russian Information Office

- Taiwan

And that's not all. Among Burson-Marsteller's other U.S. clients that have been in the news recently:

- **Blackwater Group:** the hired guns in Iraq. Blackwater's CEO, Erik Prince, hired Burson's lobbying subsidiary, BKSH, to prep him for his congressional testimony—helping him to explain glibly why the civilian cowboys who work for him have been involved in 195 shooting incidents. After news reports about the controversial representation, Burson-Marsteller ran screaming from Blackwater, describing it as only a "temporary" engagement with no involvement by Penn. And the Clinton campaign affirmed its support for Penn.
- Then there was **Countrywide Financial,** the beleaguered subprime mortgage lender that's reportedly under federal investigation for securities fraud regarding its subprime mortgages. Countrywide had the largest portfolio of subprime mortgages, and by the end of 2007 almost one third of them were in default. Facing disaster, the company was recently rescued by Bank of America—after its CEO, Angelo Mozilo, walked off with more than $120 million in compensation.
- **Microsoft** is a longtime client.
- **Exelon Corporation** paid Burson-Marsteller more than $230,000 fees related to advocating a nuclear power plant in New Jersey.
- **Philip Morris,** now renamed Altria, is a longtime client of Burson.

These and other Burson-Marsteller clients could be looking for something from Congress in the future. And they will likely be looking for something from the next president and new administration.

Penn isn't the only top Clinton aide who's either a lobbyist or tied to a lobbying firm. Howard Wolfson, her communications director, is a partner in Glover Park. He's got a good connection to the office of Speaker Nancy Pelosi—his wife, also a former Glover Park alum, is Pelosi's chief of staff. And Hillary's political director, Harold Ickes, has his own lobbying firm, Ickes and Enright, which specializes in representing New York entities that are looking for earmarks, such as the Abyssinian Baptist Church in Harlem, which received a more than a million dollars in Clinton earmarks. Calvin Butts, the pastor of the church, publicly endorsed Hillary Clinton. According to opensecrets.org, Ickes is also well paid by the Alliance for Quality Nursing Home Care, a coalition of for-profit nursing homes that fight government regulation and standards of care. The group was indicted in 2004 for making illegal campaign contributions in Texas. And Howard Paster, Bill Clinton's former White House lobbyist, currently an executive at WPP, joined the Clinton campaign in 2008.

It's no wonder that Hillary refused to accept John Edwards's challenge to promise to keep lobbyists out of her administration if she becomes president. She can't; she's surrounded by them.

Here's a simple rule: political consultants should not be straddling the campaigns of presidential candidates and lobbying firms representing domestic and foreign clients.

That goes for John McCain's consultants, too.

THE McCAIN LOBBYISTS

As already mentioned, Charlie Black, a BKSH partner until Apil 2008, is working for the McCain campaign. Unlike his old boss, Mark Penn, Black has now completely separated himself from his lobbying firm, BKSH. But before that, and while he was working on the McCain campaign, BKSH represented the foreign clients of Armenia, Greece, Cyprus, Pakistan, and Colombia, as well as General Electric, AT&T, Occidental Petroleum, Cummins, GlaxoSmithKline, General Motors, Bristol-Myers Squibb, Lockheed Martin, JP Morgan Chase, United Technologies, and Virgin Atlantic.

John Green, another McCain campaign adviser, recently took a leave of absence from the Loeffler Group, a lobbying firm that represents Airbus, Saudi Arabia, Toyota, Yahama, UST, and the Pharmaceutical Manufacturers of America. Last year, over a six-month period, the Saudi account paid more than $2.5 million. But Tom Loeffler is still working the halls of Congress and helping out McCain.

Green did the right thing; other lobbyists in the campaign should follow suit.

Again, it's puzzling that a man like John McCain, who has always railed against lobbyists and special interests, would surround himself with lobby-ists at the highest level of his campaign. It's time for them to make a choice: step away from their lobbyist affiliations or from John McCain's campaign.

HOW LOBBYISTS FOR FOREIGNERS WORK

When a foreign government hires a lobbying firm, it's often seeking to prod Congress and the federal government to pass a specific measure—such as a free trade bill—to benefit its region or trying to gain approval of a foreign investment in a U.S. company (one of the fastest-growing job openings for well-connected lobbyists). More and more, however, foreign governments are hiring Washington insiders to improve their images, to attract foreign aid and support, and to attract American investors.

In most cases, lobbyists for foreign entities aren't paid simply to moni-tor congressional action and present the client's point of view to relevant staff, committees, and members. Their clients want a lot more than that.

It used to be enough for top lobbyists to have a giant Rolodex full of use-ful contacts in both Congress and the executive branch who could help out their clients.

Not anymore. The new political consultant-lobbyists offer much more. In effect, what they often promise is to try to move the policies of the U.S. government to the position sought by the foreign entity. So if a group of Central American countries is interested in a NAFTA-like trade agreement, for instance, the lobbyist tries to convince high-level decision makers to adopt that position. Often, he or she tries to accomplish this by creating pressure from the media and the public to support the group's goals. Some-times, all that's needed is to mute criticism of its plans.

The classic image of a special-interest lobbyist is that of a cigar-smoking backroom wheeler-dealer, wining and dining a member of Congress to pave the way for a special appropriation for a client or to stop a bill that might have a negative impact on a corporation.

But those uncomplicated days are over. In the first place, recent lobbying reforms now prohibit lobbyists from buying meals for congressmen, so business isn't done over meals anymore. But that's only a small part of the fundamental changes that have evolved in today's sophisticated lobbying campaigns for foreign countries and foreign corporations.

The new lobbying contracts aren't necessarily limited to a specific issue or a specific bill. Instead, foreign clients—from Dubai to Pakistan—hire lobbying firms to run long-term public relations campaigns to improve their images with Congress, the media, and the American public.

Whenever a person or firm becomes an agent of a foreign government, a registration form must be filed with the Department of Justice in Washington. Such forms offer an inside view of just how things are done; they are probably the only way to ascertain what the lobbyists are really up to. Lobbying disclosure forms for domestic clients offer the barest minimum of information, but when a lobbyist represents a foreign country or company, the filing requirements by the U.S. Department of Justice Office of Foreign Agent Registrations are quite stringent—and failure to comply can, at least in theory, trigger criminal penalties.

Is there any rational reason that we allow American lobbying firms to intervene in the American political process on behalf of foreign interests?

The practice has been going on for a long time. Concerns about it were first raised in 1938, when Congress, concerned about evidence of Nazi propaganda efforts, passed the Foreign Agents Registration Act (FARA), which established strict registration and reporting requirements for any persons or businesses paid by a foreign government, political party, or business to provide lobbying or public relations services in the United States. Since then, all contracts must be filed with the Justice Department; today, they're available for review online at www.usdoj.gov/criminal/fara.

FARA had its origins in the 1930s, when the German munitions company I. G. Farben retained the American public relations guru Ivy Ludbetter Lee for $25,000 a month—ostensibly to advise the firm on potential boycott issues but in fact to help improve the Nazi government's image in the United States. Lee was a prominent adviser to John D. Rockefeller who was credited with changing the oil magnate's image from a "corporate monster into a benevolent old philanthropist." But the disclosure of his secret representation of the Nazis outraged America, and he eventually canceled the contract. Soon afterward, Congress enacted FARA, which requires any person or entity acting on behalf of a foreign country, company, or political party to register and disclose the terms of the engagement, the services to be provided, and the amount to be paid. The U.S. Department of Justice is charged with ensuring compliance of the act.

It was a worthy piece of legislation. But in the years since 1938, there have been very few enforcement actions—and most lobbyists know they have little to fear from FARA. The foreign propagandist business is alive and flourishing; just take a look at the list of persons and firms that have registered with the Department of Justice over the years.

We need much stricter regulation and supervision of all lobbyists—and we need to explore ways to limit lobbying for foreign entities. Whatever becomes of them in the 2008 presidential race, let's hope that John McCain, Barack Obama, and Hillary Clinton will all help lead the charge.

The Case of the Ivory Coast

. . . U.S. State Department condemns human rights abuses in the Ivory Coast, where death squads, rigged elections, and censorship of the press are a part of life . . . Ivory Coast hires former Clinton White House counsel Jack Quinn as lobbyist and image maker at $512,000 for six months to convince the United States and its allies to support the questionable incumbent regime.

When the government of the strife-ridden African nation République Côte d'Ivoire sought international backing for its not exactly democratically elected president, Laurent Gbagbo, it hired Jack Quinn of Quinn Gillespie & Associates, the D.C. lobbying firm headed by the mega power brokers Jack Quinn, a former counsel to President Clinton, and Ed Gillespie, a former chairman of the Republican Party and counselor to President Bush. Remember Jack? He's the one who brokered Bill Clinton's last-minute pardon of Marc Rich, the fugitive who had renounced his U.S. citizenship after his indictment for selling oil to Saddam Hussein during the oil embargo.

The Ivory Coast's goal in hiring Quinn Gillespie was to package and sell Gbagbo as a prodemocracy leader and to convince the United States and its allies to support his questionable regime.

This was not to be done by diplomacy. Rather, it was to be accomplished through the efforts of Quinn and Gillespie's high-profile and expensive lobbying firm to hype the media and government officials about the controversial leader's record and intentions.

The most important reason for hiring Quinn was to keep Gbagbo in office in the face of claims that his election had been rigged. Quinn's primary task was to use his influence with the media and government officials to spin Gbagbo's questionable efforts at maintaining democracy, highlight his calls for "free" elections, and rebut negative news articles about the president, his government, and his wife.

That was a tall order. Gbagbo is no knight in shining armor. Despite his call for ostensibly "free" elections, Gbagbo's government bears little resemblance to democracy. In 2005, a "confidential" U.N. report found that Gbagbo's wife, Simone Gbagbo, had directed a "death squad responsible for killing rivals of her husband's government." The first lady's involvement had been widely reported for several years, but it wasn't until the report was about to be leaked to the American press that Gbagbo sought the help of the American lobbyists. (Gbagbo, of course, denies any involvement in the killings by either him or his wife, or even by any of his supporters.)

The Ivory Coast's death squads have been around for a while. According to an earlier U.N. report, which compared the killings in the Ivory Coast with genocide in Rwanda, the death squads were "quite well organized," working from "lists of people to execute." As one press report noted, "Their victims have included General Robert Guei, the former military ruler, and 18 members of his family; Emile Tehe, leader of a small opposition party; several ethnically northern business leaders, including the owner of the main supermarket chain; a Muslim cleric; and Yerefe Kamara, a popular comedian with a weekly television show."

In its most recent report on human rights in the Ivory Coast, the State Department noted there were continued "credible reports of numerous cases in which the use of excessive force by security forces resulted in deaths. Such cases often occurred when security forces apprehended suspects or tried to extort money from taxi drivers and merchants. For example, the UN reports that on January 2, 2006, several summary executions were committed by security forces and Jeunes Patriotes (Young Patriots), a youth group with close ties to the ruling FPI Party." In the Ivory Coast, the phrase "security forces" often refers to government police officers, who routinely kill innocent people.

The 2006 U.N. report also documented the lack of a free press, the continued violence toward the opposition, and the absence of free elections. Unlike in previous years, it noted, there had been no new reports of death squads. Some progress. And the latest report on 2007 indicated continued state terrorism towards its citizens: "Security forces continued to commit extrajudicial killings with impunity, and pro-government militia groups were responsible for the harassment, killings, and disappearances. These crimes often went unreported or underreported due to fear of reprisals."

There is no freedom of the press in the Ivory Coast. The government, which abhors unflattering media stories, is unfriendly to the local press and has frequently imposed jail sentences on journalists who write favorably about the opposition. One French reporter who was investigating corruption disappeared and has never been found.

The government has also been accused of inciting riots and hatred. In 2006, Gbagbo's supporters rioted in response to state radio "hate messages" that called them into the streets and destroyed $3.6 million of U.N. peacekeepers' property and equipment. U.N. Secretary General Kofi Annan sent the regime a bill, but he probably never got paid.

These are not nice folks. So why do we permit them to circumvent diplomatic channels and hire American advocates to take their case directly to the press, the American people, and the federal government?

The only Americans who benefit from this practice are the highly paid lobbyists themselves, many of whom will take business from anyone with a checkbook.

Take Quinn Gillespie & Associates, for example. According to the terms of their $510,000, six-month contract, Ivory Coast president Laurent Gbagbo wanted help in "strategic planning." His country was in the midst of a civil war, and Gbagbo wanted U.S. assistance in securing international backing for his position against the rebels. He also wanted major help in improving his tarnished image. To do that, half a million dollars of government money was a small price to pay.

Gbagbo's 2000 election was described by the State Department as "marred by violence and significant irregularities," including the exclusion of two major political parties. In 2002, a failed coup attempt resulted in a violent and continuous civil war and an actual physical division of the country. Rebel forces successfully seized control of the northern cocoa-producing region. Although Gbagbo's term expired in 2005, no election was held because of the continued conflict in the region. Eventually, the United Nations supported the continuation of his regime until elections are feasible—a decision no doubt influenced by Quinn's successful propaganda efforts. (Elections are now planned for sometime in 2008.)

Jack Quinn was the principal lobbyist on the Ivory Coast account, assisted by four other lobbyists and several consultants. They definitely had their work cut out for them. Here's what the Quinn Gillespie contract called for:

> PUBLIC IMAGE: The parties to this agreement recognize that Côte d'Ivoire is a nation at war and faces many internal and external challenges. The purpose of this agreement is to engage QGA to help to defend Côte d'Ivoire's socio-economic, political, and cultural interests, to improve Côte d'Ivoire and President Laurent Gbagbo's public image and to identify and assist in recruiting political, diplomatic, and economic partners to assist in Cote d' Ivoire's peaceful development.

Assist in recruiting diplomatic partners? Is that Washington-speak for trying to find countries to support the Ivory Coast president's questionable side in the war? Is this an appropriate role for U.S. lobbyists?

The agreement, filed with the U.S. Department of Justice, specifically defines the role to be played by Jack Quinn and his team:

"LOBBYING"

Strategy: QGA will use its commercially reasonable efforts to formulate strategies with the goals of:

- increasing the pressure on the international community to disarm the rebels and laying the groundwork for free and democratic elections in 2005.
- improving the image of the client and its president in the U.S. media and among the general public, and attracting international economic aid investment to the client.

Action:

- Organize a U.S. visit by President Laurent Gbagbo to Washington D.C., and potentially to other U.S. cities.

- arrange meetings with key U.S. policy makers; lobby for U.S. government support of the actions of the Gbagbo government and President Laurent Gbagbo.

- arrange meetings with the U.S. media to establish a "Client News Bureau" at QGA to monitor American media (and, as possible, international) and internet reports and formulate responses to those reports as necessary.

- organize visits by U.S. public figures.

- identify potential allies of the Gbagbo government with a view toward persuading them to support the Gbagbo government on specific issues of importance, and underscore and publicize President Laurent Gbagbo's determination to hold free and fair elections.

- Publicize the results of any research related to events in the Cote d'Ivoire since 2001 to appropriate political, diplomatic, media and other audiences.

For the most part, Quinn Gillespie serviced the client by setting up meetings with State Department, National Security Council, and Trade Office officials and members of Congress. Most of the activities involved calling reporters at *The New York Times, The Washington Post, The New Republic,* Voice of America, and various other media outlets. Here's how Quinn Gillespie reported to the Department of Justice on its work for the Ivory Coast and its president from January through June 2005:

During the six-month reporting period, the contacts listed below were made in support of the foreign principal's representation of the République de Côte d'Ivoire. These contacts were all consistent with the terms contained in the retainer agreement on file with the FARA Registration Unit as an attachment to the appropriate Exhibit B of the Registration Statement. Meetings consisted of discussions regarding U.S. strategic interests in the République de Côte d'Ivoire, reconsideration of eligibility for the African Growth and Opportunity Act, peace negotiations, and implementation of the Disarmament, Demobilization and Reinsertion agreement.

2/2/05   Call to Colum Lynch, *The Washington Post*
2/2/05   Call to Kate Ackely, *Roll Call*

2/2/05   Meeting request to Walarigaton Coulibaly, Grant Godfrey, and Maria Zometsky, National Democratic Institute

2/2/05   Meeting request to Florizelle Liser, Assistant U.S.T.R. Africa

2/2/05   Meeting request to Tom Woods, Deputy Secretary of African Affairs, U.S. Department of State

2/2/05   Meeting request to Cindy Courville, Special Assistant to the President and Senior Director for African Affairs, National Security Council

2/3/05   Meeting with Walarigaton Coulibaly, Program Assistant; Grant Godfrey, Program Officer, Marla Zometsky, Program Officer; National Democratic Institute

2/4/05   Call to Silvia Aloisi, Reuters

2/14/05 Meeting with Florizelle Liser, Assistant, U.S.T.R. Africa

2/22/05 Meeting with Tom Woods, Deputy Secretary of African Affairs, U.S. Department of State

2/23/05 Meeting with Cindy Courville, Special Assistant to the President and Senior Director for African Affairs, National Security Council

3/19/05 Meeting with Ambassador Aubrey Hooks, U.S. Ambassador to Côte d'Ivoire, Abidjan Embassy

3/28/05 Meeting with Polly Trottenberg, Legislative Director, Senator Charles Schumer, U.S. Senate

3/29/05 Meeting with Jeremy Kahn, Reporter, *The New Republic*

4/7/05   Meeting with Andy Olson, Foreign Affairs Legislative Assistant, Senator Bill Frist, U.S. Senate

4/11/05 Meeting with Michael Phelan, African Affairs Staffer, Senator Richard Lugar, U.S. Senate on Foreign Relations Committee

4/11/05 Call with Jeremy Kahn, Reporter, *The New Republic*

4/11/05 Email—Lydia Polgreen, Reporter, *The New York Times*

4/15/05 Call with Jeremy Kahn, Reporter, *The New Republic*

4/18/05 Call with Gus Constantine, Reporter, *The Washington Times*

4/18/05 Call with Jennifer Ludden, Reporter, National Public Radio

4/18/05 Call with Pamela Constable, Africa Desk Editor, *The Washington Post*

4/18/05 Call with Dinesh Mahtani, Reporter, *Financial Times* and *The Economist*

4/22/05	Call with Gus Constantine, Reporter, *The Washington Times*
4/22/05	Call with Lydia Polgreen, Reporter, *The New York Times*
4/25/05	Call with Gus Constantine, Reporter, *The Washington Times*
4/27/05	Faxed letter to Gus Constantine, Reporter, *The Washington Times*
4/28/05	Email—Richard Kaminski, Country Officer (Cote d'Ivoire), U.S. Department of State
4/28/05	Email—Richard Kaminski, Country Officer (Cote d'Ivoire), U.S. State Department
5/2/05	Faxed letter to Tom Woods, Deputy Secretary of African Affairs, U.S. Department of State
5/3/05	Phone call with Jennifer Ludden, Reporter, National Public Radio
5/3/05	Phone call with Pamela Constable, Africa Desk Editor, *The Washington Post*
5/4/05	Phone call with Barbara Schoetzau, UN Bureau Chief, Voice of America
5/4/05	Phone call with Peter Heinlein, UN Correspondent, Voice of America
5/4/05	Email—Nico Colombant, Abidjan Correspondent, Voice of America
5/4/05	Email—Damian Fowler, Abidjan Correspondent, BBC News
5/10/05	Voicemail—Mark Silva, International News Correspondent, *The Chicago Tribune*
5/10/05	Voicemail—Gwen Dillard, VOA Africa Division Director, Voice of America
5/10/05	Phone call with Idrissa Dia, La Voie de L'Amerique Program Director, Voice of America
5/10/05	Phone call with Pamela Constable, Africa Desk Editor, *The Washington Post*
5/11/05	Phone Call with Jeremy Kahn, Journalist, *The New Republic*
5/10/05	Voicemail—Gus Constantine, Journalist, *The Washington Times*

As it happens, Quinn Gillespie was especially punctilious about its filings; as a result, they offer a rare window into how such contracts with foreign governments work, and the services the lobbyists provide. But Quinn Gillespie wasn't the only recipient of the Ivory Coast's largesse. At the same time, the beleagured country contracted to pay another $550,000 per year for lobbying services—this time to the Whitaker Group, a firm run by Rosa Whitaker, a former assistant U.S. trade representative to Africa under both the Clinton and Bush administrations and an aide to Congressman Charles Rangel. The Whitaker Group has renewed its contract every year and currently represents the government on trade issues.

And the Ivory Coast—like Hugo Chávez, like so many other foreign countries and corporations—just keeps doing business as usual, even as it avails itself of the services of all-too-willing American lobbyists to carry its water.

THE DUBAI-ING OF AMERICA

An authoritarian, anti-Semitic, antiwoman, antiworker nation is masquerading as a modern, sophisticated, cool new destination for tourists, while using its vast petrowealth to buy up large stakes in American companies.

Welcome to Dubai.

It's become almost impossible to open a travel magazine or the business page of any newspaper without seeing a myriad of carefully planted articles extolling the virtues of the tiny Arab state of Dubai.

Suddenly, Dubai is everywhere! The nation is spending billions to buy American businesses and stakes in major U.S. corporations. During the past few years, Dubai has been in acquisition overdrive, investing in American companies like Nasdaq (20 percent stake) and DaimlerChrysler (2 percent stake); strategically placed New York landmarks like the Essex House Hotel (now the Jumeirah Essex House) on Central Park, the Knickerbocker Hotel on Times Square, and the Helmsley Building astride Park Avenue; the Barneys and Loehmann's clothing retailers; and more than a billion dollars' worth of U.S. real estate. It even bought the *Queen Elizabeth 2* ocean liner and plans to turn it into a floating hotel in Dubai. Recently, it entered the gambling business by putting $5 million into the MGM Mirage in Las Vegas. And Dubai's getting into the defense business, too: several years ago, it bought Doncasters, a British company operating plants in Connecticut and Georgia that make precision parts used in engines for military aircraft and tanks. Doncasters has since purchased several aircraft-related U.S. companies.

So Dubai is gobbling up American businesses in lots of different sectors at a record speed. And part of its American acquisition agenda is to market itself as an attractive, modern country.

During the past few years, there's been a concerted international PR campaign to promote Dubai as a tolerant new mecca of Middle East moderation and amazing economic growth. And it's working. Halliburton, the largest military contractor in Iraq, is moving its headquarters from Houston to Dubai; the Louvre, the most famous museum in the world, is opening a branch in the emirate. Tourists are flocking to Dubai's luxurious hotels and entertainment parks, which include indoor skiing and man-made islands in the shape of palm trees.

One of the nation's biggest tourist attractions is the Dubai World Cup, a horse race that attracts more than 60,000 tourists each year. Established by the emir of Dubai, Sheikh Mohammed bin Rashid al-Maktoum, the cup attracts some of the best Thoroughbred horses in the world. This year, the sheikh provided the $21 million in prize money. Dubai takes the event seriously: several years ago, when torrential rains flooded the track with more than three feet of water, government military helicopters were dispatched to fly over the track for several days until the water had evaporated from the heat of the helicopters, and the race went forward.

It must be nice to have such control over events.

But don't be fooled. Dubai, which is one of the seven princedoms of the oil-rich United Arab Emirates (UAE), is anything but tolerant and progressive.

To put it bluntly: it doesn't like Jews. So don't try to go to the Dubai World Cup if you're Jewish. It won't let you in.

In fact, Dubai, like the rest of the UAE, is blatantly anti-Semitic. It bars Israeli citizens from setting foot in the country. People from other nations whose passport has a stamps indicating they've even visited Israel must notify Dubai immigration authorities of the stamp before entering. Now, why would the country want that information?

Dubai is also actively involved in the Arab boycott of Israel: it bans all products made in Israel, even ones with *parts* made in Israel. Make no mistake about it: this is a very serious issue for it.

But Sheikh Mohammed bin Rashid al-Maktoum understands the value of using prominent Americans to legitimize his country and burnish its image in the American media. And he's gone out of his way to make friends with prestigious Americans who can subtly endorse Dubai.

That's why former presidents George H. W. Bush and Bill Clinton have been the objects of Dubai largesse. Their Dubai friends have given millions to each of their presidential libraries. And Bill Clinton has raked in more than $1.2 million for several speeches that he's given in Dubai and the UAE.

Dubai's PR machine went into high gear after 9/11—in part to distract attention from the extensive use the terrorists made of the emirate. More than half of the 9/11 hijackers traveled to the United States via Dubai. Even more damning, the 9/11 Commission noted that $234,500 of the $300,000 wired to the hijackers and plot leaders in America came via Dubai banks—notably the Standard Chartered Bank, in which the Dubai government owns a stake. Some of the money was used to buy the terrorists' airline tickets on 9/11, including Mohammed Atta's ticket for the plane he crashed into the World Trade Center.

So Dubai's image was in bad need of rehabilitation after 9/11. In response, the sheikh began reaching out to high-profile Americans.

BILL CLINTON, YUCAIPA, AND THE EMIR

Just four months after 9/11, Dubai's newest best friend began his public association with the country. In January 2002, Bill Clinton gave his first speech in Dubai—for the princely sum of $300,000. He's been trying to legitimize the country ever since.

Clinton was the rainmaker who introduced the emir to his friend and employer, Ron Burkle, the owner of the Yucaipa Companies and a major fund-raiser for Bill and Hillary.

And last year, Yucaipa, Clinton, and the emir formed a new company for their joint ventures. Yes, that's right: former president Bill Clinton, the husband of a sitting U.S. senator and major presidential candidate, is apparently one of only three investors in what can only be described as a quasi-sovereign wealth fund. Clinton's interest is in a business funded by a country that blatantly discriminates against women, abuses workers in violation of international law, outlaws unions, deports strikers, and bans Israelis and their products from ever entering the country.

As of today, there is no sign of what the Dubai/Clinton fund has invested in. The Clintons won't disclose anything about it.

Senator Hillary Clinton has publicly criticized sovereign wealth funds—the enormous funds run by foreign governments with little or no controls. Commenting on the foreign investments in Citibank—such as the $7.5 million outlay by Abu Dhabi—she told *The Wall Street Journal* that this was "a source of concern" and that such foreign funds "lack transparency" and could be used by foreign governments as "instruments of foreign policy."

Helloooooo! Has Hillary noticed where those large deposits into her checking account come from? And does she recognize that, as a U.S. senator, she has been ensnared by her husband in a huge potential conflict of interest—exacerbated by her own lack of transparency?

The Clintons have refused to reveal how much the former president pocketed for setting up this deal—except to report on Hillary's Senate disclosure form that it was "more than $1,000."

Indeed: according to *San Francisco Examiner* columnist P. J. Corkery, Bill Clinton makes $10 million a year from Yucaipa.

QUESTION: Is it at all appropriate for the spouse of a senator who is also a leading presidential candidate to be in business with a foreign leader who often seeks favors from the U.S. government and whose economic and national security interests may be inapposite to ours?

ANSWER: NO!

The potential conflicts are obvious. Dubai frequently needs favors from our federal government that may not be in the best interests of American workers, business, or government policies. The UAE's oil interests may be in conflict with our energy and national security policies. And the possibility of a disguised—and illegal—backdoor campaign contribution is always there.

That's why Senator Clinton needs to release her tax returns for the last six years, so voters can see who is paying her husband—and how much he's getting from foreign governments and other interests.

Those issues may seem obvious to us. But apparently they didn't concern Bill and Hillary enough to keep them away from the deal. Then again, they've both proven to be very good at taking the high road in speeches—while taking the low road in their own conduct.

Throughout her campaign, Hillary Clinton has repeatedly highlighted her ardent feminism, her lifelong advocacy of workers' rights, her consistent support for unions, and her love of Israel.

But those principles can go right out the window if there's money involved. When it comes to lining their pockets, the Clintons have a double standard. While Hillary chastises American corporations and employers for layoffs and opposition to greater union organizing rights, Bill pockets big bucks—which presumably end up in his joint accounts with Hillary—to legitimize and promote an Arab state that is anti-Semitic, antiworker, antiunion, and antiwoman.

Even as the Clintons have been making millions from Dubai, the average worker in the Dubai and the UAE construction industry makes about $177 per month—not enough to support a family. According to the State Department, 98 percent of the workforce in the UAE is made up of foreigners, whom Human Rights Watch described as "indentured servants, with no right to form unions or hold strikes." About 20 percent of them work in the Dubai construction industry. Most of these workers are illiterate and were obliged to pay huge fees (usually by taking loans from their future employers) to get the job. It is routine practice in Dubai for employers to withhold paychecks for several months and to hold the workers' passports as "security."

Here are the other conditions that prevail in Dubai:

There is no minimum wage.

There is no right to organize for collective bargaining—for foreign workers *or* domestic workers.

There is no right to strike. Those who dare are either deported or banned from working for a year.

There is no right to move freely from job to job—unless the current employer agrees to provide a letter of "no objection" or the worker leaves the country for six months.

Workers' safety is not an important matter; there are only eighty inspectors to monitor more than 250,000 employers.

The standard workweek is six days. The workday is eight hours, but employers frequently require overtime—without extra pay. Workers labor in 104-degree temperatures in the summer with a only a two-and-a-half-hour break in the hottest, most punishing hours of the day—a break recently cut down from four and a half hours.

Many of the lowest-skilled workers live in horrible conditions. The U.S. State Department report on human rights in the UAE notes that:

> low-skilled employees were often provided with substandard living conditions, including overcrowded apartments or lodging in unsafe and unhygienic "labor camps," often lacking electricity, potable water, and adequate cooking and bathing facilities. Some low-paid workers did not receive these benefits, even if stipulated in their contracts.

While Bill collects checks from antiworker Dubai, Hillary righteously lectures about workers' rights. Last year, she spoke at the convention of the Communications Workers of America, urging its members to contact Republican senators about prounion legislation:

> Let them know this is a voting issue; this goes to the real heart of whether we're going to be a country that stands on a principle that every person should have the right to join a union, to be part of a bargaining unit that will stand up for your income.

Hillary doesn't have the same interest in the workers whose employers enrich the Clintons: she apparently has no objection to the Dubai dollars or Dubai's disgraceful treatment of workers.

Our own government has recognized the severity of the abuses in Dubai: "Since 1995 the country has been suspended from the U.S. Overseas Private Investment Corporation (OPIC) insurance programs because of the government's noncompliance with internationally recognized worker rights standards."

But that's no big deal for the Clintons.

It's not just Bill's $1.2 million in speaking fees from Dubai that have enriched the Clintons. And it's not just the million-dollar contribution the emir of Dubai made to the Clinton Presidential Library or Dubai's financial commitment to Bill Clinton's charitable foundation that has endeared the Islamic monarchy to them.

It's much more than that: Bill Clinton was personally responsible for delivering the ruler of Dubai and prime minister of the UAE, Sheikh Mohammed bin Rashid al-Maktoum, to a partnership with Ron Burkle's Yucaipa Companies.

Given that the sheikh is one of the richest men in the world, that deal was worth a fortune. Ron Burkle is understandably grateful.

And the emir is happy, too. Can you blame him? He's a business partner with the former president of the United States who is also the husband of a U.S. senator.

Lately, at long last, there have been some signs that political concerns may be giving Bill Clinton second thoughts. *The Wall Street Journal* recently reported that Clinton was negotiating to sever himself from the Dubai fund in order to avoid criticism if Hillary should become the Democratic nominee.

Clinton purportedly wanted $20 million to go away. Not a bad fee for an introduction. But don't jump to conclusions: as of this writing, there's been no announcement that Bill's gone his own way. And given the faltering state of Hillary's campaign, the emir and the former president may well keep up their cozy relationship.

But Bill isn't alone in legitimizing Dubai. Other Clinton pals—including disgraced former national security adviser Sandy Berger, former secretary of state Madeleine Albright, and Al and Tipper Gore—have attended highly publicized events there. Former senator George Mitchell publicly compliments the country. And former House minority leader Richard Gephardt and former congressman Thomas Downey have registered to lobby for Dubai's interest. William Cohen, Clinton's secretary of defense, organized a dinner for opinion leaders to meet the sheikh.

On the Republican side, former senator Bob Dole joined the nation's lobbying team, and Bush 41 chief of staff John Sununu, the president's brother Neal Bush, and Rudy Giuliani have all participated in high-profile conferences in Dubai.

Everyone loves Dubai!

And as the country's commercial presence in the United States continues to grow, Dubai needs help in Washington. So the emirate and the UAE have hired a gaggle of lobbyists to watch out for their various interests. The Glover Park Group—the home of Hillary Clinton spokesman Howard

Wolfson, former President Clinton press secretary Joe Lockhart, and numerous Clinton White House staff, as you'll recall—lobbies for numerous Dubai interests. And the megalobbying and law firm DLA Piper, whose employees have contributed more to Hillary Clinton than to any other candidate, has represented the sheikh. George Mitchell and Dick Gephardt make their homes at DLA Piper, which represents Dubai and the sheikh. DLA Piper likes Dubai so much, it has even opened an office there!

The lobbyists watch out for Dubai, making sure that there's no problem with its interests. Remember when Dubai wanted to buy a company that would control U.S. ports in a number of major cities? Many members of Congress—including Hillary Clinton!—loudly opposed the deal. Of course, she never mentioned that her husband was working with Dubai. Word leaked out that Bill had been advising Dubai on how to handle the crisis, though, and he had recommended his favorite lobbying firm, Glover Park. At first Joe Lockhart denied that his firm had been hired by Dubai. But then, shortly thereafter, Glover Park was retained by a Los Angeles law firm that handles U.S. real estate deals for Dubai. With the law firm and not Dubai named as the client, it was harder to trace the Dubai dollars. And the law partner in charge? Raj Tanded, the brother of Hillary Clinton's longtime policy adviser.

What a coincidence!

Now Glover Park represents Dubai-owned Doncasters and has also represented Dubai Aerospace in the acquisition of Landmark Aviation, as well as several companies in which Dubai has a stake, namely Airbus and Standard Chartered:

THE GLOVER PARK GROUP: DUBAI-RELATED CLIENTS

Client	Amount Paid
Doncasters	$200,000
Standard Chartered Bank	400,000
Airbus	620,000
Dubai Aerospace	250,000
Total	$1,470,000

Dubai also hired the Clintons' pal Jack Quinn's firm to help out on the Landmark Aviation deal and on the Airbus contract:

QUINN GILLESPIE & ASSOCIATES: DUBAI-RELATED CLIENTS

Client	Amount Paid
Dubai Aerospace	$240,000
Airbus	360,000
Total	$600,000

But Dubai's biggest lobbying dollars were spent trying to get rid of an embarrassing lawsuit—one that accused the emir, his brother, the minister of interior and culture, and other ministers of Dubai of abducting and enslaving thousands of young boys to train as camel jockeys.

THE EMIR, HIS BROTHER, THE CAMEL JOCKEYS, AND THE LAWSUITS

In September 2006, Sheikh Mohammed made a quick trip to Kentucky, where he dropped $20 million in one day buying Thoroughbreds. As he was about to board his plane, he was served with a lawsuit filed in Miami, Florida, accusing the emir and his family and political allies of systematically kidnapping and abusing ten thousand young boys. The complaint alleged that "boys as young as two years old were stolen from their parents, trafficked to foreign land and put under the watch of brutal overseers in camel camps throughout the region."

As NBC News reported, the "U.S. State Department has condemned the practice of using young boys as camel jockeys in the Gulf states, including the UAE. In the State Department's Trafficking in Persons Report last year, for example, it said that 'thousands of children, some as young as three or four years of age, are trafficked from Bangladesh, Pakistan and countries in East Africa, and sold into slavery to serve as camel jockeys. These children live in an oppressive environment and endure harsh living conditions.' "

The suit was filed in Miami, the plaintiffs asserted, because the sheikh holds millions of dollars in assets and properties in Miami.

One can imagine how upset Sheikh Mohammed was when he was served with the papers. After carefully crafting his own and his country's image in the United States and around the world as a modern monarch, he was suddenly described as a backward barbarian who abused small boys.

Dubai insisted that it stopped using camel jockeys in 2005. But that didn't solve the sheikh's problem: he had to get rid of the lawsuit.

The sheikh went into high gear and assembled a damage control team. DLA Piper was hired to help with the litigation and to lobby the Bush administration to intervene in the litigation and ask the court for a dismissal. According to filings with the Justice Department, DLA Piper represented the sheikh and others:

> DLA Piper US LLP will represent Sheikh Mohammed Bin Rashid Al Maktoum, Prime Minister and Vice President of the United Arab Emirates; Sheikh Hamdan Bin Rashid Al Maktoum, Minister of Finance and Industry of the United Arab Emirates; and The Executive Office (Dubai) in connection with the defense of the lawsuit entitled Mother Doe I et al. v. Sheikh Mohammed Bin Rashid Al Maktoum, et al., and in connection with government affairs services related to the defense of the litigation.

The law firm's filings dramatically document the full-court press that Dubai put on the State Department, National Security Council, and other senior government officials to convince them to file a "statement of interest" with the court that would urge the Florida court to dismiss the lawsuit. DLA Piper lawyers and lobbyists deluged Jonathan Schwartz, the deputy State Department legal adviser, with more than twenty phone calls and numerous meetings. Elliott Abrams, the deputy national security adviser, was called frequently and met several times with the sheikh's representatives. Calls were made to Secretary of State Condoleezza Rice, and calls and meetings were held with Senators Hatch, Pryor, Nelson, Clinton, and others. The meeting with Clinton was arranged by two DLA Piper lobbyists who are bundlers for Hillary Clinton.

No stone was left unturned.

What does it say about how Washington works that high-level officials in the State Department and National Security Council would spend so much of their time with lobbyists over a private lawsuit involving the quasi-dictator of a small country?

Is this how they should be spending their time? All this to get a "statement of interest" by the United States? Who cares if the sheikh is sued? Let him go to court just like everyone else who is sued within our borders.

And should senators really be getting involved in meetings to discuss this not very important matter? Especially a senator whose husband is a partner with the defendant?

DLA Piper was reportedly paid $3.7 million for its work. The firm sub-contracted with the lobbying firm of Johnson, Madigan for $800,000. That firm worked to get the State Department to make favorable comments about Dubai. It succeeded, and the report was filed with the court.

Ultimately, the suit was dismissed after the U.S. government issued a statement of potential interest.

It pays to have friends in high places.

Having gotten rid of the annoying lawsuit, Dubai is back to promoting its record of enlightened moderation. And its message is getting through. Major U.S. business leaders populate the many conferences sponsored by Dubai and its industries. The nation's purchases of major stakes in U.S. companies have gone uncriticized.

Once again, Dubai is everywhere you look.

All of this attention helps legitimize Dubai. And it distracts from its little problems with Israel, workers, women, and human rights.

Bill Clinton has even created a Dubai Scholars Program at the American University in Dubai under the sponsorship of the William Jefferson Clinton Foundation. It's the only foreign scholarship program that the foundation sponsors. And Laura Tyson, who chaired Clinton's Council of Economic Advisers, created a similar Dubai study program at the University of London.

Is Dubai really the best place to establish a program for American students?

Fortunately, not everyone is blind.

The University of Connecticut correctly abandoned plans to open up a campus in Dubai after serious complaints about Dubai's state-imposed discrimination based on people's national origin and religion and its documented violations of human rights. (For example, Human Rights Watch has said that Dubai abuses tens of thousands of migrant workers from India and Pakistan.)

The Clinton Foundation certainly wouldn't sponsor a program in America that banned Israeli students. It shouldn't sponsor one in Dubai, either.

It's time to stop legitimizing an anti-Semitic, antiworker state.

THE PLASTIC FLEECE:
Credit Card Company Abuse

It used to be that organized crime had a monopoly on loan sharking in this country. But these days who can blame the mob for charging outrageous interest rates—when our credit card companies are almost as bad?

When it comes to fleecing consumers, credit card companies make Mafia enforcers—and Shakespeare's Shylock—pale by comparison. With Americans owing $850 billion in consumer debt, the plastic fleece has a special impact on the average family. Our wallets and pocketbooks now house 690 million credit cards, and we charged $1.8 trillion on them in 2005. Our national average credit card debt per household more than tripled in fifteen years, rising from $3,102 in 1996 to $9,659 in 2006.

IN HOCK: CREDIT CARD DEBT PER U.S. HOUSEHOLD

1996	$3,102
2001	8,234
2006	9,659

Source: *USA Today.*

Credit card companies, raking in cash with their usurious interest rates and other gimmicks, posted a combined profit of $30 billion in 2004. Here's how they made it:

HOW CREDIT CARD COMPANIES MADE A $30 BILLION PROFIT BY RIPPING YOU OFF

- Raising their interest rates to more than 20 percent
- Tripling their late fees between 1994 and 2004
- Tripling their penalties for exceeding your credit limit
- Hiking your interest rate to 30 percent if you pay late
- Charging you extra fees to pay by phone
- Confusing you with multiple interest rates
- Charging you interest on debts you've already paid
- Punishing you for problems with other creditors even if you're current with them
- Sending out bills later to encourage late payment so they can charge more interest
- Changing their rates on existing balances of debt in midstream
- Charging you interest on your average balance even if you charged nothing in a given month

Feeling fleeced? Here's how they work their scams:

• The plastic fleece starts with the basic interest rate credit card companies charge. Though half of all card users pay their bills in full at the end of the month, those who don't carry an average balance of $13,000. You might think a 20 percent interest rate—punishing as it is—would satisfy the avarice of credit card companies. Think again: it doesn't even come close.

• Since 1995, credit card companies tripled their late fees. According to a Government Accountability Office (GAO) study, the average late fee in 2005 was $34—up from $13 ten years earlier.

- They've also more than doubled the fee they charge when you exceed your credit limit. Over-the-limit fees now average $31—up from $13 in 1995.
- Penalty interest rates now average 30 percent. You can be hit with these charges for any number of infractions: exceeding your credit limit; paying late, even just once; even for charging too high a percentage of your credit limit! As Consumer Action's 2005 annual credit card study showed, at least one bank has even raised its penalty rate to *35 percent*!
- Card companies often charge between $5 and $15 to pay a bill by phone—a charge they sometimes don't disclose to consumers. Paying by phone actually makes it easier for credit card companies to collect their money right away, but they charge large fees for simply allowing an electronic transfer.
- Card companies have as many as three different interest rates for different transactions, often charging one rate for purchases and another for cash advances. It's almost impossible to keep track of which rate is which.
- Even paying your bill often doesn't stop the interest from accumulating. The GAO study gave this example: A cardholder charges $1,000 and then pays $990 at the end of the month. Instead of paying interest on the $10 of outstanding balance, he could end up paying it on the full $1,000—even though he has paid 99 percent of that amount! Talk about getting fleeced!
- What are credit card companies to do if a consumer makes all of his or her payments on time? How can they add to their bottom line by jacking up his interest rate? To solve this inconvenient conundrum, the companies invented the concept of "universal default." According to Consumers Union, "your interest rate can skyrocket if your credit score declines because of your behavior with other creditors even if you always pay your credit card on time and never miss a payment. Some card issuers will [also] raise your rate if you inquire about a car loan or open a new credit card."

According to the consumer advocate Herb Weisbaum, universal default means that "if you have problems with one of your credit cards—miss a payment, pay late, or go over your limit—you could see rates skyrocket on your other cards." Weisbaum reports that half of credit card companies use universal default to jack their rates up to as high as 30 percent.

Oh, and as Weisbaum points out, sometimes the higher interest rate triggered by universal default can be retroactive—applying even to past bills!

• If the credit card company doesn't like the terms of its agreement with you, it can just change them anytime it wants. As Consumers Union warns, read the fine print on your contract, and "chances are you'll find this disclosure: 'We reserve the right to change the terms (including the APRs) at any time for any reason.' A fixed rate is fixed until the bank gives you at least 15 days notice that it isn't. If you want to keep your account open, you'll pay the higher new rate on your existing balance."

Travis Plunkett of the Consumer Federation of America asks the reasonable question "What business in America is allowed to change the price after you buy something, except the credit card industry? How can they possibly justify that?"

Responding to such criticism, Citibank, at least, is mending some of its ways. According to MSNBC, the bank said that "it would no longer reserve the right to change the terms on an account 'at any time for any reason.' Rather, the bank will wait till the card's expiration date."

• Some cardholders are confident that if they pay the minimum amount specified by the credit card company, that will satisfy their obligation and protect them from higher charges. But Consumers Union notes that "if you pay the minimum payment every month, you'll end up paying a lot more than what you charged and you could be on the hook for a very long time."

• To stimulate late payment, according to Consumers Union, credit card companies "are systematically mailing statements closer to the due date, giving customers less turnaround time. You can be hit with a late fee even if the payment is mailed on time. And late payments cause your interest to rise by between 7 and 27 percent." And when you are hit with an increased interest rate to punish you for a late payment or two, the higher rate applies not just to your late payment but to your entire outstanding balance.

Linda Sherry, director of national priorities for the California group Consumer Action, asks the right question: "Does the punishment fit the nature of the crime? If you are one day late does it really warrant a 20 percent interest rate hike?"

• Sometimes you have to pay even if you didn't charge a thing! Card companies often calculate your bill based on your average daily balance. They call this dubious practice "double-cycle billing." So even if you have a month during which you carry no credit card balance—either because you made no charges or because you paid off the balance in full—you can still be hit for interest based on your average balance over two billing cycles. The GAO reports that two of the six largest card issuers use double-cycle billing.

• Cash advance interest rates and convenience checks typically trigger higher interest rates than credit card purchases.

• Once upon a time, credit card companies refused to honor charges over a cardholder's credit limit. Now they tend to pay them so that they can charge a fee as high as $39 every time you charge over the limit.

• Consumers Union also reports that many card companies charge "a fee to issue what used to be free year-end summary statements"—and also charge a fee for purchases made abroad.

• Many credit card companies systematically apply payments from customers to the accounts bearing the lowest interest rates, leaving the higher-rate balances undiminished.

In all, the GAO report found that one third of active credit card holders of the six largest card issuers paid at least one penalty fee in 2005, averaging $33.64.

Senator Carl Levin (D-Mich.) points out that the usual victims of many of these charges for late payment or exceeding the maximum allowed balance are the poor, who need the money most. And they're precisely the ones who end up paying more because of the exorbitant fees card companies charge. Levin says "credit card companies must be stopped from preying on the most vulnerable Americans with unfair and confusing practices."

In 2007, Demos, a New York–based think tank, reported that "cardholders [with] household incomes between $25,000 and $50,000 are almost two times as likely as households earning more than $50,000, and four times more likely than households earning over $100,000, to pay interest rates above 20%."

Some credit cards seem specifically designed to fleece the poor. *USA Today* reported on one Chicago woman who got a solicitation offering a card with a "credit limit of up to $1,500." But the actual credit line, when the special charges were deducted, was only $250. The card required her to pay a $9 "processing fee," which she had to send back with the application. Then "the card issuer tacked on a $119 'acceptance fee,' a $50 'membership fee' and the first $6 installment of a $72 annual 'participation fee.' " By the time the scam was over, the Chicago woman's card would have $75 left in purchasing power and she would be stuck with bills to pay for all the fees.

One woman described another completely unfair practice. She applied for and received an HSBC credit card with a $300 credit limit. Intending to use the card up to the credit limit, she arranged online to make automatic payments of $250 per month. But when she didn't use the card for a while, she noticed that there was a credit balance of almost $900 on the card. Even though HSBC had held almost a thousand dollars of her money for several months, the allowable credit limit stayed at $300. It simply kept the payments. After she complained, the money was refunded—without interest, of course. The worst of the credit card practices is the so-called "interchange fee," which the card companies impose on merchants as a prerequisite to letting them sell goods and services on their credit cards. The fees now are estimated to total 2 percent of the purchase price of all goods and services that can be bought by credit card in the United States—a total of $36 billion in 2006.

The Merchants Payments Coalition, backing legislation to regulate interchange fees, notes that "with a collective market share of approximately 80 percent, Visa and MasterCard operate like price-fixing cartels, each one imposing oppressive credit card interchange fees and rules on merchants on a 'take-it-or-leave-it' basis. Credit card industry policies and practices make it practically impossible for merchants to know how much they are really paying in credit card fees or why."

Mallory Duncan, chairman of the Merchants Payments Coalition and senior vice president and general counsel of the National Retail Federation, says that "interchange fees are the biggest credit card fee you've never heard of. The $36 billion in interchange fees paid by retailers and consumers in 2006 dwarfed most other credit card fees put together, including late fees, over-the-limit fees, annual fees and inactivity fees."

But all of these fees and high interest rates beg the question: How did credit card rates get so high? What happened to the old concept of legislation, particularly at the state level, to prevent usury?

THE PLASTIC FLEECE | 169

The answer goes back to 1979, when the U.S. Supreme Court ruled that the laws of the state where the lender does business takes precedence over the state where the borrower lives. "At first," wrote Steve Diggs of www.crosswalk.com, "no one paid too much attention. But before long someone in South Dakota said, 'Hey if that's the case, why don't we change our usury laws and allow higher rates? After all, it might bring employment to South Dakota from the big banks in New York.'"

And move the banks did—to states with looser usury regulations. This race to the bottom quickly pitted states against one another to see who could offer consumers the least protection and have the best chance of attracting credit card company headquarters.

The 1979 Supreme Court ruling rendered state regulation of credit card interest rates totally ineffective. As long as there was one state willing to sell out, the other forty-nine could pass all the laws they wanted; the credit card companies would simply move to that one low-regulation state, leaving the other state regulators helpless to protect their borrowers.

Why hasn't Washington done anything about this? Congress has been a joke on the issue. Only recently have a few brave souls, such as Carl Levin and Congressman Barney Frank, begun talking about federal regulation of credit card practices. In the meantime, the credit card industry, awash in profits, has lavishly distributed money to key senators and congressmen to prevent any federal regulation or protection of consumers.

As we recounted in *Outrage,* commercial banks contributed literally millions of dollars to members of the Senate Banking Committee during the 2005–2006 election cycle alone. Among them were Richard Shelby of Alabama, who cleared $370,000 from the banks; Elizabeth Dole of North Carolina, who cleared $312,000; and Tom Carper of bank-rich Delaware, who came in at just under $300,000. Members of the House Financial Services Committee are similarly endowed. They received a total of $2.8 million in that election cycle from commercial banks alone and a total of $12.2 million from the broader finance, insurance, and real estate industry.

The Federal Reserve has proposed new regulations to help fill the void. Empowered to act under the Truth in Lending Act, *MarketWatch* reports, the Fed has proposed new rules "to improve the disclosures that consumers receive for their credit cards by making the information timely and understandable. Disclosures with credit-card applications and solicitations would highlight fees and the reasons penalty rates might be applied. Further, creditors would be required to summarize key terms at account opening and when terms are changed, and periodic statements would break out costs for interest and fees."

When the Democrats gained control of Congress, there was some hope that federal credit card regulation might be in the offing. Given the campaign contributions they've received from the industry, though, don't bet on it.

In May 2007, Senators Carl Levin and Claire McCaskill (D-Mo.) introduced the "Stop Unfair Practices in Credit Cards Act." This act would:

- Prohibit banks from charging repeated fees for a single instance of exceeding a credit card limit. So if in one month you charged $300 more on your card than you were allowed, you could be hit with a penalty fee only once. If your balance remained $300 over the limit for several months, you could not be charged a repeat penalty fee unless you made a new purchase while you were already over the credit limit. It would also prohibit charging interest on penalty fees and would ban the imposition of a penalty if a penalty fee pushed you over your card limit.

- Ban charging a fee for paying your bill by phone or online.

- Prevent retroactive increases in your interest rate. The banks could not charge you a higher rate than what was in force when you first made the charge.

- Prohibit the card issuer from raising your interest rate by more than 7 percent to punish you for a late payment or for exceeding your credit limit.

The Stop Unfair Practices bill would not ban universal default—raising your interest rate because of a problem you had with another creditor—but two other congressmen, Representative Mark Udall (D-Colo.) and Representative Emanuel Cleaver (D-Mont.), have introduced another bill that would.

ACTION AGENDA

Why should interest rates as high as 20 percent or more be allowed? With credit card companies socking away $30 billion in profits each year, it's high time that we take back some of the power and revive the old concept of usury laws, which limited interest rates to reasonable, below-loan-shark levels. The state laws used to be enough to prevent such punitive rates—but now that the Supreme Court has made it impossible to enforce them, we need Washington to fill the void.

The feds should limit interest rates on credit cards to a reasonable level, tied to the prime interest rate. That way, the limits would not be a straitjacket, hampering the free flow of credit, but would rise and fall with market rates. It might be a good idea to allow credit card companies to charge ten points over prime—and permit only five additional points as a maximum penalty.

This isn't just a matter of giving something back to the consumer. The massive credit card debt our consumers are carrying is a major threat to America's economic viability. We should prevent credit card companies from adding to that burden with their usurious interest rates.

Competitive market pressures can never do it alone. In 2004, six credit card issuers—Citibank, Chase Bank USA, Bank of America Corporation, MBNA America Bank, Capital One Bank, and Discover Financial Services—controlled 80 percent of the card lending in this country. With a handful of companies controlling the marketplace, genuine competition is unlikely—and collusion on high rates is almost inevitable.

What can you do to protect yourself from the abuses of the credit card industry? Plenty. And as a citizen you can do even more to make your public servants act in *your* interest, instead of serving the interests of the credit card companies.

What You Can Do as a Cardholder

You can start by making sure your credit card company doesn't have a policy of raising interest rates based on "universal default." In 2007, Citigroup announced that it was abandoning the practice, and with luck, others will follow. To find out if your card issuer sticks people with higher interest rates under universal default, go to www.cardratings.com.

Gerri Willis of CNN advises consumers to "check your cardholder agreement by looking at the area that mentions 'default pricing.' If that section indicates your default pricing is based on any information in your credit report, that's a red flag your card issuer has a universal default policy."

Next, be sure that your credit card company doesn't charge interest based on double-cycle billing—charging you interest even when you didn't make a purchase in that particular month (or did and paid it off). Curtis Arnold of cardratings.com advises people to check to see if the phrase "average daily balance" appears on your agreement—that's a tip-off that the issuer is ripping you off with double-cycle billing. In 2007, Chase pledged to stop double-cycle billing, limiting its interest charges to a single billing cycle.

Even if you find a credit card company with better policies, be careful not to get soaked when you switch your business to your new favorite. Credit card companies use balance transfer fees to get you coming and going. These charges used to be capped at about $75, but, as cardratings .com reports, "more often credit card companies are getting rid of caps on balance transfer fees or increasing the fees."

Gerri Willis of CNN explains how it works: "If you're transferring $10,000 to a card with a lower interest rate, and [the balance transfer] fee is 3 percent, that transfer will cost you $300. To find out if you may fall victim to high balance transfer fees, look at your credit card agreement. If there is a reference to a minimum fee for a balance transfer, but there's no reference to a maximum balance transfer fee, chances are, there are no limits to how much money you may be on the hook for."

If you're paying your credit card bills late because you don't have the money, there's not much you can do to avoid late fees. But many cardholders are just a few days late because they don't always pay their bills on the exact due date. Credit card companies love to take advantage by sending out their bills right before they're due, almost guaranteeing a late payment. The best way to avoid this problem is to arrange to pay automatically online; as Gerri Willis notes, "you can even set up your payments months in advance."

What You Can Do as a Citizen

The Supreme Court has made state regulation of credit card charges and fees virtually impossible. One weak state, tempted by the lure of credit card company jobs—or campaign donations—can sell out by passing lenient rules and vitiate any actions by the other forty-nine states. But federal legislation is a very good idea—and long overdue.

As noted above, the feds need to step in and control interest rates on credit cards, which were regulated by the states until the Supreme Court made that impractical.

The legislation now pending before Congress is decent, but its scope is pretty limited. Demos, the New York think tank, has described what an ideal bill should do:

- Eliminate universal default by requiring that any penalty or interest rate increase imposed on a cardholder be directly related to that specific card.

- Provide at least thirty days' notice before imposing a penalty on a consumer.

- Ban retroactive rate hikes. Increases in interest rates could be applied only to purchases or cash advances made after the increase was imposed.

- Impose fair grace periods and billing procedures that don't encourage late payments (such as sending out bills at the last minute).

- When offering cardholders the option of making only a minimum payment, clearly tell them how long it would take them to pay off their balance and how much extra they will have to pay if they just send in a check for the minimum.

We would add a number of other elements that should be included in reform legislation:

- Ban charges for paying by phone or online.

- Cap late fees and penalties for exceeding your credit limit and tie them to the extent of the delay or of the overdraft.

- Simplify interest rates and make it easier to understand what the card company is charging for what service.

- Permit interest charges only on the unpaid portion of a balance, not on the entire sum when part of it has been paid.

- Require bills to be mailed no later than thirty days before they are due.

- Ban double-cycle billing, which lets card issuers charge you for your average daily balance over two months rather than the actual amount you borrowed during that particular month.

- Ban card companies from honoring charges more than a certain amount over the customer's credit limit. Permitting these charges just entices consumers into acquiring debt burdens they can't discharge.

We badly need the federal government to crack down hard on the credit card companies' unfair practices—and it's our duty as citizens to pressure our representatives in Congress to make it happen. The most important people to target with your letters, phone calls, and e-mails are the members of the U.S. Senate Committee on Banking, Housing, and Urban Affairs, and of the House Financial Services Committee. Here are the chairmen and their addresses. Happy hunting!

U.S. Senate Committee on Banking, Housing, and Urban Affairs:
Senator Christopher J. Dodd, Chairman
448 Russell Building
Washington, DC 20510
Phone: (202) 224-2823

Senator Richard Shelby, Ranking Member
110 Hart Senate Office Building
Washington, DC 20510
Phone: (202) 224-5744

House Financial Services Committee:
Congressman Barney Frank, Chairman
2252 Rayburn House Office Building
Washington, DC 20515-2104
Phone: (202) 225-5931

9

TEACHERS ARE LEAVING THE PROFESSION—TOO MUCH STRESS, TOO LITTLE PAY

We are fleecing our kids. We spend too little on education. We don't pay teachers enough. What money we do spend rewards mediocrity and drives good teachers out of the profession. And we're running out of teachers—especially good ones!

The U.S. Department of Education says that 269,000 of America's 3.2 million public school teachers quit in the 2003–2004 school year—that's 8.4 percent of all the teachers we have! And only a third of these teachers left the profession because they were retiring; more than half said they left "to pursue another career or because they were dissatisfied."

According to Thomas G. Carroll, the president of the National Commission on Teaching and America's Future, "the problem is not mainly with retirement. The problem is that our schools are like a bucket with holes in the bottom, and we keep pouring in teachers."

Carroll's commission says that a third of all new teachers "leave the profession after just three years, and that after five years almost half are gone."

One of the biggest fleeces in our society is the way we undervalue and underpay our teachers, particularly the good ones. And because the teachers' union is deadly opposed to paying better teachers more than we pay those who aren't as good, the best teachers are quitting and the bad ones are sticking around—the opposite of what we want.

These new teachers—the ones who are leaving—are more qualified than those who are staying. From 2002 to 2005, new teachers "scored higher on SATs in high school and earned higher grades in college than their counterparts who [became teachers] in the mid-1990s," *The New York Times* reported.

Forty percent of the teachers who signed up between 2002 and 2005 had a college grade point average above 3.5, compared to only 26 percent of those who entered the profession in the 1990s. And only 20 percent of the more recent arrivals had a grade point average below 3.0, compared to 32 percent a decade ago.

But it's precisely these new, good, fresh teachers whom we're losing by the bushel.

The basic fact, of course, is that we're not spending enough on our schools. Compare health care and education: We spend about $2.2 trillion on health care but only about $500 billion on education. There are far more children than there are sick people—and educating them is the most important thing we can do.

Why? We can think of one reason: kids don't vote and sick adults do.

SICK VERSUS SMART: EDUCATION VERSUS HEALTH CARE SPENDING

(Per Year in the United States)

Education	Health Care
$500 billion	$2.2 trillion

Sources: *Pittsburgh Post-Gazette* and myhealthinsurancenews.com.

And with the teachers' union opposed to merit pay, taxpayers are reluctant to approve pay hikes for all teachers, good and bad. As a result, teachers' pay hasn't risen any faster than the cost of living. In 1989, we paid our teachers $47,354 in current dollars (adjusted for inflation). Now guess what? We pay them only $47,750—*an increase of only $400 in twenty years!* In the meantime, spending on schools has doubled. Even adjusted for inflation, it has gone up by 27 percent since 1990—but the teachers haven't seen any of it.

The teachers' union is part of the problem, not part of the solution. It won't let us increase the pay of good teachers unless we increase the pay of the bad ones, too. Imagine telling a company that it has to raise the pay of those who aren't producing in order to give those who are enough money to keep them at work and motivated!

But now good teachers are forcing the issue of merit pay with their feet—by leaving the profession in droves. This revolving door is costing the schools a bundle: $7 billion a year, according to the commission. That's enough to raise every teacher's pay by more than $2,000 a year—five times what they've received over the past two decades.

School districts are setting up bonus programs to hire teachers, particularly in special education, math, and sciences, where the shortages are especially great. For example:

- New York City offers a housing incentive to new teachers that includes $5,000 for a down payment on a home or apartment. It also recruits new teachers who are "midcareer professionals from fields like health care, law, and finance."

- Los Angeles offers a $5,000 bonus to teachers who agree to work at low-performing schools.

- In Guilford County, North Carolina, turnover has become such a problem that the school district is offering $10,000 bonuses to teachers who take hard-to-fill jobs.

The exodus of teachers from public schools has less to do with the difficulties of low pay and high stress than with the allure of other, more remunerative careers. But, of course, the attraction of alternate careers for would-be teachers merely makes it more apparent that teachers' pay and working conditions must improve if the profession is to become competitive.

But clearly it's the pull of higher salaries (and greater opportunities for women) in the business world, as well as the push of low teacher pay, that is driving educators to leave the system—and making young college graduates decide not to enter it.

Teaching is still largely a woman's profession. *The Washington Post* reports that "three quarters of the nation's . . . public school teachers are women, a figure that has changed little over four decades." As the paper notes, however, "in that time, women have become more educated, with more career choices than ever. So far, schools are not faring well on the open market."

Three times as many women graduated from college in 2000 as in 1964, but the proportion that went into teaching dropped by more than two thirds, from 50 percent to 15 percent over the same period of time. While the current crop of teachers, as noted, have better academic records than those hired in the past decade or two, the long-term trend has been to draw fewer teachers from the top of their classes. *The Washington Post* reports that "although in 1964, 1 in 5 young female teachers graduated in the top 10 percent of her high school class, the ratio was closer to 1 in 10 by 2000."

But as the quality of teachers has dropped, standards for teachers have increased—thanks to the No Child Left Behind Act, which we consider the most important advance in public education in fifty years. As the *Post* notes, the act recognized "widespread research that shows teacher quality helps drive student achievement." It required "teachers to have college degrees, full state teaching licenses and demonstrated proficiency in their subjects. The requirement is intended to keep school systems from relying on emergency credentials or assigning teachers to subjects they are not certified to teach."

These new, higher federal standards have created a projected shortfall of 280,000 qualified math and science teachers by 2015, and schools are scrambling to find qualified educators, often by hiring "working professionals rather than relying on traditional teacher-preparation programs."

To add to the woes of America's public school systems, the baby-boomer teachers, born after 1945, are retiring at increasing rates. *The New York Times* reports that "California is projecting that it will need 100,000 new teachers over the next decade from the retirement of the baby boomers alone."

To solve the problem of departing teachers, we must first understand the reasons they're leaving. In 114 school districts in North Carolina, 9,392 teachers quit in the 1997–1998 school year; that's about 12 percent of the total teacher pool. A detailed survey asked them why they left.

WHY THEY QUIT: THE REASONS TEACHERS ARE LEAVING NORTH CAROLINA PUBLIC SCHOOLS

(Of those who resigned)

Family responsibilities, child care	25%
End of contract	25%
Left teaching	20%
Not renewed	20%
Took other school jobs, not teaching	15%
Left to attend school	15%
Death or health problems	15%
Job dissatisfaction	10%

Source: North Carolina survey.

But each of these reasons raises a more fundamental question: Couldn't we hold on to some of these teachers, particularly the good ones, by paying them more? The pressures of family, the attractiveness of other employment opportunities, health issues, job frustrations, and the desire to extend one's education loom large over every workplace in America. In other fields, though, employers who want to hold on to their best people raise their pay, change their duties, reward good performance, and use other strategies to get them to stay. Why can't the American educational system do the same?

The North Carolina survey asked school administrators what they felt needed to be done to hold on to their teachers. The consensus, not surprisingly, was: pay them more!

WHAT COULD MAKE THEM STAY?

Higher pay 95%

Cut class size, cut extra duties, more time for planning	39%
More power to schools to make better decisions in school leadership	33%
Safety, better student discipline	23%
More parent involvement, community support, respect for teaching	21%
More benefits, better facilities	19%
Mentor support for new teachers	17%
Better teacher training	17%
Better housing, child care resources	15%

Source: North Carolina survey.

Of course, every item on this list of improvements would be a change for the better. But—no surprise—it all comes down to one key issue: compensation.

So what's the problem? It's simple: Our hard-pressed school districts have to dole out their pay increases with a thimble. Why? Because they cannot raise *some* teachers' pay; union rules mandate that any pay raise *must apply to everyone equally.* Until now, the teachers' unions have fiercely resisted any notion of paying teachers according to their ability or performance.

But particularly when schools are faced with massive teacher turnover, it's clear that we need to single out those good teachers, and spend what it takes to keep them. Unless school districts are prepared to raise teacher pay wholesale, across all categories—and most are not—selecting key teachers to keep and paying them enough to hold on to them is the best strategy. Until then, we're just refilling the bucket despite the holes in the bottom.

Fortunately, there are some glimmers of hope that the teachers' unions may be loosening their opposition to merit-based pay, provided that they have input into defining what constitutes "merit."

The New York Times writes about the change in the unions' attitudes: "For years, the unionized teaching profession opposed few ideas more vehemently than merit pay, but those objections appear to be eroding as school districts in dozens of states experiment with plans that compensate teachers partly based on classroom performance."

One of the most impressive of the new merit pay experiments is going on in Minneapolis, where Republican governor Tim Pawlenty is actually working with teachers' union leaders to design and sell a merit pay program to teachers.

The result of this collaboration is Minnesota's $86 million teacher professionalization and merit pay initiative, which is now being applied in dozens of the state's school districts. The plan got a lift in 2007 when teachers voted overwhelmingly to expand it in Minneapolis. One major reason that it's prospering, Pawlenty said in an interview, is that union leaders helped develop and sell it to teachers.

"As a Republican governor, I could say, 'Thou shalt do this,' and the unions would say, 'Thou shalt go jump in the lake,' " Pawlenty said. "But here they partnered with us."

The New York Times reports that Professor Allan Odden of the University of Wisconsin, an expert on teachers' compensation, believes that "a consensus is building across the political spectrum that rewarding teachers with bonuses or raises for improving student achievement, working in lower income schools, or teaching subjects that are hard to staff can energize veteran teachers and attract bright rookies to the profession."

Odden adds optimistically, "It's looking like there's a critical mass" for such merit pay initiatives. The trend "is still not ubiquitous, but it's developing momentum."

Denver has one of the most advanced merit pay systems in the country. Teachers in hard-to-staff schools (many of them minority or special education schools), and those whose students show great improvement, can get bonuses averaging $5,000 a year.

The program was approved by Denver voters, who even approved a $25 million tax increase to pay for it. With electorates rejecting school tax increases across the country and teachers' pay stagnating, merit pay may be the best way to put dollars in teachers' pockets, union opposition or not.

In Denver, merit pay has worked—and even earned the applause of the teachers' union. *USA Today* reports that Kim Ursetta, the president of the local affiliate of the NEA, said the merit pay "system works in Denver because it is based on student test scores and several other factors, such as whether a teacher signs up for professional development or has a good annual review." Ursetta has pointed to "greater collaboration and more of a focus on raising student achievement" as benefits of the merit pay plan. "We never sat down before as teachers to talk about where our students were," she concedes. "[Merit pay is] forcing continual conversation about student learning."

Even in New York City, where teacher unionization first took hold, the unions are cooperating with the Board of Education in awarding school-wide bonuses to schools that perform especially well. A committee heavy with union representation will determine how the bonus money is to be spent. But allowing bonuses at all represents progress.

But the schoolchildren of New York got hit with a body blow by the New York state legislature when it voted to ban the use of student test scores in determining teacher pay. Imagine that! It's illegal in New York state to pay teachers more or less based on how well they do their job according to objective, standardized tests. Subjective judgments? Meaningless seniority? Favoritism? Sure, go ahead: those are all legal. The only thing that's not is basing pay on objective testing!

Many unions still oppose merit pay for teachers. Similar plans were defeated in Texas, Florida, and New York in 2007. In Minnesota, however, the Federation of Teachers grew concerned when Republicans began making inroads in the state legislature. Union president Louise Sundin says, "We realized we were going to have to embrace some things that would get money into teachers' pockets in nontraditional ways."

It's about time.

Of course, it won't be easy to gain nationwide approval for merit pay. Chester E. Finn, Jr., a longtime advocate of merit pay and other major educational reforms, says that sometimes unions agree to merit pay "only after reshaping the programs so thoroughly that student achievement is one of many factors by which teachers are judged, reducing the programs' effectiveness." But the federal Department of Education, which embraces merit pay, has awarded $80 million in grants to schools and districts in nineteen states that have developed incentive pay plans. Some school districts are now offering bonuses of up to $10,000 to outstanding teachers.

The New York Times reports that private groups are also involved in promoting merit pay. "The Milken Family Foundation of Santa Monica, Calif., for instance, which helped create the Minnesota program, has channeled money and expertise into similar plans that include incentive pay at 130 schools in 14 states and the District of Columbia."

Florida, where the unions rejected a merit pay plan based entirely on individual teacher performance and test scores, has passed—and Governor Charles Crist has signed—a merit pay plan that can reward teams of teachers rather than just individuals.

USA Today relates how merit pay worked at Meadowcliff Elementary School in Little Rock, Arkansas. The effects were quickly noticeable: "Increasingly, cafeteria workers sat with students to chat about school work. Even more startling, the janitor began taking his breaks in the cafeteria reading a book, just to serve as a role model."

"And when test scores arrived at the end of the year showing improvement, [School Principal Karen] Carter heard whoops of joy from teachers whose bonuses would help pay off their college bills. The better each of their students did, the bigger their bonuses. The janitor and other support staff were rewarded for the school's overall gains. Such is the power of 'merit pay,' a concept long opposed by teachers and their unions."

At Meadowcliff, the teachers' bonuses (funded by a private backer) ranged from $1,100 to $5,100 per year, depending on how well their students fared on tests; support staffers got between $500 and $2,000 if the children succeeded. Overall, test scores at Meadowcliff, which *USA Today* describes as "a poor and urban school," rose seven points more than in similar schools without merit pay.

The NEA, the larger of the two teachers' unions, has derided merit pay based on evaluations of teacher performance, whether through their students' test scores or by using other criteria, as "inappropriate." But the American Federation of Teachers, whose members are mainly in large urban areas, is showing a bit more flexibility—as it has in approving the New York City schoolwide bonus system.

The president of the New York United Federation of Teachers, a union under the American Federation umbrella, said she was willing to negotiate with the city of New York on the merit pay program because it was based on "schoolwide bonuses for sustained growth in student achievement." Her attitude is a refreshing change from that of her predecessor, Albert Shanker, who famously said that "when school children start paying union dues, that's when I'll start representing the interests of school children."

The New York Times says that the New York union "opposes plans that allow administrators alone to decide which teachers get extra money or that pay individual teachers based solely on how students perform on standardized test scores, which they consider unreliable. But it encourages efforts to raise teaching quality and has endorsed arrangements that reward teams of teachers whose students show outstanding achievement growth."

Unions tend to oppose merit pay, in part out of concern that it will lead to arbitrary decisions by those in authority. *The Olympian* noted that their concern "stems partly from failed efforts of the 1980s. In those cases, principals generally were given the power to decide who would get the additional dollars"—the same way a boss does in the private sector.

Susan Moore Johnson, a professor at the Harvard Graduate School of Education, recounted that previous merit pay plans "often had no basis of any objective measure of performance. So what sometimes happened is there would be different awards made to different individuals and they would become public, and people would be appalled at the individuals who were given the awards or not given [them]."

But a pay plan that doesn't have teachers' approval won't fly, so school boards have to negotiate with the unions to structure the merit pay programs so that they work.

The key to the attractiveness of current merit pay plans is that they're typically based on objective improvement or deterioration in a student's test scores. Though unions and education purists complain that this system leads to "teaching to the test," that's a whole lot better than not teaching at all!

The tendency of critics of merit pay, or of the No Child Left Behind Act, to say that the reform is ineffective because it hasn't improved student performance ignores a fundamental fact: until the power of the teachers' union is broken and administrators can hire, fire, promote, and demote teachers as they please—the way they do in the private sector—student performance is likely to remain low.

But the critics of merit pay are still vocal. As Deborah Torres-Gore, a second- and third-grade teacher in California, says, "When I look into the eyes of a student who I have taught in the past—or I stand at the door in the morning and my students say 'Mrs. Gore, I love you' or 'Mrs. Gore you're such a good teacher'—am I effective or not? I think I am effective."

Okay, Mrs. Gore, you probably are effective. You'd probably get a bonus yourself. But how about some objective measurement of your good work on standardized student tests?

Chief among teachers' worries is that they'll be passed over for bonuses because of factors beyond their control. " 'Can you account for the child's emotions? Can you account for whether their parents are getting them to school on time?' asked Sharon Vandagriff, a third-grade teacher near Chattanooga, Tenn[essee]."

As longtime pollsters, we share an enthusiasm for merit pay, a confidence that stems from our experience in survey sampling and research. When merit pay bonuses are based on measurable changes in students' performance on standardized tests from the beginning to the end of the school year, there should be no need to account for a "child's emotions" or "getting them to school on time"—because such factors are usually constants, no more influential in June than in September. Of course injustices will occur, and those will rankle and animate controversy in the teachers' lounge. But making seniority the sole basis for compensation—as most schools now do—is not fair or even logical, it is simply consistent and predictable.

Typical of teachers' critiques of merit pay are the comments of Sandy Hughes, a high school English, French, and Latin teacher in Tennessee. She says that those who advocate merit pay based on standardized testing are "looking at this as if we're manufacturing automobiles. With children, you're working with unique individuals, all of whom have unique qualities. Our variables are so extensive."

Extensive? Yes. But when the same teacher is teaching the same class in June that she did in September, why isn't it fair to pay her based on how much better or worse her students do on a standardized test?

One person who has it right is Sandi Jacobs, the vice president of the National Council on Teacher Quality. "In most professions," she told the Associated Press, "people earn salaries based on merit, not based on formula schedules." Jacobs feels, according to the AP story, that "measuring teacher effectiveness, and paying educators accordingly, would bring public education in line with other professions." We couldn't agree more.

ACTION AGENDA

Our schools are in trouble. The signs are all there: a heavy retirement rate among baby boomers, high federal standards, a rapid turnover of young teachers, and a souring voter mood where education budgets are concerned. Now that women have other options, our local school districts must be attractive to new teachers or they'll soon be unable to staff their classrooms. Asking new teachers to wait in line behind senior faculty for pay raises will alienate the teachers the districts need to keep, driving them out the school door in droves.

Raising starting salaries for teachers is a good idea, but it won't stanch the teacher exodus if ongoing pay raises don't make the profession attractive in the early years.

With school boards and state legislatures unable or unwilling to appropriate the funds for across-the-board pay raises, schools must zero in on the top teachers they need to keep by offering pay hikes based on merit. The systems must be objective—based on test scores—and they must compare apples with apples by rating teachers based on the performance of their students from the beginning to the end of the school year.

But the political consensus—that pay raises are best doled out according to merit—will probably drive labor policy. With luck, the unions, faced with the alternatives of no or low pay raises or higher raises based on merit, will begin to see the light. As they do, we can only hope that their interest shifts more to meeting the needs of newer, better teachers rather than those who have accumulated seniority but may also have lost their edge.

Congress can help by increasing funding for merit pay and by requiring merit pay systems—to be negotiated locally—for schools found to be failing by standardized testing.

On a broader front, Congress must resist pressure to water down the No Child Left Behind Act. It's not perfect, but it is a vast improvement over the education policies previous to its passage. Now, at least, we are assessing our schools objectively. Even if its measurements are sometimes flawed, or penalize non-English districts, or cause teachers to teach to the test, introducing objective measurement into the system is a big gain over the subjectivity of teacher-awarded grades, the only previous yardstick of school improvement (and one that grew or shrank according to each teacher's self-congratulatory grading).

Pressure to weaken the act will come from many sources. Conservatives object to the program because it increases federal intervention in local control of education. But such national objective standards are vital. Many parents aren't sufficiently educated themselves to judge their child's progress in school, so they rely on outside evaluations. The practice of relying on report cards made out by teachers eager to prove their own merit has led to decades of self-deception, as parents concluded that their schools were succeeding because their children got good grades. And when conservatives speak of returning control over schools to the communities, what they're really doing is giving them over to the unions who dominate the state legislature and the local school boards!

Unions don't like the law because it shows how little the public schools have improved under their rule. Diane Ravitch, an assistant secretary of education in the Bush 41 White House, calls the act "fundamentally flawed" because national test scores did not rise. But she forgets that without the law, there would be no national test scores in the first place! And she seems oblivious to the fact that our children's scores are sagging not because we're measuring them but because we haven't accompanied them with the reforms that are necessary. Blaming the No Child Left Behind Act—a measuring tool to spotlight problem areas—for the lack of improvement is like criticizing a thermometer for showing that a patient has a fever! If the diagnosis isn't followed by medication, what's a thermometer to do?

The formula for success in public education is clear:

- Give parents the option of sending their children to charter schools that are free of union control.

- Pay teachers in public schools based on the degree of improvement in their students' test performance. And weaken teacher tenure to allow administrators to get rid of incompetent or burned-out teachers.

- Finally, where charter schools do not solve the problem, give private and parochial schools a crack at doing so by issuing tuition vouchers.

If we want to keep from shortchanging our kids, that's the only way to do it.

RELEASED FROM GUANTÁNAMO, THEY KILL AGAIN

Surely, being required to pay for the same service twice constitutes "fleecing." And when the price is paid not in money, but in American blood, that fleecing becomes both contemptible and unendurable.

That's just what's happening to us in the war on terror. Battle-weary American and NATO troops are being asked to put their lives on the line to kill or capture terrorists whom we once held in custody at the Guantánamo Naval Base in Cuba—until we released them and sent them back, at our expense, to their native countries. Now these terrorists have rejoined the ranks of our adversaries—and we're being forced to spend both blood and treasure to bring them to heel once more!

Records reveal that dozens of terrorists who have been released from custody at Guantánamo Bay have rejoined their terror gangs and gone back to their day job killing our soldiers. Estimates differ on how many enemy combatants have rejoined the fight against our troops, but the number may be as high as one in ten. In July 2005, Commander Jeffrey Gorden, a Pentagon spokesman, said that "our reports indicate that at least thirty former Guantánamo detainees have taken part in anti-coalition militant activities after leaving U.S. detention. Some have been killed in combat in Afghanistan and Pakistan." By June 2007, *The Washington Post* was reporting that "possibly as many as fifty former Guantanamo detainees have returned to the battlefield to fight against the United States and its allies."

How do we know? A Pentagon official explained that every detainee is fingerprinted and photographed. "We build up pretty extensive biometrics on these guys. There are a lot of different ways we could know that someone we'd captured or killed had already been in our custody."

These men were captured by American troops—soldiers who were risking their lives to bring them in—because they posed a threat to the United States. Yet after holding them, we have let them go, so that they could return to the ranks of our adversaries.

Let's remember that these men are not in prison because of some crime they committed for which they are to serve a determined sentence and then be released, their debt to society paid. These inmates are enemy warriors captured in battle. They must be held until the fight is over, lest they simply reappear in combat fighting against us.

So how did they get out in the first place?

Under pressure from human rights advocates, liberal Democrats, European do-gooders, and even the U.S. Supreme Court, the terrorist prison at Guantánamo Bay now has a revolving door that is being used by terrorists to rejoin their terror gangs and go back to fighting our soldiers.

The exploits of those whom we once had safely locked up in cells at Guantánamo should be sobering reading for those who lobbied so hard for the release of the prisoners we had taken in Afghanistan and Pakistan.

TERRORISTS WE RELEASED—SO THEY COULD ATTACK US AGAIN

- **Abdullah Mehsud,** a thirty-one-year-old Pakistani, spent more than two years at Guantánamo. Mehsud was something of a celebrity in terrorist circles, having lost a leg in a land mine explosion a few days before the Taliban conquered the Afghan capital of Kabul in September 1996. At the time, he was second in command of a Pakistani Taliban group.

  In December 2001, Mehsud was captured by Afghan forces and turned over to American authorities. He was held at Guantánamo until March 2004, when we let him go.

How did he get out? He hid his identity. When he was first captured, he was carrying a false Afghan identity card; according to *The Washington Post,* "while in custody he maintained the fiction that he was an innocent Afghan tribesman."

Mehsud boasted to reporters that U.S. officials never realized he was a Pakistani deeply involved with terrorist organizations. "I managed to keep my Pakistani identity hidden all these years," Mehsud boasted to *Gulf News.* We never discovered who he was—despite the fact that "Pakistani newspapers have written lengthy accounts of Mehsud's hair and looks and the powerful appeal to militants of his fiery denunciations of the United States."

After he fooled us into letting him go, Mehsud "took up arms again and soon became the Taliban commander of South Waziristan, a tribal area near the border with Afghanistan." In 2004, he kidnapped two Chinese engineers working on a hydroelectric dam. One was killed and the other was freed by government forces.

Mehsud's enthusiasm for terrorism was, if anything, stoked to a fever pitch by his years at Guantánamo. "We would fight America and its allies until the very end," he declared in an interview after his release.

He got his wish on July 24, 2007, when he blew himself up to avoid arrest by Pakistani government forces. Reuters reported that "a counter-terrorism squad acting on a tip-off raided the house belonging to a senior official from the pro-Taliban Islamist party of Fazal-ur-Rehman, leader of the opposition in the [Pakistani] National Assembly."

"We asked them to surrender but they opened fire," reported Mira Jan, the chief administrator for the area. "The shooting lasted for about half an hour and then we heard a blast from inside the house." Mehsud blew himself to bits to avoid capture.

- **Maulvi Abdul Ghaffar,** described by the Associated Press as "a senior Taliban commander in northern Afghanistan," was arrested roughly two months after the American invasion. The AP notes that Ghaffar "was held at Guantánamo for eight months, then released, and was killed Sept. 26 [2004] by Afghan security forces during a raid in Uruzgan Province. Afghan leaders said they thought he was leading Taliban forces in the southern province."

After his release from Guantánamo, Ghaffar led a force of men that, according to *The Washington Post,* "ambushed and killed a U.N. engineer and three Afghan soldiers."

(continued)

Incredibly, however, Major General Eric Olson, the number two commander of U.S. troops in Afghanistan, defended Ghaffar's release—saying that there was no alternative to releasing prisoners from Guantánamo. The Ghaffar case, he said, "has not led to any soul-searching about the release program."

• The Associated Press also reported that another "released detainee killed a judge leaving a mosque in Afghanistan." The information was provided by Lieutenant Commander Flex Plexico, a Pentagon spokesman, who declined to give the terrorist's name.

• **Mullah Shahzada,** a Taliban field commander, was released in the spring of 2003 after confinement in Guantánamo. According to *Insight* magazine, he "appears to have become active [as a terrorist] again almost immediately following his release." He is reported to have been either killed or recaptured.

• Another released Guantánamo prisoner—whom the Pentagon won't name—"is still at large," according to *The Washington Post,* "after taking leadership of a militant faction in Pakistan and aligning himself with al Qaeda." Now that he is out of our custody, however, he's talking. "In telephone calls to Pakistani reporters, he has bragged that he tricked his U.S. interrogators into believing he was someone else."

• *The Washington Post* also reports that "another returned [Guantánamo] captive is an Afghan teenager who had spent two years at a special compound for young detainees at the military prison in Cuba, where he learned English, played sports, and watched videos. . . . After almost three years living with other young detainees in a seaside house at Guantanamo Bay, he was returned in January [2004] to his country, where he was to be monitored by Afghan officials and private contractors. But the program failed and he fell back in with the Taliban." U.S. officials released him because they "believed they had persuaded him to abandon his life with the Taliban." Apparently not. "The young man, now 18, was recaptured with other Taliban fighters near Kandahar, Afghanistan." A military spokesman said "Someone dropped the ball in Afghanistan." No kidding.

Republican Congressman Porter Goss (R-Fla.), a former chairman of the House Intelligence Committee, likened the Guantánamo releases to the weekend furlough granted the lifer Willie Horton by the Massachusetts prison system in the 1980s. Horton, in jail for murder and rape, used his furlough to kill and rape again; his release became a key issue in sinking the 1998 presidential bid of the former Massachusetts Democratic governor Michael Dukakis. "[W]e've already had instances where we know that people who have been released from our detention have gone back and have become combatants again," Goss has said. "It's the military Willie Horton."

The military goes to great lengths to defend its review process, which determines who to let go and who to keep locked away. Mark Jacobson, a former senior Pentagon official who helped design the review policy at Guantánamo, says that the process is "pretty meticulous." Told of five former detainees who have picked up arms against us again, he said that "even if five got through, that's still an 'A' grade." He conceded that the process was "not foolproof" but persisted in defending it as "pretty thorough." Though he claimed that the military "errs on the side of caution," Jacobson admitted that "mistakes are going to be made."

Jacobson explained the difficulties involved. "These people don't have driver's licenses. They don't even have birth certificates. Some of them are trained in deception and counter-interrogation techniques. One guy had 13 aliases."

But all this raises the question: Why are we releasing Guantánamo inmates if we can't be sure they won't take up arms against us again?

In all, at least 425 detainees have been released from Guantánamo. As of February 9, 2008, 275 remained in custody.

And don't be fooled; those we've imprisoned at Guantánamo—and, in many cases, released—are not innocents. One study of Guantánamo detainees confirmed that these detainees "included fighters of Al Qaeda, veterans of terrorism training camps and men who had experience with explosives, sniper rifles and rocket-propelled grenades."

Why have we released more than half of those we captured, even though the war on terror continues at a high intensity?

The short answer is that the Bush administration is bowing to global liberal media pressure to shed itself of Guantánamo detainees as quickly as possible.

One defense official who helps to oversee Guantánamo prisoners implied as much to *The Washington Post* in late 2004: "We could have said we'll accept no risks and refused to release anyone. But we've regarded that option as not humane and not practical, and one that makes the U.S. government appear unreasonable."

The international media pressure for releasing detainees at Guantánamo began building almost as soon as terrorists started arriving there in the wake of the U.S.-led invasion of Afghanistan.

Soon after September 11, 2001, the administration refused to treat captured terrorists as prisoners of war under the rules of the Geneva Convention. These prisoners wore no uniforms, represented no government, and were members of no army: by that logic, they were not entitled to POW status. The international community was outraged.

As the liberal online magazine *Slate* wrote, "It would be a gross understatement to say there was 'blowback' from this decision. . . . After a half-century as the world's leader on international law, the U.S. was quickly earning the status of the world's brigand. Politicians, lawyers, activists, and even editorial cartoonists lambasted the Bush administration for its Guantánamo policy, calling the camp a 'black hole' for the law. The pictures of hooded and shackled detainees wearing orange jumpsuits at Gitmo came to symbolize American policies toward terrorism and the Middle East more generally."

All the international reaction might have been an acceptable price to pay for the ability to have a free hand in interrogating terrorists, but the Bush administration got squishy as a result of the international outcry. As *Slate* notes, "In response to this blowback, the Bush administration slowly back-pedaled from its initial policies with respect to the detainees."

Thus began a long process of retrenchment by a panicked administration in which hundreds of terrorists were released back to the battlefield— where a great many returned to their previous roles as enemy soldiers in the terrorist war against the United States.

The process began in October 2002, when the Pentagon sent Guantánamo detainees back to their native countries—"usually with assurances that they would be tried and detained at home." Given the porous nature of the criminal justice systems in nations like Pakistan, where the war on terror raged, these repatriations often amounted to releases.

Once the Guantánamo inmates are released to their native countries, they are usually freed on arrival. France, supposedly an ally in the war on terror, tried six men released from Guantánamo on charges of terrorism and convicted five of them, French citizens all: Brahim Yadel, Khaled ben Mustafa, Nizar Sassi, Mourad Benchellali, and Ridouane Khalid admitted that they had spent time at military training camps for terrorists in Afghanistan. Arrested in late 2001 by U.S. forces in Afghanistan, all served at least two years at Guantánamo before they were handed over to France in 2004 and 2005. All were convicted of "criminal association with a terrorist enterprise," and sentenced to four years in prison—but three of the years were suspended, one counted as time served, and all five terrorists were released at once.

MSNBC noted that "the ruling in France capped proceedings that seemed at times like a trial of the U.S. prison camp itself with the prosecutor lashing out at the 'Guantanamo system' and saying the prison violates international law."

But the real pressure came from the U.S. Supreme Court, which held in the summer of 2004 that Guantánamo detainees could petition in federal court for their release. Stuart Taylor of *The National Journal* observed that the Bush policies on Guantánamo had triggered the Supreme Court's intervention. "By refusing to give even the minimal hearings [to detainees that] most agree were required under international law," he said, the court was "being asked to put its imprimatur on violations of international law that had caused world wide outrage."

As one defender of the administration's detention policies observed, the court's decision "left everything quite confused." The justices had made it clear that some form of review of the detentions was necessary but failed to spell out how it should work.

Under the Court's prodding, the Pentagon, according to *Insight on the News*, "began work on a more structured review process for detainees, under which an annual hearing would consider whether they still posed a threat." But, faced with the prospect that the court decision might trigger "an avalanche of litigation from the 500-plus detainees" held at Guantánamo by the end of 2004, the Pentagon began putting the "process of sorting through the detainees . . . into overdrive," according to Elisa C. Massimino, the director of the Washington office of Human Rights First. The court decision led the Pentagon to institute a system of Combatant Status Review Tribunals to decide which detainees to hold and which to release.

The increasingly large number of enemy combatants with Guantánamo degrees we face on the battlefield today confirms that this review process was flawed.

Slate is correct when it points out that the problems that led to the pressure to release inmates from Guantánamo were of the Bush administration's own making. "International law would have allowed the United States to warehouse the Gitmo detainees until 'the cessation of active hostilities' and to interrogate them too. But by rejecting the Geneva Conventions' restrictions on Gitmo detainee operations, the United States also rejected its benefits—creating the situation we have today in which paroled detainees have returned to the fight against us."

Declaring the Guantánamo inmates the "worst of the worst," former defense secretary Donald Rumsfeld rejected all efforts to limit interrogation techniques or other procedures to those permitted by the Geneva Convention. But the question of whether we should have had to release any detainees still persists. Mark Jacobson, the former Pentagon official who helped to set up the Guantánamo protocols, submits that "it would have been wiser to treat the detainees captured in Afghanistan as prisoners of war right off the bat . . . rather than leaving them in the legally murky situation of unlawful combatants." As Jacobson notes "that way, the only question is 'when is the conflict over?' [and] the courts don't get involved."

The liberal activist Massimino of Human Rights First agrees. "It makes much more sense," she said, "to do Article Five [of the Geneva Convention] hearings on the front end than get into complex review procedures afterward." (Under Article Five of the convention, the hearings screen those captured to check that they really are combatants, not just bystanders caught up in the fighting.)

The administration usually justifies its decision not to treat its terrorist prisoners under the Geneva Convention by saying that it needed a free hand to interrogate them. But Marine Lieutenant Colonel William Lietzau, who worked on detainee issues in the Defense Department's Office of General Counsel, contradicts this view: "There were very good reasons not to designate the detainees as prisoners of war, but the claim that they couldn't be interrogated was not one of them." Lietzau maintained that detainees could be as easily and effectively interrogated under Geneva rules as outside them.

"More important," *Slate* asserts, "the Geneva Conventions already contained the solution to the paroled detainee problem. . . . Article 118 of the treaty establishes the rule for repatriation at the end of hostilities. Had the administration followed Geneva all along, it could have simply invoked the provisions of this time-honored treaty to support its policy of holding the Gitmo detainees indefinitely, or at least until the insurgency abated in Afghanistan, from where the majority of Gitmo detainees came."

With U.S. policy operating outside the Geneva rules, however, the judicial harassment of the Pentagon has only gotten worse. In July 2007, a federal appeals court ordered the administration "to disclose virtually all its information on Guantánamo detainees"—a step our top intelligence officials say could cause "exceptionally grave damage to the national security."

The three-judge appellate panel said "that it was not possible to review the decisions of Pentagon tribunals 'without seeing all the evidence.' "

Acting as if the Guantánamo cases were like normal criminal proceedings, Susan Baker Manning, a lawyer who handled the case that led to the July ruling, has said that "if we're going to hold people possibly for the rest of their lives, it should look eminently fair that we should look at all the evidence to see if they are or are not the people who should be at Guantánamo."

But this kind of judicial review, which would be out of the question in prisoner-of-war cases, "would reveal counterterrorism activities," according to a brief filed by intelligence officials including the directors of the CIA, FBI, and NSA. The agencies noted that it "could disrupt intelligence gathering" and that the work of processing the information was already proving "so time-consuming that the effort had distracted the agencies from terrorism investigations."

General Michael V. Hayden, the director of the CIA, said that complying with the court order would force him to turn over to the lawyers for the terrorists "information about virtually every weapon in the CIA's arsenal" and would "severely restrict the U. S. government's ability to collect information and wage the war on terrorism."

With the courts, defense lawyers, international human rights activists, and liberal lawmakers closing in on Guantánamo, however, the military is being forced to release ever-larger numbers of enemy combatants—who are heading right back to the front lines in attacking U.S. troops.

ACTION AGENDA

The Bush administration and the Pentagon must stop the massive releases from Guantánamo. There are only two conditions under which we should be releasing detainees: either because they were wrongly imprisoned in the first place or because they have been rehabilitated and can be safely returned to their native lands.

In the case of Guantánamo, the first possibility is patently absurd. Though a few mistakes were undoubtedly made—and have been widely publicized in the liberal media—the vast bulk of those shipped to the Cuban base were indisputably terrorists at the time of their capture.

The second alternative, too, defies credibility. Our ability to turn these fanatics away from lives of terrorism is very, very limited. It would be astonishing if the experience at Guantánamo succeeded in converting these warriors into friends of the United States. It is far more likely that these cunning prisoners deceive military interrogators into believing that they have changed, only to reappear on the battlefield shortly after their release.

With the legal and political pressure for quick and frequent releases, military interrogators have seemed only too happy to believe these terrorists' tales and let the prisoners—who are causing such political, bureaucratic, and legal grief—go their own way.

It's ironic to reflect that the support for the Vietnam War was undermined, in part, by Americans who worried about the fate of our servicemen held prisoner at the Hanoi Hilton. Today, in contrast, the Iraq War is losing popularity because people are worried about the fate of our enemies held in our own prison!

America needs to wake up and realize that the people we're holding at Guantánamo are dangerous. Rumsfeld wasn't wrong to call them the "worst of the worst." In past wars, releasing prisoners would have been unthinkable until the war ended. Can we imagine releasing hundreds of thousands of German Wehrmacht soldiers in the middle of 1944 and flying them to Germany? Or flying Japanese POWs to their Pacific island of choice so they could take up arms again?

The inmates we have in detention at Guantánamo are a dangerous bunch. It would be fooling ourselves to believe that we have the knowledge, background, or skill to differentiate those who will return to terror if we release them from those we have reformed—especially when the terrorists themselves are content to deceive us to obtain their release.

Any prisoner of war can be counted on to try to escape. At Guantánamo, they don't need to tie sheets together and slide down them to freedom. They just have to con our military interrogators into believing they're innocuous.

Even if we credit soldiers with an incredible ability to spot the liars and separate them from the truly rehabilitated, they still wouldn't be making the decision on their own. The pressure by defense lawyers, American courts, international observers, the terrorists' native countries, and the U.S. Congress is forcing us to release more and more detainees.

Can the Bush administration—let alone the next administration—resist that pressure?

The shadow of Abu Ghraib hangs heavily over Guantánamo. The photos of American soldiers humiliating their captives—and the stories of innocent Iraqis swept up into detention without reason—made a deep impression on people all over the world.

But there is no comparison between the Iraqis held at Abu Ghraib and the prisoners at Guantánamo. The inmates in the Cuban prison are hardcore terrorists, usually captured in combat. They are a far cry from the thousands who were swept up in the early days of the coalition invasion in Iraq. As loose as the evidentiary standard appears to have been for incarceration at Abu Ghraib, those sent overseas to Guantánamo were generally shooting directly at American or coalition troops at the time of their capture or were highly wanted terror suspects.

Regrettably, it's now clear that neither the Bush administration nor the Pentagon has the stomach to resist calls for continued Guantánamo releases.

But if the administration is going to ask young men and women from the United States and our allies to risk their lives to kill or capture terrorists, the least it can do is to keep those whom they have bagged in prison until this war on terror is over. And, if that takes a long time, that's just too bad.

HOW HEDGE FUND BILLIONAIRES LIVE OFF TAX BREAKS

Why do the rich get richer? For one thing, because the U.S. tax law helps them to!

The billionaires who run hedge funds and equity firms have amassed their great wealth, in part, because they pay only 15 percent of their income in taxes—while the rest of us have to pay up to 35 percent!

Should partners in hedge funds and equity firms get special treatment when it comes to taxing their income? Right now, some of the most highly paid business executives can take advantage of a tax loophole that saves them millions of dollars.

Take Stephen A. Schwarzman, one of the cofounders of the Blackstone Group, a private equity firm that went public in 2007. Schwarzman has a stake in the company of almost $11 billion, according to *The New York Times.* Under capitalism, let him take what he can get. But let's not give him a special reduced tax rate! The *Times* also points to hedge fund manager James Simons, who earned $1.7 billion last year, and to two other managers who earned more than $1 billion each. In 2006, the combined income of the top twenty-five U.S. hedge fund managers exceeded $14 billion.

Why should they receive this preferential treatment? Apparently because they think they deserve it.

In a quotation that could rival Marie Antoinette's "Let them eat cake," the British buyout figure Nicholas Ferguson—who benefits from similar tax treatment in the United Kingdom—said that he and his associates "pay less tax than a cleaning lady."

But here's one important difference: a cleaning lady doesn't contribute millions of dollars to political campaigns, and hedge fund managers do.

In the first half of 2007, the Democratic Senatorial Campaign Committee, chaired by Senator Chuck Schumer (D-N.Y.), raised nearly $2 million from executives and employees of private equity and hedge funds such as Blackstone, according to an analysis by the Center for Responsive Politics. After years of splitting their funds evenly between the political parties, in 2006 these investors guessed right and gave more than two thirds of their money to the Democrats, who swept Congress that year.

In return, the Senate Democrats, led by Schumer, have blocked legislation to make these hedge fund managers pay the same tax rates as the rest of us. John G. Gaine, the president of the Managed Funds Association, the trade group for hedge funds, called Schumer a "guardian of America's capital market and, more parochially, New York's economic interest."

Fortune magazine wrote, "In another era, this might be a slam dunk for populist-minded Democrats: A new class of billionaires doesn't pay the same tax rates as ordinary Americans, leaving tens of millions of dollars more in their pockets to spend on private helicopters and ivy-clad boarding schools and Nantucket summer homes. What better example of Republicans favoring the rich? But wait: These new Greenwich/Manhattan billionaires happen to be donors, friends, and constituents of Democrats—not Republicans."

The New York Times highlighted Schumer's role, noting that "June was a busy month for Senator Charles E. Schumer. On the phone, at large parties and small gatherings around the nation, he raised more than $1 million from the booming private equity and hedge fund industries for the Democratic Senatorial Campaign Committee, of which he is chairman."

The story continued, "But there is another way Mr. Schumer has been busy with hedge fund and private equity managers. . . . He has been reassuring them that he will resist an effort led by members of his own party to single out the industry with a plan that would more than double the taxes on the enormous profits reaped by its executives."

Schumer has considerable power on tax issues. He is the only Senate Democrat who sits on both the banking and finance committees. And he is the number three ranking member of the Senate majority leadership.

In most respects, Schumer is a certified and consistent liberal Democrat. But he defends his opposition to raising taxes on hedge funds by pointing to his obligation to support one of his home state's biggest industries: Wall Street. Schumer told the press that "he was torn between the need to protect an industry vital to his home state and the need to generate revenues to finance government programs [and that] a tax increase on private equity and hedge fund executives could lead to an exodus of jobs and companies from New York, and even from the country. . . . He worried that the industry was being unfairly singled out."

Question: Why would a federal tax that simply *evened out* the tax treatment cause an exodus from New York?

Apparently, Schumer wants to be prepared for anything: he summed up his views by saying "unintended consequences often occur when you do major tax work. And you have to be careful." Doubtless he meant that raising taxes on hedge funds might drive them out of New York or out of the country altogether. But isn't it possible that the "unintended consequences" he's worried about might also include a reduction in campaign contributions to the Democratic Party? After all, without those funds, how can Democrats continue portraying themselves as opponents of vested privilege and defenders of the average American?

Senator Charles E. Grassley (R-Iowa), the ranking Republican on the Senate Finance Committee, said that Schumer's explanation did not tell the whole story: "They [private equity firms] contribute most of their money to the Democrat Party, and he [Schumer] wants to protect the [party's] income. It's completely contrary to the position he took in the last election, when he was leading the Senate Democratic campaign committee and he talked about the inequity of the tax system."

As a result of Schumer's efforts coupled with solid Republican opposition, all efforts to reform the tax treatment of hedge fund managers or other partnerships died in Congress in 2007–2008. It failed despite the support of both Senate Finance Committee Chairman Max Baucus (D-Mont.) and ranking member Grassley.

One lobbyist expressed surprise that his clients had emerged from the congressional session unscathed. "We did think until fairly recently that the . . . legislation [taxing hedge funds more] would get enacted."

One possible reason for the success of hedge fund partners in escaping fair taxation? *The Hill* reported that the Blackstone Group, a huge private equity firm, spent $3.74 million on lobbying fees in the first half of 2007. "Meanwhile, the hedge fund industry has given $5.4 million to federal lawmakers this election cycle, up from $4.8 million last year, according to OpenSecrets.org."

Private equity firms, also called hedge funds, raise money "from investors, including institutions, pension plans and wealthy individuals, and use the money, combined with loans, to acquire companies in hopes of selling them at a profit."

The managers of these funds are paid by two streams of revenue. They typically receive 2 percent of their fund's total value (taxed as ordinary income) and 20 percent of its profits (taxed as a capital gain called "carried interest").

Should the managers' share of these colossal profits be taxed as a capital gain (at 15 percent) or as ordinary income (at 35 percent)?

A capital gain generally refers to investment income—as distinguished from wages and salary, which are considered earned income. The reason investment income is taxed at a lower rate than earned income is that you've already paid taxes on the principal you invested, so you should pay a reduced tax on the money your principal earns.

Everybody agrees that the fund managers' return on their actual investment should be treated as a capital gain—but what about the 20 percent of the portfolio's profit that they receive as a fee for managing the investment?

The fund managers make the case that that 20 percent fee should be treated like a return on any other investment and taxed as a capital gain. They point out that the income is speculative, depending on whether or not the fund turns a profit, and goes up or down based on the fund's profits.

The Private Equity Council, the lobbyist for the fund managers, also says that this carried interest should be taxed as a capital gain like other investments. "Under the law today," says Douglas Lowenstein, the president of the organization, "private equity is taxed in exactly the same manner and at exactly the same rate that applies to every other investor that takes an entrepreneurial risk, expends time, energy and effort, grows the value of an asset over time and earns a profit."

The risk, the speculative nature of the investment, the variable rate of return, and the fact that their fee is tied to the value of the asset all argue for capital gains treatment. But we think carried interest for private equity firms should be treated as income. Why? Because the profits these private equity firm managers make are *not* based on returns on their actual financial investment. The managers of these funds typically contribute only a very small portion of the money the fund invests—so, although the return on their actual investment should be taxed as a capital gain, the remaining 20 percent of the profits that they take as a fee amounts to ordinary income. And it should be taxed that way.

After all, the theory of taxing capital gains at a lower rate is to reward an investor for taking a risk. But the only risk these hedge fund managers have is that *other people* may lose money because of any mistakes they make.

Part of the theory of capital gains taxation is that the government is taxing the earnings of after-tax money. The cash the taxpayer invests has already been through the IRS wringer; he's investing what is left. But the fees paid to investment fund managers have never been taxed—and there's no justification for taxing them as anything other than ordinary income.

As Senator Max Baucus (D-Mont.), the chairman of the Senate Finance Committee, says, "there is little difference between a large private equity firm and a Wall Street investment bank. Both offer a wide array of investment strategies for their clients. But only one claims that the income from an active business is passive and is subject to capital gain treatment."

Paul Krugman, the Princeton economist and *New York Times* columnist, compares private equity management fees to book royalties. Alan Binder, another Princeton economist, has noted that although the profits the private equity firms make come from capital gains, it's someone else's capital, not the fund manager's.

So what is Congress doing about this abuse?

No surprise: it's playing political games. The Democrats aren't anxious to fix this problem, even though they have the votes to do so. Why? One reason may be the massive campaign contributions they're receiving from private equity funds. But there's another reason: they have their eyes on bigger game.

The Democrats want to raise taxes if they take the White House in the 2008 election. They plan to raise income taxes, take the cap off Social Security levies, raise the inheritance tax, and double the capital gains and dividend tax. To pass the largest tax increase in history—by far—they will need political cover. So rather than close the hedge fund loophole before the 2008 election, they'll wait until afterward, so they can showcase this popular tax measure and hope to hide the rest of their package behind it. They're saving up this particular perk so that they can use outrage at its injustice to arouse support for the rest of their tax package.

And Chuck Schumer no doubt wants one more round of campaign contributions from the hedge funds to pay for the 2008 election. To make sure the loophole for capital gains by private equity partnerships isn't closed before the election, Schumer is insisting on a "poison pill" to kill the bill: he says he wants to eliminate capital gains treatment for *all* partnerships, not just private equity firms. His proposal would hike taxes on real estate, oil and gas, and other partnerships. He knows such a broad bill won't pass, so he's pushing it to make sure that private equity firms keep their loophole wide open as the 2008 election approaches (in the hope that their wallets will also be wide open for the Democratic Party).

Some halfway reforms that have been introduced in Congress seek to take the capital gains benefit away from private equity firms—but only those that have gone public. It would keep the benefit intact for privately held partnerships. But the only real difference between publicly traded firms and private partnerships is that the public ones have to reveal how much money they are making and thus they trigger public outrage. The privately held firms are likely making just as much.

No one is really sure how much money the federal government would reap from closing the private equity fund loophole. As Politico.com reports, "Private equity and hedge fund managers control trillions of dollars. Their lobbyists, hired from some of the top shops in town, wield influence worth billions. But neither group can get its hands on the most important piece of information in the hottest tax debate on Capitol Hill: the number of billions a new tax on private equity would bring into government coffers."

Whatever the sum turns out to be, it's sure to be substantial.

Private equity firms defend their tax break by crying crocodile tears for union and state pension funds, which they claim will lose vast sums of money if their cozy little tax loophole is repealed. They argue that the overly generous tax treatment the federal government accords their earnings gives them an incentive to work to build the value of the companies in which they invest. Without that incentive, they say, they wouldn't work nearly as hard to add value to these companies. This compromise in their work ethic, they maintain, would reduce the value of the stock in these companies and cut the returns to all those who invest in the company, particularly institutional investors such as pension funds.

Is there anyone who doesn't see through this argument?

"I don't buy it at all," says Michael Musuraca, the designated trustee for the $42 billion New York City Employees Retirement System. "I don't buy that their paying additional taxes will limit their incentives to make money for themselves or their pensioners. I think they have enough incentives to do their business."

The bottom line is simple: for the rest of us, keeping 65 percent of our income after the taxman leaves is adequate incentive to send us to work each morning. So why do private equity fund managers feel they deserve 85 percent?

The answer, most likely, is simple: they're bold enough to demand it.

For the moment let's put the issue of incentive aside and look at another question: Couldn't the private equity funds simply pass the extra tax cost along to their investors, so that the increased federal tax bite would come at their expense, the same way it does with pension funds? Obviously, they would like to, but can they? Senator Max Baucus of the Senate Finance Committee says he doesn't believe that increasing taxes "would significantly affect pensioners because of the competitiveness of the marketplace for investments by pension funds." Baucus says, "The data says to me that hedge funds and private equity funds may need pension funds more than pension funds need private equity or hedge funds. And that means that hedge funds and private equity funds may not have the economic power simply to pass along increased costs to pension funds."

Private equity fund managers are even saying that they'll take their money offshore if their tax break is repealed. As Congressional Budget Office Director Peter Orszag points out, however, moving offshore wouldn't help them much. "The United States taxes the income of its citizens even if they are located overseas, meaning that fund managers would have to forfeit U.S. citizenship to avoid tax increases." Orszag notes that in fact many funds are already headquartered offshore.

ACTION AGENDA

For once, we think the liberals are right. It's fleecing of the vilest sort to make regular taxpayers dig deeper into their pockets to cover tax breaks for people who make a billion dollars a year. If a regular tax rate leaves enough of an incentive for the average American, it should for fund managers as well.

Congress will have to fix this law eventually. But first the politicians want to milk the cow once more to use it to raise millions of dollars for the 2008 election. The fact that two thirds of the cream from this particular source is going to the Democrats is neither here nor there. The loophole needs to be closed right now—we shouldn't have to wait for it to fund one more round of suspicious election contributions.

The American people should challenge their elected representatives to act on the principles they proclaim from the rooftops.

It's an odd twist of fate that two of the leading liberals in Washington, Senator Chuck Schumer and Congressman Charles Rangel, both of New York, are the key players who will decide the fate of reform legislation. Rangel, at least, supports closing the loophole; Schumer opposes it and has used his poison-pill strategy of roping in other industries to help his efforts to quash it.

So, if you live in New York state, please write or call Senator Schumer and let him know how you feel about giving tax breaks to billionaires. His phone number is (212) 486-4430, and his office address is 757 Third Avenue, Suite 17-02, New York, NY 10017. And tell him we sent you!

HOW THE TEACHERS' UNION RIPS OFF ITS MEMBERS

Just as the worst sinners in Dante's *Inferno* occupy the hottest places in Hell, so those who fleece people of their retirement money deserve our special condemnation. When the perpetrator of the fraud is a labor union that its members rely on for guidance, support, and good-faith advice, the sin is especially heinous.

But the fact is that America's largest teachers' union, the National Education Association (NEA), with its 3.2 million members—along with a number of smaller local teacher unions—actively induce their members to invest in high-cost annuity policies that squander their savings and sap their retirement nest eggs in return for millions of dollars a year paid to the unions from the companies pushing the plans.

The union payoffs come in a number of ways: outright cash from the annuity companies; donations to favored NEA causes; paid exhibitions at union events; and a host of other goodies all induce the union to betray the confidence of its members and steer them to investments that drain their retirement savings.

Because of this scam, thousands of teachers, who implicitly trust and eagerly follow the union's recommendations, invest their life savings with companies that cream off as much as 5 percent a year (and sometimes even

more) for various administrative charges. In relying on union endorsements, teachers have every reason to expect that products endorsed by their
union have some special advantage for them and that the power and pres-
tige of the union make it possible for them to get the best product at the
very best prices.

But that's not the case with the NEA. It gets the best deal for the union
coffers, not for the members' pockets.

Let's take a look at the basics. An annuity is a contract with an insurance
company to provide regular payments to a worker after his or her retirement. Fixed annuities grow at a set interest rate. Variable annuities are tied
to the performance of a mutual fund. Tax-deferred annuities, which most
teachers buy, also have a death benefit that assures the teacher's heirs of
continued payments after his or her death.

The problem is that the insurance companies selling the annuities typically charge investors high fees (sometimes up to 5 percent a year) that
come right out of the money their savings earn. So if a particular plan
makes $5^{1}/_{4}$ percent a year, that's pretty good. But if a fee of 5 percent is
charged against the earnings, the net earning is only $^{1}/_{4}$ of 1 percent. And
that's definitely not good!

It gets worse. Unfortunately, the annuity investors are often trapped—
they usually can't move their money out of a fund without paying high
penalties.

Obviously, teachers aren't forced to buy the annuities; they could buy
low-fee mutual funds instead. Or they could purchase term life insurance that would ensure their beneficiaries of income after their death.
But many teachers are attracted by the convenience and simplicity of
having their savings, investments, and insurance wrapped up in a single
financial package—and, in many cases, automatically withheld from their
paycheck. More important, the union endorsement means a lot to them.
Unfortunately, the price they pay in fees is sometimes exorbitant, leaving
them with far less in retirement savings than they would have if they invested, instead, in alternatives.

Take a look at the following example:

FLEECING TEACHERS

Here's how the annuity fees rob teachers of their savings:

Teacher A contributes $500 per month . . .

. . . earns 10 percent a year . . .

and has $379,684 after twenty years.

Teacher B also contributes $500 per month . . .

. . . also earns 10 percent. . . .

But the annuity company deducts 4.85 percent for its fee

. . . leaving her with only $209,114 after twenty years!

DIFFERENCE: $170,570 LESS FOR TEACHER B! *THAT'S LESS THAN HALF AS MUCH!*

Source: *Los Angeles Times.*

In an extensive article for the *Los Angeles Times,* which was pivotal in unearthing these union shenanigans, business writer Kathy Kristof cited the unfortunate experience of Art Dawe, an English teacher from Middletown, New York. Dawe purchased an Opportunity Plus variable annuity from ING, citing "the state teachers union's endorsement" as the "key factor in his decision."

According to Kristof, Dawe was stunned at the utter failure of the NEA-endorsed investment to live up to his expectations. In reviewing the dismal performance of his account, he found that after the administrative and other fees charged by ING were deducted from the return on his savings, he had earned a net average of only 1.6 percent since 1990! "By comparison," Kristof points out, "U.S. mutual funds overall grew [at] an average of 8.4% a year during that period." As Dawe lamented, "I could have fared better with Atlantic City slots."

And the paltry return wasn't because ING didn't invest Dawe's money wisely; it was that it took the bulk of his earnings back for itself. As Kristof reports, "he paid ING 3.59% of his assets each year in fees. Of that, 0.67%

went to operating expenses for his annuity. An additional 1.92% was taken out for management fees for the mutual funds he chose. Finally, 1% was deducted to pay for the death benefit [to his heirs]."

After that, there wasn't much left in the profit column.

HOW TO RIP OFF A TEACHER

(Based on Art Dawe's experience)

Average annual percentage paid to Dawe: 5.19%

Total deducted from his earnings each year and returned to ING: 3.59%

Comprising: 0.67% for operating expenses

1.92% for management fees

1% for death benefit

Net paid to Dawe each year: 1.6%

Source: *Los Angeles Times.*

It doesn't have to be that way. There's no reason for annuity fees to be so prohibitive. Most mutual funds charge only a small fraction of what the union-recommended annuity policies do. The *Los Angeles Times* reports, for example, that the T. Rowe Price Group offers a "plan with a low-cost mutual fund that charges just 0.35% a year." Though the mutual fund does not provide insurance, an investor would save a lot of money by purchasing a term policy on his own. And paying 0.35 percent a year for administration is a lot better than paying either 3.59 or 4.85 percent!

How could Dawe—or any teacher for that matter—possibly amass a nest egg at that ridiculous rate of return? It's just not possible.

Let's face it: Dawe was shafted. But guess what? ING did fine—it made more than Dawe did. And the union did okay, too. We don't know exactly how much it was actually paid for Dawe's account—or even how much it received from all of the annuities combined. But federal law does require it to disclose the total amount it received from all endorsement deals. According to the *Los Angeles Times,* "the most recent disclosure on file with the

[United States] Labor Department shows that the NEA received $49.6 million from . . . endorsed companies in 2004." (This presumably includes companies providing credit cards and other financial products in addition to the annuities.)

So, for all we know, the union may have done better than Dawe, too.

It's not just the NEA that's trying to quietly make a buck on its members' investments: local teachers' unions are also climbing aboard the gravy train. The *Los Angeles Times* again: "local unions that help promote NEA-endorsed products [also] get a share of the royalties. The Florida Education Assn., for example, collected $140,000 in 'program royalties' last year, federal records show. The Illinois Education Assn. received $178,148, while the Maine Education Assn. was paid $33,610."

So everyone is doing well on the annuity scheme—except the union members.

It's a huge market. According to Margaret E. Haering of the *New Haven Register,* 7 million public school, hospital, and university employees have about $560 billion invested in annuity plans. These policies, called 403(b) plans after the section of federal law authorizing their formation, are like the more familiar 401(k) retirement plans in that employees contribute to them monthly, select investment options, and accumulate gains tax-free until they take out their money. Haering explains that "originally, insurance company products called annuities were the only investments permitted in 403(k) plans. Although the law was changed in 1974 to include mutual funds as allowable investments, annuities still account for more than 80 percent of 403(b) assets."

As Haering notes, however, the problem is that "participants who invest in annuities typically pay two to three times higher administrative and other costs than those who invest solely in mutual funds. For the privilege of possibly annuitizing their retirement savings in the future, teachers and other participants are subjected to mortality and expense fees, excess administrative charges, and the prospect of paying a surrender fee if they change their minds. Excess fees are a drag on investment growth in 403(b) plans."

Most teachers, trusting in their union, don't have the faintest idea that they're being fleeced out of their retirement savings because of the secret deals that benefit the union. The federal Government Accountability Office

(GAO) recently announced that "retirement plan participants . . . needed clearer information on fees" paid to unions by sponsors of annuity plans.

Dan D. Otter is one teacher who's trying to supply that vital information to his colleagues—through www.403bwise.com, which educates teachers about the high fees their annuity plans charge. He says that his efforts are to counter the high-pressure tactics used to sell these questionable plans to unsuspecting teachers.

Poor Art Dawe, the New York teacher fleeced by his union, told the *Los Angeles Times* that "he couldn't understand why the union had endorsed the annuity—until he read about ING's payments to the union on Otter's Web site. 'I was under the impression that because it was from the union, it would be in my best interest—because they're in my best interest,' he said. 'Now, I kick myself in the butt for buying it.' "

Dennis Tompkins, a spokesman for New York State United Teachers, told the *Times* that the union endorsement of the ING plan Dawe purchased was "good for members because it helps underwrite the union's benefits department and other services."

Ronald Mentzer, treasurer of NEA Member Benefits, told the *Times* that the endorsement money "pays the salaries of 110 union employees." In addition, endorsed firms sponsor NEA conferences and donate to favored NEA causes. One wonders if Dawe appreciates that his union was using his life savings to subsidize its benefits department. Perhaps it might have asked him if that's what he wanted to do with his retirement money. And let's be clear—it's not union employees who are servicing these accounts. The insurance company takes care of all of that.

Consider the scope of the benefits paid to the NEA by all its financial endorsements: $50 million a year. Last year, the NEA annual budget was estimated at slightly more than $300 million. So this windfall is no small matter to the union.

Perhaps that's why it supports the programs so vigorously. Tompkins defended his union's endorsement of the ING policy by citing the value of the financial advice its planners and agents give to investors as ample justification for their higher fees. "A lot of our members are beginning investors who need a lot of hand-holding and guidance," he said.

But these folks aren't high school dropouts. They are teachers, all college educated, and many with master's degrees. If they were, in fact, high school dropouts, it might be worth some of their savings to get "hand-holding and guidance." But they're not; they're teachers. Are they really the financial ignoramuses their union leaders pretend they are in order to try to justify this sweetheart deal?

The strength of the union's endorsement is such that teachers usually sign up for the annuities it recommends even if it means paying higher fees. According to the *Los Angeles Times,* "ING offers a lower-cost retirement plan for New York teachers, called Opportunity Independence, that does not include financial advice, a death benefit or other annuity features. But the vast majority choose the Opportunity Plus annuity."

Why? Kathleen Murphy, ING's group president for institutional financial services, claims that "overwhelmingly, the teachers have chosen the higher-service model because they want help, education and advice." But is that really so—or is it that the teachers' union gives priority to selling the Opportunity Plus annuity and the salespeople employed by ING push it aggressively?

And why would the "help, education and advice" teachers got from ING be important anyway? Mutual funds and annuity plans are identical in that they both make investment decisions on behalf of their investors. Satisfied to know that they investments are being well managed, few investors in either fund want to worry about which stocks to buy and when to sell. In fact, many annuities subcontract their investment decision to mutual funds. So how would such special expertise justify the high fees the annuities charge?

It seems that the one kind of expertise they really have is in fleecing the teachers' union members.

Members do get an advantage in that they're guaranteed an annual payment under an annuity. But investing in federally guaranteed products would provide the same sort of security without the high administrative fees. And, as noted, term life insurance would provide just as satisfactory a way of protecting beneficiaries as an annuity does.

But the unions aren't getting away with their ripoff! Thankfully, a number of lawsuits—by teachers, public interest groups, and state attorneys general—have emerged to threaten the cozy, mutually profitable relationship between the teachers' unions and their favorite annuity providers—a relationship that's good for everyone but the people who pay for it.

Recently, two NEA members, who invested in annuities sold by Nationwide Life Insurance Company and the Security Benefit Group, sued the teachers' union for endorsing the policies.

Their suit, filed in federal court in Washington state, charges that the NEA took millions to endorse annuity plans from two firms that charged teachers particularly high administrative fees. The suit charges that the NEA was more than just an endorser, and therefore violated its fiduciary obligations to its members: "NEA, through its NEA Member Benefits subsidiary, took on the role of a retirement plan sponsor, which must put its members' interests ahead of its own." The plaintiffs contend that "by taking fees from the two companies whose annuities NEA Member Benefits recommended to its members, the NEA breached its duty to them."

It's not clear exactly how much the NEA has been paid by Nationwide and Security Benefit since 1991, when the NEA began to endorse the specific annuities. But one newspaper reported that "a recent Security Benefit prospectus indicated that fees paid to NEA Member Benefits might exceed $2 million a year. That prospectus said Security Benefit paid the NEA subsidiary $510,000 a quarter."

The lawsuit alleges that these payments were not disclosed to the plaintiffs and that the union said it had selected the vendors based on "competitive criteria." Apparently the only thing that was truly competitive was which annuity was willing to give more money to the union.

The lawsuit charges that NEA members have invested more than $1 billion in these annuity policies, known as Nationwide Valuebuilder plans. Once again, there was more value built in for the union than for the individual. The *Los Angeles Times* documented the costs: "The NEA-endorsed . . . Valuebuilder [plan] charges 0.9% to 2.6% a year in fees and expenses—not including management fees for the mutual funds available through the plan. When the fund fees are added, investors pay a minimum of 1.73% of their account balances each year."

That's way too much.

The plaintiffs in the Washington state lawsuit contend that "the fees levied in the Nationwide and Security Benefit annuities 'far exceeded' those of comparable retirement vehicles available elsewhere. . . . The fees in one of the annuities recommended for the Valuebuilder plan reached 10.62 percent, according to the suit, making it exceedingly difficult for investors to make money in the plan."

Compare the Valuebuilder annuity plan endorsed by the NEA and sponsored by the Security Benefit Life Insurance Company with mutual funds with similar investment strategies offered by Vanguard Group:

THE VALUEBUILDER/NEA RIPOFF

After five years in each program, here is how the returns would compare if you invested $10,000:

In Foreign Stocks

Valuebuilder/NEA	$11,892
Vanguard Global Equity	$18,167

In Stocks and Bonds

Valuebuilder/NEA	$12,618
Vanguard Wellington	$14,050

Source: *Los Angeles Times.*

So here's the clear message: the Valuebuilder/NEA Fund is a loser. And the teachers are catching on!

The same law firm that represents the Washington state teachers, Keller Rohrback, has also sued the New York State United Teachers Member Benefits Trust on similar grounds.

When Eliot Spitzer, until recently the governor of New York, was the state's attorney general, he went after the New York state teachers' union. Spitzer's investigation revealed that the union "got almost $3 million for endorsing retirement products offered by a single insurance company." Spitzer found that the union's role in promoting the plans was widespread, including that "the teachers' union allowed insurance company employees to staff its benefits office and telephone lines and concealed the fact that the union was getting paid for allowing the insurer to sell products to members." How were teachers supposed to uncover this? There was no way they could be expected to figure this out on their own.

Spitzer's office reached a settlement with the union in 2006. As the *Los*

Angeles Times reported, the union agreed to "change the way it markets individual retirement plans to its members, ending what authorities called a 'silent partnership' with insurer ING Group that saddled teachers with high-cost investments that provided scant benefits."

The ING annuities "carried fees and expenses of as much as 2.85% a year, or about three times the cost of many popular mutual fund investments." David D. Brown, chief of the attorney general's investment protection division, said that "under the guise of giving objective advice, the union not only endorsed this product, they steered people to it. They ultimately became a sales arm of the insurance company."

Under the settlement, the union agreed to disclose its endorsement payments and promised to work with state authorities "to hire an independent consultant to suggest alternative investments to union members and to pay $100,000 to cover costs of the state investigation. In addition, the union agreed to provide members with annual access to free and objective investment advice and allow the 53,000 people who purchased retirement products it endorsed in the past to roll their balances into a newly endorsed product at no cost."

Unfortunately, the Spitzer settlement didn't require the union to end the practice of receiving payments in return for endorsing annuity products to its members. It merely has to disclose the fact that it's doing so and offer access to competing plans.

But the Spitzer lawsuit and other publicity about such practices—notably in the *Los Angeles Times*—may be having an impact on the teachers' union leaders. Richard C. Iannuzzi, the president of New York State United Teachers, told the *Times* that "your exposure, and others who started to raise questions about the insurance and financial industries, led me to ask questions about how we handled the issue of disclosure here. Your article in particular played an important role in our understanding of the issue."

Did Mr. Iannuzzi really need a lawsuit by the New York state attorney general and an exposé in one of the country's leading newspapers to figure this one out?

Helloooo?

We doubt it. If anything, Mr. Iannuzzi probably knows better than most about the origins of the $3 million check that shows up in the bank account he controls—money that permits him to add to the union's bureaucracy.

And was he surprised to find out that the people who were hawking the funds in the union offices were actually employees of the insurance company masquerading as union employees with the best interests of the members at heart?

Well, you be the judge: he's the one who okayed the deal.

Note to Mr. Iannuzzi: remember Harry Truman's famous admonition, "The buck stops here"!

The *Times* reports that the Los Angeles teachers' union "has also begun to reexamine its endorsement deals." Steve Schullo, a Los Angeles teacher who has been critical of the union, said it recently "played a key role in getting Los Angeles Unified School District officials to make low fees a required component for a new supplemental retirement savings plan that may be offered to teachers next year."

It's about time.

The *Times* also notes that the National Education Association "said it had [also] begun working on adding a low-cost investment option for its members."

But don't hold your breath waiting for it to stop publicizing high-cost options—not as long as that gravy train is still rolling.

ACTION AGENDA

If you're a teacher—in which case, thanks for all you do—your union is counting on your ignorance of its annuity fund ripoff. So write the National Education Association and complain about the administrative fees on the annuity plans it endorses!

In responding to the lawsuits, note that the unions never promise to end the practice of endorsing plans or of taking fees from those it recommends. They merely promise to reveal the fact that they are getting money from the plan to their members.

What kind of a response is that?

In effect, they're saying "Yes, we are recommending a higher-priced plan that robs teachers of their retirement savings. Yes, we know there are lower-cost options available. And yes, we admit that we're being paid to recommend the plan—but we'll push it on the teachers anyway so we can make more money, even if it costs them their retirement savings."

The unions' argument that teachers don't know enough to read a balance sheet or that they need some kind of special investment advice assumes that they're dunces (in which case one wonders why the union wants them teaching anyway). If teachers chuck their high-cost annuity plans, it doesn't mean that they need to become Wall Street mavens and figure out how to beat the market. It simply means that instead of letting the annuity plan choose which mutual fund to invest in, the teachers should be allowed to make the choice themselves. Even if they make a big mistake, they can't do any worse than they're doing now, with the annuity folks taking 2 to 5 percent of their investment each year as a fee!

So raise a little hell. Let the unions know you don't appreciate their high-handed tactics and they need to change their ways.

Specifically, all the lawsuits and complaints should aim at a few basic policy goals:

- All teachers who are locked into a high-fee annuity scheme should be able to opt out without any penalty. It's not their fault that they were suckered by their union and the insurance company into signing on the dotted line.

- The union should stop taking money from plans it recommends. That is a clear conflict of interest!

- The union should, for once, side with its members—as opposed to its own financial interest—and educate them on the virtues of low-cost investment options, which would allow members to build their retirement nest eggs without enriching the insurance companies in the process. If teachers are indeed as naive as the union makes them out to be, they need all the help the union can give them not to be trapped into giving away their savings in administrative fees.

- The details of all fee arrangements with insurance companies and other businesses should be prominently disclosed on all union materials and Web sites.

If you're not a teacher but you know one: please give him or her a call and explain how he or she may be getting ripped off. It's the least we can do to show our gratitude to the dedicated men and women who educate our children!

RE-REBUILDING LUXURY SECOND HOMES IN FLOOD AREAS AGAIN AND AGAIN—AT OUR EXPENSE

Having to pay for the same thing twice would fall into anyone's definition of being fleeced. But that's exactly what American taxpayers have done in the aftermath of hurricanes, storms, or flooding. Even though many of the homes that are rebuilt with our tax money are luxurious second or vacation beach homes that have been flooded or even washed away at least once before, the government still comes up with new money to rebuild them again and again.

These flood insurance claims, while relatively small in total numbers, account for a disproportionately high amount of the total claims paid. Indeed, *USA Today* reports that although "properties with repetitive flood losses—two or more flood claims within ten years—make up only 2% of all flood insurance policies, [they] account for nearly one-quarter of all payouts."

That's one quarter of our money!

Here's how it works: People build homes in areas known to be suscepti-ble to extreme flooding. As could be expected, their homes are wiped out when a storm passes through. They collect their taxpayer-subsidized flood insurance payouts—and then turn around and rebuild their homes in ex-actly the same spot—usually without taking any extra precautions. When a second catastrophe hits, they begin the process of milking the taxpayer all over again.

Maybe you're thinking, Well, that's no big deal. Let the government pay them to rebuild their homes. Washington can afford a scattering of luxury homes every year—they can't cost us much in the big picture, can it?

Well, first of all, remember this: we're not talking about the many unfor-tunate people who lose their primary homes to storms or other catastro-phes each year—who are left with nothing and genuinely need help. Our hearts go out, of course, to the many millions who have been wiped out by storms or floods, who deserve our assistance to get back on their feet. But some of those who milk our flood insurance program don't deserve our tears. Take a look: you might be surprised to learn who's really collecting the most from repeated federal flooding insurance payments.

First, we're talking about expensive homes. Close to half of them are worth more than half a million dollars. The average value of the properties that have been rebuilt under the insurance program is twice the average value of homes in the United States. In fact, a report by the Congressional Budget Office indicates that "the median value for single-family homes in the [fed-eral flood insurance] program range from about $220,000 to $400,000 com-pared to the average U.S. home value of $160,000." In fact, 40 percent of the homes covered by subsidized federal flood insurance are worth more than $500,000 and 12 percent are valued at more than $1 million.

WHO RECEIVES FEDERALLY SUBSIDIZED FLOOD INSURANCE?

Average value of flood-insured homes	$220,000–$400,000
Average value of all homes in the United States	$160,000

Percentage of flood-insured homes that are worth $500,000 or more	40 percent
Percentage of flood-insured homes that are worth $1 million or more	12 percent

Source: Congressional Budget Office.

It's one thing to have a pricy home rebuilt by federal flood insurance. It's quite another to rebuild it in the exact same place in the exact same way, wait for the next storm to pass through and destroy it—and then expect another bailout. According to the Federal Emergency Management Agency (FEMA), at the end of 2004 there were 11,706 properties with federal flood insurance that had either "four or more losses or two or three losses that exceeded the value of the building."

Take the example of Dauphin Island, a barrier island off the coast of Alabama. The island was known as "paradise" to locals—at least until Hurricane Katrina destroyed 350 of its homes. Since then, the government has spent more than $30 million to repair the damage from the storm. Part of the money was used to build a huge nine-foot sand dune to prevent future flooding "that has already been breached by the Gulf of Mexico's waters."

But the storm and flood damage hasn't deterred people from rebuilding their destroyed homes in the same exact place. One homeowner who owns a bed and breakfast told USA Today that her home had been damaged six times in the past seventeen years. Another island resident described the havoc that the storm damage has done: she has spent less time living in her house than waiting for repairs to be completed. Another couple who had five properties had no problem rebuilding the two damaged and three sunken homes that were Katrina victims. This wasn't their first experience in recovering from storm damage—but they're so stubborn that they're even considering building additional waterfront homes!

Does this make sense? If you're the homeowner, it might. But as taxpayers, do we want to support a public policy that constantly pays to rebuild houses—even if they're almost certain to be knocked down by the next storm?

From the homeowners' point of view, it's not an expensive proposition.

Despite the high prices of the homes involved, FEMA says that the policyholders have to pay only 35 to 40 percent of what they would pay if there were no government subsidy. FEMA reports that the average annual subsidized premium is $721 per year as opposed to the approximately $2,000 it would be at full market prices.

But behind the rebuilding program and the federally subsidized flood insurance that pays for it lies a basic conundrum: low-cost, taxpayer-subsidized flood insurance gives homeowners and developers all the incentive and protection they need to build on prime beachfront properties that are likely to be struck by damaging storms. As these homeowners enjoy their barefoot strolls in the sand, they realize that should a storm come—and it inevitably will—their flood insurance policy, paid in part by Uncle Sam, will give them the money to rebuild—in precisely the same spot!

A study by the Century Foundation pointed out that insurance generally creates "a well-known problem by blunting the consequences of risky behavior"—such as building in a hurricane zone. But where "private companies offer insurance, such risk is well under control" because the more risk people incur, the higher their premiums go. But with the federal government offering not only insurance but subsidized insurance, a homeowner has the freedom to take as much risk as he wants because Washington will foot the bill. If the worst happens, his premiums will go up by only 10 to 15 percent a year.

The study explains the concern: "the problem with [how federal flood insurance] accommodates repetitive losses is that it undermines the incentive to avoid building and rebuilding in high-risk locations. As risks grow, with fiercer hurricanes and rising sea levels destroying some of the most expensive property in the country, federal flood insurance may become a bulwark *against* the exercise of good sense."

The federal flood insurance program started in 1968. As one report detailed, it began "with the idea that it would offer subsidized rates in communities that adopted minimum building and zoning requirements." Since then, however, the influence of politics has taken its inevitable toll on the original goals of the program. "Over time, the subsidized rates have done far more to encourage development than the very minimal requirements have done to restrict it."

For decades, public pressure has successfully kept insurance premiums for flood insurance down, allowing policyholders to make repeated claims for damage from storm after storm without paying higher premiums. Although there have been some minor efforts to reverse this policy, they haven't been successful. A 1982 law attempted to put some "uniquely vulnerable undeveloped land off-limits to flood insurance," but congressional earmarks have repeatedly cut into the reserved areas and made those homes eligible for subsidized insurance, too.

The reason we needed to pass federal flood insurance in the first place was because the high risk of flooding in some areas made it so unprofitable for private insurers to cover the risk that Washington had to move in to fill the vacuum. But the feds never charged full fare for their insurance. As the Century Foundation study concluded, "federal flood insurance may be called insurance, but since the beginning, it has involved a subsidy to property owners."

The flood insurance program, which is run by FEMA, is virtually the sole provider of flood insurance in the United States. There are currently more than 5 million policies in effect, and a quarter of them are subsidized by the taxpayers. Coverage goes up to $250,000 for homes and an extra $100,000 for furniture and appliances. Premiums run to about $400 annually for each $100,000 of coverage. The Associated Press reports that "the rates typically do not reflect the real risks and therefore shift costs from policyholders to taxpayers generally."

The program is hugely expensive. Critics have warned for years that the full potential costs of the flood insurance program could be daunting—but their arguments remained theoretical until the twin hurricanes Katrina and Rita hit. Those two ladies generated $23 billion in claims, an amount far beyond the ability of the premium payments to meet. FEMA had to borrow $17.5 billion to meet the burden—a debt that will be passed on to future taxpayers.

As storm damage claims soared in the wake of the two hurricanes, private insurance companies raised their premiums sharply. According to USA Today, "a typical homeowner's policy that once cost less than $4,000 per year, now costs even more than $10,000. And many companies aren't even writing new policies."

But political considerations stop the feds from following suit and raising rates. On July 27, 2007, the House Financial Services Committee passed the Flood Insurance Reform and Modernization Act of 2007, raising premiums by only 10 to 15 percent annually and giving the program the authority to borrow more money to fund its operations. These token increases in premiums lag far behind the rate rises in the private sector. And it's the American taxpayers who will have to fund the difference.

So it fell to Maryland Republican Congressman Wayne Gilchrest to ask the question "Why should the people of Iowa, Colorado or Maryland have to subsidize some poor ignorant sap who is going to build a home on shifting sand that's going to be destroyed every five years?"

And well he should wonder. About half of the $30.6 billion paid out in the history of the flood insurance program has gone to three states: Louisiana, Florida, and Texas, mostly for homes the average American could not afford.

STATES WITH REPETITIVE FLOOD LOSSES

State	Buildings Lost a Second Time
Louisiana	24,175
Texas	15,875
Florida	14,940
New York	7,898
New Jersey	7,871
North Carolina	6,634
Pennsylvania	6,150
Mississippi	4,915
Alabama	4,038
Missouri	3,927

Source: *USA Today.*

Congressman Richard Baker, a Republican from Louisiana, has stuck his neck out against the interest of part of his home state and proposed that Congress pass a "Two Floods and You Are Out of the Taxpayer's Pocket Act," which would limit repetitive claims.

He's on the right track.

As the Century Foundation study charged, "It is both wasteful and unfair to ask average taxpayers to subsidize trophy houses on barrier islands, McMansions in flood plains, and other risky property developments by wealthy property owners."

Unfortunately, the legislation passed by the House committee in 2007, which would have phased out subsidized insurance rates for vacation or second homes, did not pass the Senate. So we're back to square one.

We can only hope that when the next Congress takes up the matter, it will also focus on the key issue: requiring better building codes and upgrading of the antiflooding construction as a precondition of new insurance. Without that, the flood insurance program will become a bottomless pit.

If property owners insist on rebuilding the same houses in the same places with the same designs as the homes that were washed away, the federal government should not offer subsidized insurance premiums and should probably deny any coverage at all.

Some people are getting the message. *USA Today* reports that "economic reality is already beginning to dictate a different kind of development. Near Biloxi[, Mississippi], high-rise condominiums, which can be engineered to better endure storms and spread insurance costs, are replacing single-family homes."

The newspaper asks why "people in Kansas or Colorado should be compelled to help foot the bill for others to live near the beach." *USA Today* echoes the point, noting that "Gulf Coast residents deserve the nation's sympathy and assistance in putting their lives back together. But the answers lie . . . in new kinds of construction and innovative building codes that reduce risk; in returning vulnerable seashore to a natural state; and in aid to the thousands still displaced by the storm. Subsidizing everything to be as it once was or inviting reckless development will only ensure a new catastrophe with the arrival of the next great storm."

And it won't be long in coming.

Climate change is warming the ocean, particularly in tropical areas. The warmer the water, the more of it evaporates, the harder it rains, and the more it floods.

As the Century Foundation study found, "Among the likely consequences of climate change are rising sea levels and increasingly extreme weather events. As a result, many homes and businesses near the sea and rivers face a growing threat of flooding. . . . As sea levels rise and storms become more frequent and more violent, flood losses can be expected to increase."

The Century study sees no alternative: "If we are going to prepare for the consequences of climate change, we must modify our institutions to roll with nature's punches."

To "roll with nature's punches," the foundation urges, "rules against repetitive loss must be strengthened, enforced, and funded. Whenever a claim is made in an area deemed [to be at] high risk for repetitive loss, the owner should be offered a choice between a buyout and payment of the claim. After such a claim is paid, federal flood insurance should not be renewed. For buildings in high-risk areas, the goal must be to remove federal flood insurance through a buyout option."

There's another problem with the flood insurance program. While some homeowners make repeated claims on their subsidized insurance policies for luxury or vacation homes, there are many homeowners at the opposite end of the spectrum—those who have no flood insurance at all. Washington relies on private insurance brokers to spread the word and sign people up for federal flood insurance in vulnerable areas. But because the subsidized premiums are so low, private brokers don't make much of a commission on each policy they sell—and thus they're not often very aggressive in marketing the policies.

Indeed, after Katrina there were indications that many insurance brokers had been steering people *away* from federal flood insurance, pushing private policies with higher premiums and commissions instead. When the hurricanes hit, policyholders became well acquainted with the fine print in these private policies, which indicated that they covered only wind damage and not problems caused by water damage or flooding. But private insurance brokers hadn't mentioned this small point to their customers, so many never bought the federal flood insurance they needed. Indeed, only about a quarter of those who really should have flood insurance have purchased policies.

Some homeowners don't buy flood insurance because the federal maps, which designate which areas are prone to flooding, inaccurately suggest that they don't need it. But these maps are often obsolete and don't reflect the new storm conditions global climate change has ushered in.

The feds encourage flood insurance in areas within a hundred-year floodplain, meaning that they're likely to flood once in a century. But, as the Associated Press has reported, "when the storm surge from Hurricane Katrina breached levees in New Orleans, thousands of homeowners outside the 100-year flood plain who lacked flood insurance suddenly found their dwellings under water for the first time."

According to *Forbes*, "75% of U.S. flood hazard maps are outdated." Michael Bullock of Intermap Federal Services told a congressional committee that the obsolescence of the maps "greatly limits their value in reducing flood losses to lives and property." For example, *Forbes* noted that "the flood maps for much of Spartanburg County in South Carolina date back to 1984. In Cobb County, Georgia, FEMA uses maps from 1992—since then the number of housing units there has grown from 190,000 to 256,000, meaning there's less undeveloped land area to absorb runoff and more area that could flood."

In 2004, FEMA awarded a $750 million, five-year contract to convert 100,000 maps on file into a nationwide digital map in order to reduce the time required to change them. But less than a third of the job is complete, and the project is behind schedule.

The Century Foundation study also advocated completion of the remapping—but for a different reason. It urged that "maps must be updated across the nation and then used to deny federal flood insurance to any new construction in the highest risk areas."

Remapping would double the number of federal flood insurance policyholders, generating extra revenue for the program. But *Kiplinger's Business Report* notes that "developers and builders object [to the remapping], fearing that the costs would scare away potential buyers."

There are a lot of reforms needed to protect those who really need and deserve federal flood insurance and a lot of changes needed to stop subsidizing those who repeatedly use the program without making any changes to prevent yet another flood disaster.

It's high time for both.

ACTION AGENDA

The Century Foundation study hit the nail on the head: policies that *insure* storm damage also *ensure* that there will surely be storm damage, by incentivizing construction in high-risk areas and disincentivizing buildings strong enough to stand up to hurricanes. If the feds are always ready to bail out homeowners and let them rebuild again and again and are prepared to let them off with slight premium increases, there will be more and more risky building.

The basic question remains: Why should taxpayers pay so that someone can live on the beach?

We need to do three things:

- Restructure federal flood insurance so that it forces homeowners to build their new structures higher, stronger, and farther away from the beach so as to minimize storm damage—or no subsidized rates.

- Distinguish people who face personal catastrophe from flood and storm damage from the vacationing rich who want a house on the beach and also want the taxpayers to subsidize the risks they take on by building in such a vulnerable area.

- Stop subsidizing premiums for flood insurance on homes that cost a million dollars or more.

Several legislative fixes are currently in various stages of consideration in Congress, but no single bill meets all these criteria.

Obviously, we need to end any federal subsidy for any insurance premium for a second or vacation home. If the federal government is generous enough to fill the void left by private insurers who are pulling out of flood-plain areas en masse, owners of second homes should at least pay full freight for their coverage and not ask other taxpayers for subsidies.

Whether a home is a family's primary residence or a vacation home, when a storm hits, federal insurance should pay them fully for their loss. But that does not oblige us to rewrite a policy on a new home in the same spot with the same vulnerable construction, much less to subsidize the premiums with our tax money.

The coverage must be structured the next time around so as to encourage construction in lower-risk areas and to demand stronger construction. Even if local building codes—enacted by politicians elected by local homeowners—don't require adequate antiflood measures, federal flood insurance should impose those requirements as a precondition of its purchase.

Insurance premiums should be raised or lowered to encourage homeowners to protect themselves against storms and to move away from vulnerable areas.

In New Orleans, FEMA is doing the opposite. It is letting residents rebuild as long as they have three feet of flood protection—this in a city that, in many places, was under up to twenty feet of water after Katrina.

Residents can avoid even these modest elevation requirements if their homes were less than 50 percent damaged by Katrina. But, as one local homeowner noted, there was plenty of room to fudge the numbers. "We were 70 percent damaged, but we got [the official designation] down under 50 percent. You could go down and get it changed depending on what you wanted."

J. Robert Hunter, the insurance director for the Consumer Federation of America and the head of the federal flood insurance program in the 1970s, has it right: "You're not doing people a favor," he says, "by letting them rebuild in the same way" that caused the flood in the first place.

One measure we'd recommend is that no homeowner should be allowed to collect federal insurance of any kind more than twice on the same property. Two strikes and you're out! Homeowners should be able to retain their coverage, of course, if they move to a new and less risky location. But we need to end the ebb and flow of repetitive rebuilding, flooding, and re-rebuilding.

Federal flooding maps must be digitized—and updated quickly, so that all those who face flood danger can get insurance. The responsibility for informing people that they need flood insurance in the newly mapped areas should not lie with brokers. Instead, the feds should reach out directly to homeowners to publicize the need for flood insurance and should ask banks to require such insurance in all areas the new maps indicate are prone to flooding.

But once there has been a storm and a homeowner rebuilds in the same area with the same flimsy construction, future premiums should rise to market levels. Taxpayers shouldn't be required to subsidize the insurance when people are voluntarily taking the risk of living in vulnerable homes in vulnerable places. The current congressional plans to require a 10 to 15 per-cent premium increase are unrealistic. With private companies doubling their premiums, these minor increases still leave taxpayers holding the bag.

Of course, federal flood insurance should cover both wind and water damage—even if it pushes private firms out of the market. There are no dry hurricanes, and Washington shouldn't predicate its policies on being able to distinguish between wind and water damage. Readers of our previous book, *Outrage,* will remember our section on this point: the courts have ruled that these companies must cover wind damage but have let them off the hook from covering flood damage—even though policyholders pro-vided substantial evidence that they had deliberately been misled by insur-ance brokers into believing that their private polices covered both wind and water.

As a partial fix, legislation is now making its way through Congress that would allow FEMA to write policies covering both wind and water damage. With private insurance companies withdrawing in horror from writing policies of any sort in the flood-imperiled areas of Louisiana, Florida, and Texas, industry opposition to federal wind insurance is likely to be muted.

With sound public policy, we can strike a balance between compassion for those who have been flooded and for the taxpayers who are inundated each year by demands from the IRS. Americans at both ends of the transac-tion deserve our empathy. Too often, however, we forget the taxpayer in our understandable sympathy for the homeowner.

Let your members of Congress know about the changes the program needs!

THE SUBPRIME LOAN CRISIS:
Why the Greedy Are Going Free

The subprime mortgage scandal has all the elements of a proper fleecing: poor and undereducated victims, distracted government regulators, rising home prices that covered a multitude of sins, and greedy lenders who expected federal insurance to bail them out if things got tough. But in the months since the mortgage lending scam hit the front pages, most attention has been focused on how to stop our economy from drowning in a tsunami of bad debt. Some have begun looking at how to stop more borrowers from getting fleeced by subprime loans. But no one, it seems, has been taking a good look at the perpetrators—the greedy, unscrupulous con artists who made the loans in the first place.

The shady and shaky loans these subprime scammers made are threatening to send the entire world into a downward economic spiral. More than the Internet bubble of the 1990s, the savings and loan debacle of the 1980s, or the oil price shocks of the 1970s, this mass of nonperforming loans is undermining the global credit system, sending interest rates and the adjustable rate mortgages they influence rising from Barcelona to Brooklyn. In recent years, only 9/11 seems to have had a larger impact on the world's economy.

But it was not a terror attack that caused this economic mayhem—it

was a ripoff by a group of con men in the mortgage business making subprime loans to gullible people. And what an impact they have had!

In a March 2008 survey of 259 economists, all members of the National
Association for Business Economics, 34 percent ranked the financial tur-
moil caused by loan defaults as "the No. 1 threat to the economy over the
next two years."

A year ago, only 18 percent said that debts and defaults were the major
problem while 20 percent cited terrorism. Two years ago, "the credit crisis
did not even register as a chief threat."

After fifty-one months of refusing to change short-term interest rates,
Federal Reserve Chairman Ben Bernanke succumbed to fears of fading
prosperity and global economic recession and dropped the federal interest
rate by half a point on September 18, 2007. But that wasn't enough: in the
months since, he's been forced to order several additional reductions to
stave off a recession and keep capital flowing despite the shocks of the subprime scandal. From there, the rate went cascading downward as the crisis
worsened.

But those who made the bad loans that have eaten away, like termites, at
the foundations of our world economy are largely escaping culpability.
There have been no convictions, no indictments, and no real investigations
into their irresponsible conduct in making these loans in the first place.

Meanwhile, they're reaping the benefits of their own greedy conduct.
Too big to fail, the very mass of the bad loans they have made is forcing
the government, led by President Bush, to come to the rescue of their victims. But the mortgage brokers and the lenders—who made vast sums as
commissions, fees, and surcharges on their rotten loans—are happily
spending their ill-gotten winnings, confident that explicit or implicit federal guarantees will protect their profits even as they foreclose on millions
of homes.

Some homeowners are being rescued. But many more are facing the risk
of losing their investment—and their home along with it—after two or
three years of paying mortgages because the circumstances of their loans
don't happen to qualify them for the forms of relief Washington and other
national capitals can offer.

How did the subprime debacle come about?

It all goes back to the real estate market boom that began in the 1990s and continued into the first half of this decade. It was a period marked by a very high rate of home purchases—driven by what economists call "household formation." As the children of the baby boomers came of age and wanted to buy homes of their own, the demand for more housing grew rapidly. Meanwhile, their boomer parents, nearing retirement, rushed to buy vacation homes or to relocate entirely from their Frostbelt moorings to the Sunbelt. Flocking to Florida, Arizona, Texas, and California, they suddenly needed new homes—and, having made a killing in the go-go world of mergers and acquisitions of the 1980s and the Internet bubble of the 1990s, it seemed that many could afford them.

As a result, the increase of demand for housing so outstripped the supply that home prices rose out of all proportion. With values rising, homeowners refinanced their mortgages to convert their home equity into cash—and mortgage lenders did a handsome business keeping pace with their desires.

Inflation, long the fear of the bond markets, seemed tame as Federal Reserve policies held the increase in prices down year after year. Long-term interest rates declined, feeding the demand for new mortgages.

With low interest rates and rising home prices, con artists moved in—offering the poor and uneducated a chance to get in on the action. They induced millions of downscale families to buy homes they couldn't afford.

Can't come up with a down payment? they said. Don't worry, we'll fold it into the loan.

Can't afford market interest rates? No sweat, we'll lend you the money at an artificially low rate, wrapping up the interest you'd otherwise have to pay during the first three years of the loan into the principal of the mortgage. About 20 percent of all mortgage loans made these days are subprime.

So countless families bought homes this way—by putting no money down, borrowing the down payment, and paying amazingly low interest rates because they also borrowed the interest on their loan for the first few years. The folks who arranged for them to get these mortgages then added to the injury by charging "points" or fees or commissions, folding these charges, too, into the principal of the mortgage loan.

Here's how it worked:

Let's say the Smiths wanted to buy a $150,000 home. In the old days, they would have put $30,000 down and borrowed the remaining $120,000 at a fixed rate of interest of, say, 8 percent. Not anymore. Once the scam artists moved in, they offered a new kind of deal, one many people couldn't refuse:

1. They waived the down payment, allowing the Smiths to borrow the entire $150,000 with nothing down.
2. They gave the Smiths an adjustable rate mortgage (ARM). Instead of paying 8 percent for the life of the loan, the Smiths got a lower opening rate of, say, 6 percent. After two or three years, once national interest rates had gone up, theirs would go up to. More than 90 percent of subprime mortgages are based on these adjustable rates.
3. And if the Smiths couldn't afford even the 6 percent rate, the lender would lop off three more points of interest ($4,500 a year on a $150,000 mortgage) for three years. He would take this extra interest the borrower wasn't paying and fold it into the mortgage loan itself, so that the borrower was borrowing not just the principal but also the interest on his loan. As a result, when the loan-within-the-loan expired after three years, the Smiths would owe not just the $150,000 they originally borrowed, but an additional $13,500 of interest ($4,500 per year times three years = $13,500). That turned their $150,000 loan into a $163,500 commitment.
4. Then, to make a little more money for themselves, the mortgage brokers and lenders might charge $7,000 to $10,000 in fees, commissions, and "points." Of course, the Smiths didn't worry: the lenders just folded their charges into the body of the loan and hiked the amount they lent the Smiths up to $170,000! No one bothered to think about one little detail: the home was only worth $150,000 to begin with, and once home prices started dropping it would be worth even less.

THE SUBPRIME MORTGAGE SCAM

1. Mr. and Mrs. Smith buy a $150,000 house. They make no down payment, so the loan is for $150,000

2. The lender also lends them three points on their mortgage payments for three years. $150,000 x 3 percent x 3 years = $13,500

3. The lender also charges $10,000 in fees, commissions, and other charges, which he includes in the loan: *$10,000*
   Bringing the total amount the Smiths owe to: $173,500

At first, this kind of deal must not have looked too bad. The Smiths got their beautiful house, the brokers got their commission, the lenders made their fees, and everybody went home happy. Or so it seemed.

But the lenders knew the dirty little secret—that the Smiths would probably have to default after that first three-year period was up. At that point, they would be hit with a double whammy: the loan-within-a-loan that had allowed them to pay just 3 percent interest would be over and their rate would jump to the 6 percent it should have been in the first place. And because interest rates had gone up since they took out their adjustable rate mortgage, that 6 percent rate would more likely be moving up to 7 or 8 percent. So their monthly payments would double and perhaps triple.

Was this any surprise to the lenders? No way. They knew that most of their subprime customers would end up defaulting—and they certainly didn't want to be left holding the bag when the loan went south. So somebody came with a bright idea—they would start issuing paper on Wall Street based on the value of the mortgages. Calling their product a "mortgage-backed security," they went to the mortgage lenders and bought tens and even hundreds of billions of dollars of mortgages, which they then resold to investors.

At first, these mortgage-backed securities were based on pretty secure loans. But as the subprime boom got going, they became a refuge for lenders who had made bad loans—and an incentive to make more of them. By the first half of 2007, the total value of mortgage-backed securities had swollen to $17.2 trillion, of which 7 percent were subprime loans. To the lenders, this looked like a low-risk situation: after all, if their borrower defaulted, the only loser would be the investor who had bought the mortgage-backed security. The broker and lender would be long gone—spending their commissions and fees happily, with no further responsibility for the mortgage.

But even those investors were protected—because no one investor was responsible for a particular mortgage. No single investor owned the Smith mortgage, for example. Each investor held a tiny portion of the entire portfolio. And each portfolio was a mixed bag. Some portion of each portfolio was probably a very good investment; some of it was even federally guaranteed. Another portion was likely more iffy—such as the Smiths' subprime mortgage. But because no one was on the hook for any specific mortgage, nobody cared much if the Smith loan was solid or shaky.

Investors in mortgage-backed securities funds either didn't know or didn't care much about potential risks involved with any given mortgage; they figured there were enough good loans in the pile to offset any losses. And of course the Smiths didn't care—or didn't know. They just made out their monthly checks to a new company after their mortgage was sold.

The investors in mortgage-backed securities may have gotten a good deal, but the borrowers of the mortgages themselves—the Smiths in our little parable—were stuck with a time bomb disguised as a mortgage.

When the adjustable rate kicked in and the loan-within-the-loan expired, their payments would go sky-high. Even if the Smiths had been punctilious about paying their original mortgage on time, there would be no way they could afford the doubled or tripled interest rate that would kick in after three years.

So why didn't the Smiths get a new mortgage, without the pitfalls? Why didn't they refinance? Most likely because the mortgage market had gone soft over the first three years of their mortgage. The glut of new homes, built in response to the bubble of higher selling prices, had so glutted the market that home prices had begun to drop.

The Smiths' house, worth $150,000 when they bought it, was most likely falling in value—so much so that no one would lend them money to cover their mortgage. If they had put down an equity payment of 20 percent when they bought their home—so that they were borrowing only $120,000—

they would have had some leeway to offset a drop in values. But they had overborrowed themselves into a home that was nowhere near justifying that size of mortgage.

So the Smiths faced default. Unable to sell their home for a price that would cover the mortgage amount, they faced eviction from their home and the loss of any equity they had tried to build up over their three years of paying the mortgage on time.

But there were so many "Smiths" out there that many other borrowers joined them in the foreclosure docket, as a larger and larger percentage of the securitized mortgage portfolio turned bad.

And there were lots of loans to turn bad. In 2005 and 2006 alone, lenders made $1.2 trillion in subprime mortgage loans. *That's about 10 percent of the size of the whole U.S. economy.*

If the risky loans had been segregated from the rest of the lending market, they could just have been written off, leaving the investors to learn an expensive lesson in the dangers of get-rich-quick schemes. But the $1.2 trillion worth of subprime loans was mixed in with $17.2 trillion of regular loans—which were largely healthy mortgages. The increasing number of defaults on subprime mortgages cast aspersions on the entire credit structure, threatening to drag the global economy down with them.

The worst part of all is that the schemers at the root of the scandal—the unscrupulous lenders who persuaded the gullible and poor to take out the mortgages in the first place—haven't been punished. Worse yet, they haven't even been stopped. They're still at it, fleecing the public even as the subprime scandal builds. Like pickpockets working a crowd of spectators at the hanging of a pickpocket, they persist in their come-ons even as their past prey are evicted from their homes.

Undaunted by the mayhem they've left in their wake, subprime lenders keep inducing the unwary to fall into their trap, baited by low-cost mortgages. Since 2000, mortgage lenders have spent more than $3 billion on television, radio, and print advertising according to Nielsen Monitor-Plus.

And the methods of many lenders are shameless. As *The New York Times* has reported, Quicken Loans (separated from the makers of Quicken software), the nation's twenty-fifth biggest lender, runs a radio advertisement that's bound to entice unsuspecting borrowers." 'This is a rate alert,' the advertisement starts off, sounding much like a newscast. 'Slower economic growth has caused the Fed to keep interest rates flat, and the market has responded with some of the lowest mortgage rates in years.' "

But it's on the Internet that they're really coming on strong. Nielsen//Net Ratings "estimates that mortgage companies spent $378 million in the first six months of [2007] on Internet display ads, and many companies also buy search advertising."

The *Times* cites LowerMyBills.com, owned by the credit agency Experian, for its "prolific" and outrageous Web advertising, "with its impossible-to-miss ads that feature dancing cowboys and a video of a woman jumping and screaming with joy, presumably after being approved for a loan."

And ads like these work. Patricia A. McCoy, a law professor at the University of Connecticut, says that "the [mortgage] advertising has been a drumbeat to consumers, saying: 'Don't worry, you can qualify for a loan. We will approve it.' It was push marketing to reach out to these people on the sidelines who have doubts about their ability to pay a mortgage and lure them in."

Even as subprime mortgages are tanking all over the world, the lending continues at a frenzied pace. Quicken Loans, for example, wrote $18 billion in lending commitments last year—three times its 2001 total—and it planned on making more than $20 billion in 2007. It has found its borrowers—some would call them victims—by spending $37 million on mortgage ads in the first half of 2007.

Now that the subprime bill is coming due, Washington and the world are focusing on how to stop the world's credit markets from crashing and are desperately trying to keep loans flowing to sound businesses and thrifty consumers. President Bush and Congress—whether driven by compassion or politics—are moving to bail out many of the borrowers who were enticed to take subprime loans. The Bush plan, which is both reasonable and costly, would refinance the mortgages at as low an interest rate as possible for homeowners who satisfy two criteria: they must have at least 3 percent equity in their property (i.e., they must have invested 3 percent of the purchase price of the home from their own resources), and they must have a good history of making timely mortgage payments before their adjustable rate mortgage interest costs were jacked up.

The Bush plan doesn't involve any direct federal subsidy, since it capitalizes on the federal government's ability to borrow money at a lower rate than private lenders can. But—and here's the catch—if any of these new borrowers defaults, it will be we, the American taxpayers, who foot the bill.

And let's not forget that no such plan does anything to *punish* those who profited from the shady mortgage loans—or to stop the system from continuing to make subprime loans, now and in the future.

How are we supposed to apportion blame for such a monumental disaster—and fashion appropriate punishments? Let's start by identifying those who caused the crisis in the first place.

MORTGAGE BROKERS

Seventy-one percent of all subprime mortgages have been arranged by mortgage brokers—independent consultants who reach out to homeowners by ringing doorbells, making phone calls, and placing advertisements in the media. Their goal is to find customers (or, in this case, suckers) who will fall for their pitch. According to the Bureau of Labor Statistics, there are 136,000 mortgage and loan brokers in the United States—a vast increase from the 50,000 who worked in the field ten years ago.

The brokers don't actually do the lending. What they do is reel customers in and then take the potential borrowers to a mortgage company. In exchange, the lender pays them a commission for each new sucker they bring in. But the lenders are too smart to foot that bill out of their own pockets: ninety percent of the time, the broker's fee, called a "yield spread premium" (YSP)—which averages $1,800 per mortgage—is folded into the subprime mortgage loan. Once again, it's the little guy who pays.

Brokers have an incentive to steer customers into these heavily interest-deferred and therefore risky loans. Why? Because the lower the down payment and monthly payments are, the more likely they are to close a sale. Unfortunately, too few borrowers know enough to ask about what will happen down the road, when the deferments end and their interest rate reverts to its normal level—and too many brokers would rather keep them in the dark than jeopardize their fees.

The Washington Post describes the potential for abuse: "salespeople worked on commission—meaning the more loans they sold, the more bonus money they received . . . [some] salespeople tweak numbers in mortgage applications to ensure that the loans would be approved."

LENDERS

Although many mainstream banks made subprime loans—Citigroup and Lehman Brothers actually set up subprime subsidiaries—most of the mortgages flowed through nonbank lenders such as New Century Financial, Ameriquest, Option One, Countrywide, and Ocwen Mortgage Solutions. Jim Hightower, a vigorous and virtuous consumer advocate from Texas who briefly served in the state government, notes that while "brokers are on the front lines . . . the lenders are the ones who invented the scams that are bleeding borrowers."

Conventional mortgages from reputable banks typically carried a 1 percent fee for the lending institution. But Hightower reports that subprime borrowers were "commonly hit with fees (hidden in mortgage payments) totaling more than 5 percent."

Contrary to the tradition of most banks, which carefully investigate the borrower's credit history and income, these lenders did little to check out their customers. Hightower reports that one broker said, "you could be dead and get a loan."

As *The Washington Post* reports, subprime lenders have been in a "feeding frenzy" to make loans and "basic quality controls were ignored in the mortgage business, while the big Wall Street investment banks that backed these firms looked the other way."

Subprime mortgages are so profitable that although they accounted for 20 percent of mortgage loans last year, they generated 30 percent of the profits in the mortgage business. *The Washington Post* adds that "lenders also made a fortune selling subprime loans to Wall Street. Investment banks charged huge fees for packaging them into massive bonds called mortgage-backed securities. Investors received high returns for buying and selling these bonds."

In the rush to cash in, the usual safeguards were abandoned by lenders. *The Washington Post* says that "automated underwriting software that searches for irregularities and possible fraud was also supposed to stop bad loans. But industry professionals say such programs were easily manipulated. Meanwhile, some appraisers and underwriters, who examine housing values and other claims made on loan applications, say they felt pressure from bosses to let questionable loans through."

A lot of these "questionable" subprime loans were loaded with gimmicks, usually buried in the fine print of the lending agreements and couched in legal language. Some home loans were based on bloated appraisals of the value of the properties for which they were lent. In some cases, the lenders wouldn't tell the borrower about the property taxes or mortgage insurance premiums they'd be obliged to pay. Hightower notes that this practice "leads to borrower shock (and sometimes default) when the tax and insurance bills arrive separately in the mailbox. At this point, ever-helpful lenders offer to refinance the loan, thus collecting additional fees."

Borrowers who came to realize that they were headed off a cliff when the initial term of their mortgage expired could do little to avert the catastrophe. They couldn't refinance even if they found a lender who would give them the money to pay off their current subprime mortgage. Seventy percent of subprime loans include prepayment penalties with a fee of several thousand dollars for paying off the loan early. (Only 2 percent of conventional mortgages carry such penalties.)

The ever-eloquent Hightower sums up the abusive process: "What a system! Lenders mislead borrowers, collect fat fees from them, then shift the risk of any bad loans to Wall Street. The Wall Street repackagers then transfer the bad-loan risk to their rich investors, drawing even fatter fees."

The subprime lending craze led to an increase in foreclosures of 41 percent during the first half of 2006. A total of 550,000 American families lost their homes in the last year. In all, some 2 million American families may face foreclosure of their subprime loans.

One of them is Gerald Porter, a seventy-six-year-old California man who is suing his mortgage company, saying that it "conspired with a bank to commit elder abuse and fraud by arranging to refinance his home with a high-interest loan that he did not want." He charges that "Loyalty Mortgage, Inc, and the Downey Savings and Loan Association worked together to earn high fees by harassing and intimidating him into taking out an unnecessary and expensive loan."

If we take his allegations at face value, Porter's case demonstrates how far lenders and brokers will go to get people to sign up for mortgages. He says that the defendants "took advantage of him because of his age, diminished physical and mental abilities, and inexperience with financial transactions and used a campaign of repeated harassment, physical intimidation and fraud to obtain his business."

Porter says that Loyalty representatives made "incessant" calls to get him to take out a loan. He finally "gave them his personal financial information because he thought they would stop calling once they had the data." But the calls didn't stop. Indeed, a Loyalty representative, one George Lopez, "came to his home [and] stayed there for five hours, during which he used physical intimidation to obtain an electronic copy of [his] signature." Porter says he was "fearful for his life while Lopez was at his home." The complaint says that Lopez, who is "physically imposing . . . poked Porter in the chest with a rod-like electronic device used to obtain electronic copies of signatures."

Porter says "he was shocked when he received a notice from his mortgage lender . . . saying that his debt had been paid off through a refinancing loan from Downey Savings" and notes that the new mortgage has such high monthly payments that they "will leave him unable to pay all his bills."

Commenting on the subprime defaults, the president of the Federal Reserve Bank of Saint Louis, William Poole, suggested that the market is starting to punish those who made bad loans. "This year's markets punished mostly bad actors and/or poor lending practices," he said. "Lenders who made loans to borrowers without documentation, or who did not check borrower documents that proved fraudulent, or who made adjustable-rate loans to borrowers who could not hope to service the debt when rates adjusted up, deserved financial failure. As is often the case, the market's punishment of unsound financial arrangements has been swift, harsh and without prejudice. . . . I cannot feel sorry for the lenders who have gone out of business."

On the other hand, Poole continued, "my attitude is entirely different toward the relatively unsophisticated, but honest, borrowers who have lost their homes through foreclosure. Many are true victims."

And, as often happens, minority families are the hardest hit by the scandal. According to a study by United For A Fair Economy, "People of color are more than three times more likely to have subprime loans than white people." The study estimated that these families have lost between $164 billion and $213 billion in the subprime collapse.

But what about the middlemen? The brokers and their favored lenders who made bad loans, knowing they were bad, and then sold them on the secondary mortgage market as mortgage-backed securities and are now comfortably enjoying their fees and commissions? These people have gotten away free.

And some of them are showing considerable chutzpah while enjoying their gains. Having been the president of Countrywide Financial Corporation, one of the biggest subprime lenders, Stanford Kurland has now founded the Private National Mortgage Acceptance Company. Its purpose? According to the *Wichita Business Journal,* "to purchase and restructure distressed mortgages." So first Kurland makes money giving out bad loans—and now he wants to make money fixing them up!

Unfortunately, the Fed hasn't been as forthcoming with regulatory action as Poole has been with his sympathy. While the Federal Reserve Board did issue guidelines on June 29, 2007, requiring banks to stop abuses like imposing prepayment penalties, the regulations apply only to banks, not to nonbank lenders who account for most of the subprime loans.

But where was the Fed when the subprime crisis was building? Out to lunch, as *The New York Times* has noted. "An examination of regulatory decisions shows that the Federal Reserve and other agencies waited until it was too late before trying to tame the industry's excesses," the *Times* reported. "Both the Fed and the Bush administration placed a higher priority on promoting 'financial innovation' and what President Bush has called the 'ownership society.'"

The Fed finally acted on December 20, 2007, but it was too little, too late. It issued new regulations, binding on both regulated banks and other lenders, requiring them to get detailed financial information—including tax returns—from would-be borrowers and making them liable for determining prospective borrowers' ability to repay their loans. The Fed would let borrowers sue lenders who approve loans they are fairly certain they cannot repay.

But the Fed regulations are only prospective; they do nothing to punish—and therefore deter—those who made the bad loans in the first place.

One company, Fannie Mae, is hoping to use the subprime mess to resuscitate its reputation and expand its empire. In our most recent book, *Outrage,* we examined the role of Fannie Mae, the once public, now private company that still has quasi-official status and guarantees a vast number of mortgage loans. We described how Fannie Mae uses the implied, but not legally binding, federal guarantee of its debt to generate low-cost capital to buy up mortgage loans so as to let banks make new loans in the housing market.

Unfortunately, as we also noted, Fannie Mae has inclined toward empire building, using its vast lobbying and political clout to get special favors from the government. Most recently, Fannie Mae was found to have overstated its earnings by $200 million, allowing it to pay $90 million in salary and bonuses to its CEO, Franklin Raines.

As punishment for such infractions, the federal government imposed limits on how large Fannie Mae's portfolio can grow. Circling like a vulture over the subprime debacle, Fannie Mae is using its lobbying power to get congressmen to propose lifting the ceiling as a way of curing the subprime crisis.

But, given its sordid history, can Fannie Mae be trusted to lead us out of this crisis without feathering its own nest in the process? Sending in Fannie Mae to rescue the system may be like asking the wolf to indemnify the farmer for the losses in his chicken coop.

While the Federal Reserve Board buried its graying head under the sand as the subprime crisis grew, Congress has been considering a series of ever-so-limited legislative fixes to the problem. But none go to the root of the situation: how to punish the folks who gave us this crisis to begin with.

Here's the state of play on legislative fixes as of this writing:

CONGRESS TO THE RESCUE?. . . FORGET ABOUT IT!

Congress Has Passed:

- A program to build or preserve 1.5 million "affordable homes or apartments over the next ten years." Big deal! It'll take years for those homes to open their doors—while hundreds of thousands are facing foreclosure *right now*.

- A bill to make the IRS forgive taxes when a lender finds it in his heart to forgive some of the mortgage debt. Again, small potatoes.

- The House passed legislation to expand Federal Housing Administration refinancing—a little help, but not much.

- $250 million for housing counseling to those facing foreclosure. A hand-holding measure—not what we need.

And it's considering . . .

- Letting bankruptcy court judges revise mortgages to offer relief. If it passes, it'll do a lot of good.

- Legislation to curb predatory lending practices. A.K.A.: Closing the barn door after the cows have escaped.

- More oversight hearings. Just what we needed, more talk!

Most states have done nothing to deal with the subprime crisis, but a few have taken limited steps:

North Carolina recently passed a law to limit the fees mortgage brokers can charge and to stop prepayment penalties. The law also contains disclosure requirements to alert home buyers to the perils of adjustable rate mortgages.

As North Carolina's governor, Michael Easley, has said, "If Washington isn't going to act, the states are going to act." But perhaps more candidly—and less typically of a politician—he has also admitted that "I should have watched this [crisis] closer, all of us should have on the state level. We should have looked at our laws closer and made some changes."

Indeed.

The *International Herald Tribune* reports that "about a dozen states . . . are starting to make legislative and regulatory changes to protect subprime borrowers" including Maine, Minnesota, Illinois, New York, and Massachusetts.

Ohio, which has the third highest mortgage foreclosure rate in the nation (after California and Florida), now requires lenders of subprime mortgages to verify the ability of borrowers to repay loans—a key step that all states should have taken a long time ago.

But most of the states are working to help those who are facing foreclosure by instituting various schemes to refinance their mortgages at lower rates. The *Herald Tribune* reports that Maryland, Massachusetts, New Jersey, New York, Ohio, and Pennsylvania have all "rolled out mortgage programs intended to refinance loans by homeowners at risk." But these measures will help only hundreds of homeowners, a few thousand at best. Considering that half a million families have already lost their homes and many more will follow, this is scant relief indeed.

Fortunately, Congress may begin to consider seriously legislation to reform subprime lending practices. Senator Christopher Dodd (D-Conn.), the chairman of the Senate Banking Committee, had previously opposed new legislation (arguing that the Federal Reserve had all the power it needed under the Home Ownership and Equity Protection Act of 1994). But he is now reversing his position, advocating new reforms and promising to file a bill to "prohibit brokers and lenders from steering homebuyers into a more costly loan," which would stop brokers from playing "lenders and borrowers off against each other and would ban prepayment penalties."

It's another good start. But to these two objectives—reforming lending practices so the abuses will stop, and refinancing victims' mortgages to prevent them from losing their homes—we would add a third: punish those who made bad loans, making an example of them so that others aren't tempted to imitate their behavior.

ACTION AGENDA

Skilled brokers and unscrupulous lenders will always find a way around regulatory requirements. Though legislation can effectively end certain obnoxious features of the subprime mortgages—such as prepayment penalties and the exclusion of taxes and insurance from the list of monthly payments the broker must reveal to the borrower—it won't solve the basic problem. No amount of disclosure, or rehearsed or scripted statements about the perils of subprime lending or the dangers of adjustable rate mortgages, will halt the practice.

This is because every time an unsuspecting borrower meets a broker or lender who's anxious to make a buck, both sides are hot to close a deal. The borrower sees the mortgage as his gateway to middle-class living, and the broker and lender sees it as a ticket to risk-free dollar signs. Even if the lender and broker sit the borrower down and say "in three years, your rate will go up to this figure and may go as high as this other figure," the borrower is perfectly likely to disregard the warning, betting that the property value will increase and cover the extra amount, or that he'll get lucky and interest rates will fall. Or maybe that big raise will come through. Or perhaps he can switch jobs. Hope springs eternal . . .

For their part, brokers and mortgage lenders will always smile and wink their way through the disclosures, making clear that they really see them as something the government makes them read but that they don't regard as a serious danger. The implication will be: I have to tell you this, but don't you believe it for one second.

There is, however, one very good way to stop unscrupulous brokers from arranging these shaky loans: hold brokers and lenders alike responsible for any defaults by recapturing the fees and commissions they made off the deal.

The federal and state governments should create strict standards for responsible behavior and hold both lenders and brokers to them. If a reasonable lender would not have made the loan, for instance, the legislation should require the broker and lender to repay the borrower the commissions and fees they earned in the transaction. If the borrower has to go to court to enforce his rights, he should be entitled to triple damages for his pains, and his attorney fees should be included in any judgment rendered against the broker or the lender. If the broker or lender doesn't pay up following a judgment, it should cost him his state license or federal charter.

Federal and state regulatory authorities should be empowered and required to review the records of these proceedings to recapture mortgage commissions and fees and take note of individuals or companies that are repeated offenders. They should then have to take action against them for revocation of their licenses or charters.

These measures would make brokers and lenders think three times before agreeing to a loan. If the borrower defaulted, they would know that it would bring them under scrutiny for recapture of the fees they made and could possibly lead to a loss of their licenses.

Why should we let brokers make an average commission of almost $2,000 and lenders charge up to 5 percent of the face value of the mortgage as fees when the loans should never have been made in the first place? Only if we subject them to a penalty will they refrain from making loans that they shouldn't. As long as they can keep their fees and commissions, why should they care if the loan goes south? They're no longer on the hook, and the risk is absorbed into the vast, amorphous mortgage-backed securities market.

There is ample precedent for this kind of recapture of past benefits. When taxpayers use tax shelters that turn out to be bogus, they're held liable for the past taxes they have avoided paying over the previous years. We should use recapture as a way to discipline those who have obviously disregarded normal principles of sound lending and sought to inveigle gullible borrowers into committing to mortgages they can't afford.

As we write this, not one lawmaker has raised this obvious disincentive in Congress or included it in a new legislative proposal. It's not on the radar screen. We hope this book helps to put it there.

The chairman of the House Financial Services Committee, Barney Frank (D-Mass.), has introduced a bill that, according to *The New York Times*, "would for the first time let homeowners sue Wall Street firms for relief from mortgages that the borrowers never had a realistic chance of repaying."

Frank's bill would "require any mortgage lender to verify that the borrower has a 'reasonable ability to repay' based on documented income, credit history and debt level." The criterion it sets is whether the monthly payments on the mortgage, taxes, and fees amount to more than half the borrower's income.

The *Times* explains that, under Frank's bill, "people who can show that they never had a reasonable ability to repay the loans would still have to pay for their homes, but would have new statutory power to demand better deals from the lenders. They could demand that their original mortgage lender offer a better loan. Or they could demand relief from the Wall Street firm that bought the mortgage and resold it to investors."

Frank has criticized the "people who package mortgages and sell them into the secondary market," calling them "a major cause of the single biggest world financial crisis since the Asian crisis" of 1997–1998. He said, "it's unthinkable that we would leave that undisturbed."

Again, Frank's bill doesn't go as far as it should. The ones who should be responsible for the shady and unpayable mortgages are not only the Wall

Street people who packaged the mortgages and sold shares in them on the securities market but also the brokers and the lenders who conned homeowners into taking the loan in the first place. But it's a clear step in the right direction.

So write Barney Frank and Senator Christopher Dodd, his Senate counterpart, and tell them how you feel. Tell them you support Frank's mortgage lawsuit bill—and that next they should go after the brokers and lenders themselves. Here's how to reach them:

Representative Barney Frank
2252 Rayburn House Office Building
Washington, DC 20515-2104
Phone: (202) 225-5931

Senator Christopher Dodd
P.O. Box 51882
Washington, DC 20091
Phone: (202) 737-DODD (D.C.); (860) 244-2008 (Conn.)

HOW HALLIBURTON RIPS OFF THE PENTAGON

While Some Fight for Freedom, Others Use War to Get Rich

Here is a quote from the Associated Press that begs to be read and reread, it is so impossible to believe: "Corruption has long plagued Iraq's reconstruction. Congress approved more than $30 billion to rebuild Iraq, and at least $8.8 billion of it has disappeared, according to a government reconstruction audit."

Disappeared???

That's right. The sorry fact is that both the Iraqi government and American defense contractors are fleecing the U.S. taxpayer big time. As swiftly as Congress appropriates tens of billions of dollars, the Pentagon spends them—with little oversight or checks and balances. As Shay D. Assad, the director of defense procurement and acquisition policy for the Pentagon, has conceded, "In [this] combat environment, we didn't have the checks and balances we should have in place. So people who don't have ethics and integrity [have been] able to get away with things."

Apparently, this supervision gap has posed a massive opportunity for some contractors doing business in Iraq—particularly the American corporation Halliburton, its spin-off Kellogg Brown & Root, and officials and contractors in the Iraqi government.

Business fraud and siphoning off taxpayer dollars are bad enough under normal circumstances. But when it is perpetrated within the context of the heroic sacrifice so many young men and women are making to help Iraq win its freedom and escape from the grip of terrorists, it is downright obscene. Worse yet—if that's possible—is that a number of whistle-blowers who have risked their careers and, in some cases, braved incarceration to tell the truth by exposing these contractors' wrongdoing have been singled out for punishment—not rewards—by the powers that be.

We supported the invasion of Iraq and still feel that American forces are at work on a noble mission there. But Iraqi contractor fraud is not about backing or opposing the war. It is about honoring the patriotism of our armed forces by not going behind their back and stealing from taxpayers.

Halliburton, the Texas company formerly run by Vice President Dick Cheney, has been at best sloppy and at worst corrupt. According to the Committee on Oversight and Government Reform, "Pentagon auditors found $1 billion in 'questioned' costs and over $400 million in 'unsupported' costs."

THE HALLIBURTON RIPOFFS

- "The company charged $45 for cases of soda, billed $100 to clean 15-pound bags of laundry, and insisted on housing its staff at the five-star Kempinski hotel in Kuwait."

- "Halliburton truck drivers testified that the company 'torched' brand new $85,000 trucks rather than perform relatively minor repairs and regular maintenance."

- "Halliburton procurement officials described the company's informal motto in Iraq as 'don't worry about price. It's cost-plus.' "

- "A Halliburton manager was indicted for 'major fraud against the United States' for allegedly billing more than $5.5 million for work that should have cost only $685,000 in exchange for a $1 million kickback from a Kuwaiti subcontractor."

- "A Halliburton subsidiary charged $110 million for housing, food, water, laundry, and other services on bases in Iraq which had been shut down!"

- "A former manager for a Halliburton Co. subsidiary and an alleged accomplice in Kuwait [were charged in an indictment for having] defrauded the U.S. government out of nearly $4 million by inflating the price of supplying fuel tankers for military operations in Kuwait in 2003."

- The army contends that KBR, the Halliburton subsidiary, overcharged $212 million for meal services to troops in Iraq, "including [charging] for meals never served to troops." The army finally settled the dispute "by withholding $55 million of the disputed amount."

- The Pentagon's auditors found that KBR had charged double for some handling costs on "shipping containers outfitted as housing for U.S. troops." The government auditors said that KBR sought payment for "unjustified delays" and "selectively used higher priced subcontractors without justification."

KBR, a Halliburton subsidiary until the companies split in April 2007, has played a unique role in the contractor mess in Iraq. The successor of Brown and Root—the Texas powerhouse firm that funded Lyndon Johnson's rise to political power and wealth—KBR has kept its political ties polished and up to date. As *USA Today* reports, it is "by far the largest government contractor in Iraq. [It] has been paid more than $20.1 billion through last October [of 2006]—about half of all government spending on contracts in Iraq, mostly under a multiyear Army contract to provide logistical support for U.S. troops. The company also has contracts to help rebuild Iraq's oil industry."

But the contracts haven't always worked out so well. The newspaper reports that "the Defense Contract Audit Agency (DCAA) has challenged nearly $2.2 billion of KBR's invoices and cost proposals. The Army has resolved nearly $1.3 billion of those questioned costs, paying KBR only $804 million, records show."

Congressional criticism has focused, in particular, on Halliburton's $2.5 billion contract, awarded without competitive bidding, to repair Iraqi oil fields damaged or destroyed during the war. But even when the company won a competitive bid, it could not account for the money it was paid. As

The Washington Post notes, "auditors turned up $1.8 billion in 'unsupported costs' in [a] $10.5 billion logistics contract . . . which KBR won on a competitive bid. Despite those findings and a recommendation to withhold some of the payments, the Army decided last month to continue paying Halliburton in full, plus performance bonuses."

HALLIBURTON'S COST TO THE TAXPAYER

**(Results of audit of Halliburton subsidiary KBR
by Defense Department Auditors for 2003–2006,
as reported by *USA Today;*
numbers are in billions of dollars)**

Total spent	$20.1
Cost challenged by auditors	$2.2
Challenges resolved	$1.3
Challenges pending	$0.9
Challenged costs paid	$0.8

Source: Defense Contract Audit Agency.

Behind these numbers lies a story of deceit, treachery, and chicanery that should make Halliburton's executives (and Dick Cheney) blush. Media reports indicate that "federal investigators have uncovered what they describe as a sweeping network of kickbacks, bribes and fraud involving at least eight employees and subcontractors of KBR, the former Halliburton subsidiary, in a scheme to inflate charges for flying freight into Iraq in support of the war."

The convictions have already begun. One former executive for an airfreight carrier "hired by KBR pleaded guilty in federal district court to dispensing bribes and then lying to federal investigators." The subcontractor, Eagle Global Logistics, was hired to carry military goods from Dubai to Baghdad. But in November 2003, a plane "operated by a rival carrier, DHL, was struck by a missile and landed in Baghdad with its left wing in flames." Federal prosecutors charge that "Eagle executives used that incident to charge a fraudulent 'war-risk surcharge' of 50 cents for every kilogram of freight on its own flights."

To make sure that the extra charges would not raise eyebrows—or red pencils—the Eagle executives distributed "nearly $34,000 in nearly 90 gratuities 'to obtain or reward favorable treatment' in connection with the contract." The "gratuities" included "meals, drinks, golf outings, tickets to rodeo events, baseball and football games and other entertainment items." Life can get pretty dull in Kuwait.

Army Secretary Pete Geren admitted that "there have been reported cases of fraud, waste, and abuse of contracting operations, with many of the worst cases originating out of Kuwait." He noted that "we've seen more cases lately and that's a cause for concern." Geren announced that seventy-six criminal cases "related to the acquisition of weapons and other supplies for forces in Iraq and Afghanistan" have already been brought.

The real question behind these Halliburton and Kellogg Brown & Root frauds is how much the companies used their influence with Vice President Dick Cheney to get their contracts. Democrats have been quick to charge unjustified bias in the process, but there has been no proof of any such preferential treatment.

There is no doubt that Cheney received a windfall compensation package when he left Halliburton to become vice president in 2001. He got a $20 million retirement package and an additional $1.4 million cash bonus. But the key question is, What is his financial stake in the future profitability of Halliburton?

Cheney maintains that he has "severed all [his] ties with the [Halliburton] company, gotten rid of all my financial interest." In 2003, he said he had "no financial interest in Halliburton of any kind and haven't had, now, for over three years."

But Cheney's ties with Halliburton are substantial. Between 2001 and 2004, he received $740,000 in income from the company in deferred compensation. He now holds almost 500,000 shares of company stock—worth more than $17 million at current prices.

The Congressional Research Service, in 2003, said that Cheney's unexercised stock options and deferred salary "are among those benefits described by the Office of Government Ethics as 'retained ties' or 'linkages' to one's former employer."

Cheney counters that his deferred salary will be paid even if Halliburton goes broke because he has taken out an insurance policy, for which he pays annual premiums, that guarantees it. He also says that he will donate any profits or gains from his stock options to charity.

But presumably Cheney would not have to cash in his options during his government service. And afterward, he would not be obliged to give the proceeds to charity. So if Halliburton remains highly profitable until after he has left office in 2009, he would still stand to benefit.

Cheney's critics also point out that his pledge to donate the profits from any stock sale to charity are not legally enforceable. No specific charity was named, so no such organization would have any standing to sue if he reneges on his commitment. Once he is out of the public eye, having retired as vice president, he would likely be free to sell the stocks and profit handsomely—with few, if any, public repercussions.

In the meantime, during the Bush administration, the value of Halliburton's contracts with the government has increased exponentially. According to the Center for Public Integrity, "Halliburton, largely through its subsidiary Kellogg, Brown, & Root, has received more revenue from government contracts in the last year (2003) than from 1998 through 2002."

HALLIBURTON GETS RICH OFF THE IRAQ WAR

Halliburton Contracts from the Pentagon

1998–2002	$2.5 billion (five-year total)
2003	$4.3 billion (in one year)
2004	$11.4 billion (in one year)

Source: Center for Public Integrity.

The war has been good for Halliburton.

By contrast, before the Bush-Cheney administration, Halliburton wasn't doing so well on its government contracts. The Center for Public Integrity reports that "in 1998, Halliburton's total revenue was $14.5 billion; that year, the company got contracts from the Pentagon worth $284 million," a far cry from the sums it made just a few years later.

Halliburton, curiously enough, actually *reduced* the amount it spent on lobbyists during the Bush-Cheney years. While it spent $1.2 million lobbying Congress and the executive branch during the last two years of the Clinton administration, it invested only $600,000 in lobbying during the first two years of the Bush administration. As James Thurber, an American University professor (and the son of the great humorist of the same name) has noted, there's a simple reason the company no longer needs such a strong lobbying presence to ensure its access to Washington lawmakers: "They're already in." (During 2004, perhaps hedging its bets against the possibility that the Bush/Cheney team might lose its reelection bid, the company increased its annual lobbying spending back to $770,000.)

Certainly, the experiences of Bunnatine "Bunny" Greenhouse, a top contracting specialist for the Army Corps of Engineers, have fueled speculation of improper influence by Halliburton. As *Time* reports, "in February 2003, less than a month before the U.S. invaded Iraq, . . . Greenhouse walked into a Pentagon meeting [discussing] the awarding of an up to $7 billion deal to . . . Halliburton to restore Iraq's oil facilities. On hand were senior officials from [Donald Rumsfeld's] office and aides to retired Lieut. General Jay Garner, who would soon become the first U.S. administrator in Iraq."

Shortly after Greenhouse arrived, "several representatives from Halliburton entered." She asked that they leave since the meeting involved "internal discussions of the contract's terms." After the Halliburton folks had left, Greenhouse argued—reasonably—that the term of the no-bid emergency contract under consideration should be not for five years, as the draft document specified, but for only one. She pointed out that emergency conditions might have necessitated forgoing competitive bidding in the current year, but that the remaining four years on the contract should be put out to bid.

"When the contract-approval document arrived the next day for Greenhouse's signature," however, "the term was five years. With war imminent, [Greenhouse] had little choice but to sign."

Eventually, Greenhouse got her way: the Halliburton contract was divided into two and opened to public bidding in January 2004. Halliburton won the bigger contract for $1.2 billion; another company, the Parsons Corporation, won the $800 million deal.

But Greenhouse suffered for her objectivity and integrity. She was "warned to stop interfering and threatened with a demotion," *Time* reports. Major General Robert Griffin, who admonished her, "later admitted in a sworn statement that her comments on contracts had 'caused trouble' for the Army and that, given the controversy surrounding the contract, it was 'intolerable' and 'had to stop.'"

In August 2007, the Associated Press reported that Greenhouse "now sits in a cubicle in a different department with very little to do and no decision-making authority, at the end of an otherwise exemplary 20-year career. People she has known for years no longer speak to her." Her supervisors say she was performing poorly, but she insists that "they just wanted to get rid of me. I have the courage to say what needs to be said. I paid the price."

Halliburton and Kellogg Brown & Root have been politically potent for decades; they could likely chew up an Army Corps of Engineers contract officer and spit her out on their own. But it can't hurt that its former CEO for five years is now the vice president of the United States.

Our system is supposed to reward whistle-blowers, but it has done quite the opposite in the case of those like Greenhouse who have uncovered cost overruns and fraud in the Iraq War contracts. The Associated Press notes that "one after another, the men and women who have stepped forward to report corruption in the massive U.S. effort in Iraq have been vilified, fired, and demoted. Or worse."

Donald Vance, a navy veteran, and Nathan Ertel both handed the FBI evidence of arms sales by an Iraqi-owned company they worked for called Shield Group Security. Interviewed by the AP, Vance called the operation "a Wal-Mart for guns. It was all illegal and everyone knew it." He said it sold "guns, land mines, and rocket launchers—all sold for cash without receipts . . . to Iraqi insurgents, American soldiers, U.S. State Department workers, and Iraqi Embassy and ministry employees." The AP reported that "Vance supplied photos, documents and other intelligence to an FBI agent in his hometown of Chicago because he did not know whom to trust in Iraq."

Apparently, he guessed wrong. For his pains, Vance was "imprisoned by the U.S. military in a security compound and subjected to harsh interrogation methods." He was "classified a security detainee," the AP reports, held in solitary confinement for "97 days in a U.S. military prison"—Camp Cropper in Baghdad, the same prison that once held Saddam Hussein. Vance, who says he was denied an attorney during his imprisonment, has joined with Ertel, who was also imprisoned, to sue the government, saying that they were "illegally imprisoned and subjected to physical and mental interrogation tactics 'reserved for terrorists and so-called enemy combatants.'" A spokesman for detention operations in Iraq confirmed the detentions to the AP but refused further comment because of the pending lawsuit.

Vance told a congressional committee that "[U.S.] government officials blindfolded and handcuffed me and took me into detention. I was placed in isolation. I was denied food and water. I was denied sleep. I was also denied requested, and much needed, medication. I was interrogated constantly. Before each session, I would ask for an attorney. This request was invariably denied."

Vance, Ertel, and Greenhouse aren't the only whistle-blowers who have fared badly. Robert Isakson and William Baldwin turned up evidence that Custer Battles, a private contractor in Iraq for which they had worked, "cheated the U.S. government out of tens of millions of dollars by filing fake invoices and padding other bills for [Iraq] reconstruction work." They sued Custer Battles and got a $10 million jury verdict but saw it reversed in 2006 when a U.S. District Court judge ruled—outrageously—that they had "failed to prove that the Coalition Provisional Authority, the U.S.-backed occupier of Iraq for fourteen months, was part of the U.S. government."

From this sorry history, William Weaver, a professor of political science at the University of Texas–El Paso and a senior advisor to the National Security Whistleblowers Coalition, has drawn a sobering lesson: if you blow the whistle on Iraq-related fraud, "you will be destroyed. [The] reconstruction [of Iraq] is so rife with corruption, sometimes people ask me 'Should I do this? [blow the whistle] and my answer is no. If they're married, they'll lose their family. They will lose their jobs. They will lose everything."

Beth Daley of the Project on Government Oversight, an independent group that investigates corruption, agrees that the risks of crying foul in this way are extraordinary. "The only way we can find out what is going on is for someone to come forward and let us know. But when they do, the weight of the government comes down on them. The message is 'don't blow the whistle, or we'll make your life hell.' "

Incredibly, the Bush administration decided to address the issue of contractor fraud . . . but specifically exempted contracts abroad (like those in Iraq and Afghanistan)!

USA Today reports that "the Justice Department wants to force companies to notify the government if they find evidence of contract abuse of more than $5 million. Failure to comply could make a company ineligible for future government work."

But the proposed guidelines "specifically exempt 'contracts to be performed outside the United States.' "

ACTION AGENDA

The juxtaposition of contractors making billions of dollars from fraud, overcharges, abuse, and corruption while young, idealistic men and women, volunteers all, sacrifice their lives or their health to fight for freedom and against terrorism is nauseating.

There should be a special place in Hell for those who make money illegitimately from war. It's equally as sickening that almost one hundred Halliburton employees have lost their lives providing services to our troops in Iraq and Afghanistan while others in the company and its network of subcontractors have charged the taxpayers for the delivery of nonexistent meals to our troops.

Did Vice President Cheney play a role in Halliburton's getting the massive contracts it did? No one has proven that he did—but then again he probably didn't need to. Pentagon officials watch the power games above them closely; they're well aware of where the vice president used to work.

But did Cheney's influence, directly or indirectly, implied or exercised, stay the hand of those who wanted to crack down more vigorously on Halliburton's and KBR's abuses? It's hard to imagine it didn't.

A close and pervasive symbiosis binds defense contractors to the Pentagon. Relatively few firms are qualified to meet the military's procurement needs. Jet fighters and armored cars are not available from a large number of suppliers. In fact, a very small number of firms supply the vast majority of the military's needs. Their veiled collusion is one reason why the defense budget is as high as it is.

While the military supervises the contractors it hires, it also nurtures and coddles them. It's in both the Pentagon's and the nation's interest that those who manufacture our arms stay in business and prosper; otherwise we would become dangerously dependent on foreign arms suppliers.

The need to feed our defense contractors is one reason the United States leads the world in the dubious industry of arms selling. We encourage foreign countries to buy armaments from our contractors—often supplying or lending them the money to do so—so that our firms can be robust and able to meet our own needs when the time comes.

So the Defense Department has a conflicted relationship with Halliburton even apart from the vice president. It wants the Texas company to do well, as it wishes well to all of its suppliers. But with a former Halliburton CEO sitting in the second chair in the Bush administration, the relationship has become even more intimate.

And Halliburton is more than just a defense contractor. It is one of America's premier oil exploration and drilling companies. With our focus on energy independence, such companies receive lots of government benefits.

Finally, it is in the interests of the Bush White House to get the job in Iraq done and done quickly. The premium on efficiency and speed has served contractors like Halliburton's former subsidiary KBR well. In the haste to let contracts to get Iraqi oil fields up and running and U.S. troops supplied in the field, a lot of overcharging and even graft is probable.

So the combination of Halliburton's oil privileges, its status as a high-ranking defense contractor, the need for speed in Iraq contracting, and the firm's connection with Cheney all entitled it to very special consideration by this particular administration. Any hope of a fair and reasonable treatment of this company while Bush is president is far-fetched indeed.

But the next administration need not feel bound by any such loyalty. The time is ripe for a special prosecutor—outside the Defense Department—to investigate corruption and overcharges among the Iraq War contractors. The possibility that those who ripped off the taxpayer while our troops were dying may get away with it should be galling to all Americans.

And the Defense Department is just too up close and personal in its relationship with Halliburton to ensure any kind of fair investigation under any administration—even a Democratic one. The Defense Department's need to protect its contractors is so deeply felt in the bowels of the Pentagon that any kind of aggressive investigation is unlikely.

For just those reasons, we need to pay special attention to the problems of whistle-blowers—for they are our only reasonable hope of uncovering the bulk of the waste and corruption in our defense contracting system. The current de facto policy of punishing them is unacceptable and must be reversed. Laws now on the books provide for rewards for whistle-blowers, but they do not go far enough.

Rather, any attempt to obstruct or intimidate a whistle-blower who is seeking to call attention to an abuse—any attempt to punish a whistle-blower for taking such brave actions—should be a felony, punishable by jail time. Those who sidetracked Bunny Greenhouse and who held Donald Vance and Nathan Ertel in prison should be punished criminally. Only such severe action will ensure that, despite the political inconvenience, whistle-blowers have both an incentive to turn in wrongdoers and the protection they need to encourage them to do so.

Years ago, Congress passed laws to reward whistle-blowers and to entitle them to a portion of the savings the government realizes by their efforts. But now we must take the next step and protect them, by statute, from harassment by their superiors. We need them to blow the whistle—loud enough for us all to hear it!

BLOCKING TOYS THAT POISON CHILDREN FROM BEING SOLD IN AMERICA—AND BEING MADE IN CHINA

It's bad enough to fleece adults out of money. It is far worse to fleece infants and babies out of their health. Every week, it seems, we read reports of unsafe toys—many from China, coated in everything from brightly colored lead paint to the date rape drug GHB. Any child who puts such toys in his mouth and sucks off the chemical coating could sustain permanent brain damage or worse.

How do these unsafe products get into our country?

Because the agency charged with protecting us has its head buried in the sand—so much so that it has only one full-time toy tester on its staff.

The Ostrich in Chief is Nancy Nord, the head of the Consumer Product Safety Commission, who adamantly refuses to expand her staff of inspectors, increase penalties on violators, or make complaints public. This is an amazing policy on the part of someone who is charged with protecting the public. Instead of doing that, however, she protects the industry—while taking free trips paid for by those she regulates.

Protecting the American public from dangerous products is, by anyone's estimate, an enormous responsibility. You'd think Nord would *want* more staff to help her perform it. But when Congress considered legislation to give the commission more resources to protect consumers, she said she didn't want them!

Nancy Nord and her equally obtuse predecessor, Hal Stratton, are real pieces of work. *The New York Times* reports that "Ms. Nord, who is supposed to be the consumers' advocate, has more often echoed the views of manufacturers' lobbyists. She has argued that voluntary compliance by business is the only way to promote safety when an agency as small as hers . . . lacks adequate resources. [Yet] remarkably, she has been resisting calls for it to get those resources."

PLEASE DON'T HELP US! THE CRY OF THE CONSUMER PRODUCT SAFETY COMMISSION

- Don't increase funds for our agency.
- Don't let us impose higher fines on violators.
- Don't give us more staff to investigate frauds on consumers.
- Don't ban lead in children's toys.
- Don't protect whistle-blowers.
- Don't prosecute company executives for willful violations of consumer safety.
- And, whatever you do, don't make us publish the complaints we get from consumers!!!

Source: *The New York Times.*

In November 2007, Nord opposed increasing funds for her agency, even though it has faced major cuts in its budget over the past decade. That's fine with her. She's also against raising the maximum fine the commission can impose on industry violators from $1.85 million—a slap on the wrist—to a more hefty and significant $100 million.

And she opposes legislation to require the commission to make complaints public almost immediately, as the National Transportation Safety Board does. As the *Times* notes, the commission "now keeps complaints and even results of internal investigations secret while industry has weeks or longer to respond. That might work for industry, but not for the consumer."

When the Consumer Product Safety Commission (CPSC) was founded in 1973, it had a staff of eight hundred. Now it has fewer than four hundred. But this small group is tasked with policing an enormous flow of consumer products into this country from overseas. As CBS News has reported, "more than 21 million toys from China . . . have been recalled because of excessive levels of lead paint, tiny magnets that could be swallowed or other potentially serious problems." These products range from Baby Einstein Color Blocks, made by Kids II, to Thomas & Friends Wooden Railway, made by the RC2 Corporation.

The government relies on the toy industry to regulate itself—something it's demonstrably incapable of doing. The CPSC has only about one hundred field investigators and compliance personnel to inspect the $22 billion worth of toys and other products sold in the United States each year.

The bill to increase the commission's staff would push its budget to $80 million in 2009 and raise it by 10 percent each year thereafter. As Senator Mark Pryor (D-Alaska) has said, "it is very clear to me, as well as millions of moms and dads around the country, that the [commission] is failing to keep dangerous toys and products out of the marketplace."

Nord says she opposes the bill because it "could have the unintended consequence of hampering, rather than furthering, consumer product safety." CBS News reports that "she specifically complained that the additional responsibilities the bill adds [to the commission's workload] will make it more difficult for the agency to do its job."

What additional responsibilities? The obligation to tell the public when a complaint is filed about a dangerous product?

Acting more like an industry lobbyist than the head of the federal agency charged with protecting the public from the misdeeds of the industry, Nord opposed provisions in the legislation that would ban lead from any children's toys. She was against the parts of the bill that would have protected whistle-blowers who called the commission's attention to defects in the products their companies make. She objected to increases in the fines for safety violations and opposed legislation to prosecute the executives of companies that willfully violate safety standards.

Her opposition comes at a time when 13 million toys have been recalled because they had unsafe lead levels.

Nord and the Bush administration say that they oppose strengthening the commission, despite the evidence of a massive need for its intervention, because they'd rather trust the industry to self-regulate. Self-regulation has its place, but when the toys or products in question are made halfway around the world in China—a country not known for exacting quality standards, to say the least—the capacity of even the most diligent companies to police the safety of their products is sorely taxed.

The crux of the difference between Nord's position and the public interest boils down to litigation: The commission itself can go only so far in imposing penalties, although the Democrats would like to strengthen their power to enact remedies. Today, however, it's the legal system, not the commission, that's responsible for enforcing U.S. quality standards.

When the CPSC identifies an unsafe product, it publishes its findings— and then the trial lawyers go to work, seeking out the injured and lining them up as plaintiffs. Accepting the cases for free, based on a contingency fee of one third of the jury award, they use the facts unearthed by the commission in their litigation. This is why the Bush administration is so eager to prevent publication of consumer complaints and wants to deprive it of a sufficient team of inspectors—because it doesn't feel that those lawyers should be getting their facts handed to them by the commission.

This stonewalling is hardly surprising: After all, no one likes trial lawyers. They're out for themselves, eager to line their pockets any way they can. But they are the bacteria that keep our system clean. Aggressive, self-promoting, interested first and foremost in making money, these lawyers may be the only ones who can enforce our safety laws in as diverse a marketplace as we face today. The bar can punish wrongdoers very effectively if they are given the facts. (Don't count on government to do it!)

Why has Nord opposed proposals to raise the potential penalty for making unsafe products? Because, she says, the proposed increase to $100 million "may have the undesired consequence of firms, as a precautionary measure, flooding the agency with virtually every consumer complaint and incident." The commission would be so swamped, she worried, that "true safety issues would go unrecognized in the process."

But of course Nord also opposed the proposed increases in staffing and funding that might have helped her deal with an influx of new cases.

Nord also opposed giving state prosecutors the authority to enforce federal consumer safety laws. So, even as she wants to deprive her agency of the required manpower to handle its workload and police the marketplace, she also opposes giving the states the power to do the job for her.

And why doesn't she want to protect whistle-blowers? Because, she says, such a measure might "dramatically drain the limited resources of the commission, to the direct detriment of public safety." But again, she has turned down the extra money or staff that might have allowed her to protect whistle-blowers.

Nancy Nord is like the cop who doesn't want to fight crime. But why?

Here's a likely guess: Could her reluctance to staff her own agency adequately, or to empower it to impose fines that might deter future corporate misconduct, have anything to do with her cozy relationship with the industry she's supposed to regulate?

Nord was not Bush's first choice to head the agency. He first nominated Michael Barody, who had to withdraw his nomination after it came out that he was a highly paid lobbyist for the National Association of Manufacturers—a group that represents the very toy and product makers he would have been in charge of policing.

Yet Nord, Bush's second choice—and her predecessor, Hal Stratton— have both had close ties to the industries they were charged with regulating. Public interest groups sued under the Freedom of Information Act and forced the release of government documents showing that Nord and Stratton "have taken dozens of trips at the expense of the toy, appliance and children's furniture industries and others they regulate," according to *The Washington Post*. The newspaper reported that they took "nearly 30 trips since 2002 . . . that were paid for in full or in part by trade associations or manufacturers of products [the commission regulates,] ranging from space heaters to disinfectants. The airfares, hotels and meals totaled nearly $60,000, and the destinations included China, Spain, San Francisco, New Orleans and a golf resort on Hilton Head Island, S.C."

The trips included an eleven-day visit to China and Hong Kong in 2004 for Stratton, paid for by the American Fireworks Standards Laboratory. The tab for the trip? Eleven thousand dollars. There's nothing wrong with going to China. Indeed, it makes eminent sense for a commission overseeing the safety of products imported from China to survey manufacturing sites firsthand. But there's a lot wrong with letting a regulated company pay for your travel.

And guess what? After the fireworks industry paid for the trip to China, *The Washington Post* reports, it "urged the commission to adopt its safety standards, an idea that is still pending, according to an organization newsletter."

Nord's China trip wasn't her only such indiscretion. She also traveled to the International Toy Fair in New York City, this time funded by the Toy Industry Association, which paid for her rail fare, hotel bill, and meals. She even had the association pay her $51 parking bill at Washington's Union Station.

Obviously Nord needed to attend the gathering. But it's equally obvious that the government should have paid for the trip—which probably cost less than $2,000.

Former commission chairman Hal Stratton must have had a good time as a guest speaker at two annual meetings of the Gas Appliance Manufacturers Association, one in Orlando, Florida, and the other on Hilton Head Island in South Carolina. *The Washington Post* reported that "the meetings drew more than 300 manufacturers' representatives and spouses for seminars, a dinner dance, and golf."

Could the largesse of the manufacturers' association have anything to do with the fact that it represents the makers of fuel-fired heating equipment being investigated by the commission because it has been linked to three hundred deaths through fires and carbon monoxide poisoning? "While the association's manufacturers are regulated by three other government agencies," the *Post* reported, "its vice president, Joseph Mattingly, said he could not recall paying for any attendees from those agencies."

Stratton defended his trip: "My view was we needed to engage industries and not only tell them what we expected but also to learn what they were thinking. . . . You can't do that sitting in the ivory tower at the CPSC." Of course, the issue wasn't whether he should have stayed in the tower but whether he really should have accepted an industry-sponsored two-day stay at a golf resort to "engage" them. A summons to appear in his office might have been more appropriate.

And there were other such favors. In February 2007, Nancy Nord traveled to New Orleans; this time she billed the Defense Research Institute, an organization of lawyers who defend product liability cases, $2,000 for her travel expenses. When Stratton met with the same group, he did her one better: he met with them in Barcelona, Spain, and charged the organization $915 for his hotel room.

Product liability lawsuits, of course, are often based on factual findings by the Consumer Product Safety Commission. Given the largely nominal fines the commission is now allowed to impose on violating companies, such civil litigation constitutes the only real deterrent to industry misconduct. By attending the New Orleans and Barcelona conferences, Nord and Stratton were essentially briefing the lawyers for the enemy—the companies that the commission frequently finds in violation.

Government travel restrictions ban agencies such as the commission from accepting trips from private companies if they "would cause a reasonable person . . . to question the integrity of agency programs or operations."

Other U.S. government regulatory agencies ban their officials or employees from accepting travel money from industry. The Securities and Exchange Commission, for example, "does not accept host-paid travel reimbursements or in-kind payments from any organization regulated by the agency," according to an SEC spokesman. Similarly, the Food and Drug Administration prohibits its staff from taking travel payments from companies they regulate, organizations "engaged in any lobbying activities," or those that receive "more than ten percent of their income from a corporate source." The Federal Communications Commission also bans payment for travel expenses by regulated companies.

Apparently the folks at the Consumer Product Safety Commission see things differently.

Craig Holman, of the consumer group Public Citizen, says that the CPSC's acceptance of corporate paid travel is "a blatant violation of the ethics code." He said that you can't pay for a trip "if you're a private party with business pending before the agency."

Ann Brown, Bill Clinton's appointee to head the commission back in the 1990s, traveled "only at the expense of the agency or of media organizations that sponsored appearances where she announced product recalls," according to *The Washington Post.* " 'We hated to have an industry pay for our staff for anything,' said Pam Gilbert, a lawyer who was executive director of the agency under Brown."

And that's the way it should have been. Without even this kind of base-level integrity, our safety watchdog is effectively worthless.

THE CHINESE CONNECTION

Of course, the commission would have much less work to do if it weren't for the constant flow of dangerous products flooding our store shelves each year. Every Christmas, millions of mothers eagerly flock to Toys 'R' Us and other stores to keep their children supplied with gifts and games. Four out of five toys they buy are made in China. Delighted by the low prices at the checkout counter, these mothers are doubtless thankful for just how far their holiday shopping dollar goes.

But the conditions under which these toys are made are horrific. The perpetual smiles on the dolls and toys mask the misery, starvation, and brutalization of the millions of Chinese workers—including many children—who toil away in dirty, unhealthy hellholes to make the playthings. The despicable working conditions are knowingly tolerated by major American companies. And as the many safety infractions of recent years demonstrate, they threaten not only the health of the workers but the health of the American children who receive the toys as gifts.

In the past year, as noted above, more than 21 million toys, most of them made in China, have been recalled from American shelves for safety hazards. Recently, Mattel recalled China-made toys twice in one month for using lead-based paint.

American companies such as Disney and Hasbro affix their prestigious names to these products, using their sterling reputations to hide the vicious circumstances that attend their manufacture and the health threats they pose to our children. They deliberately avert their gaze from the appalling conditions that prevail in the factories of their suppliers. Meanwhile, parents, confident that these companies would never lend their brand names to covering up such abuses, innocently buy the toys that trigger such misery when they are manufactured and such danger when their children play with them.

Now, some might ask: Aren't the children and adult workers who produce these toys, dolls, games, and stuffed animals lucky to have jobs? Aren't we doing them a service by buying their products? The answer to these questions is that we want cheap toys but not toys that are stained with blood—or that threaten our kids' health. American consumers would willingly pay a few cents more to ensure that the gifts they buy are made in humane conditions by adequately paid workers and that they're safe for their children to play with.

Why are some of our top companies bringing such tainted products to our shelves? And why do they keep such intense pressure on their manufacturers to shave costs that the companies cut corners—with the inevitable result that our kids are exposed to lead paint and other hazards? Surely, if our consumers knew what was behind the smiles on the dolls and teddy bears, they wouldn't buy them.

The horror stories of exploitation in Chinese factories abound. Sandra Williams offered a vivid picture of child labor conditions in her June 2007 report, which can be found online at poverty.suite101.com:

THE LIVES OF CHINA'S CHILD WORKERS

Some children as young as 12 have been kidnapped and forced to work in slave-like conditions. Doors are bolted shut, windows barred and many of their beds are made of simple bricks. They are being beaten and whipped if they are too tired to work or try to escape. Vicious dogs are guarding the brick factories to ensure people cannot escape. Thirteen children have been reported to have died from overwork and abuse in Shanxi. Most of them are teenagers or younger and look starved and exhausted.

There are many other such stories from China:

• Duoyuan Plastic Production Company, in Shenzhen, makes inflatable toys, plastic products and furniture, supplying Hasbro and Sanrio in the United States and Japan. It requires all of its employees to work overtime, "adding three hours every day on average after their 6 P.M. daily shift. Workers earn 1,000 yuan ($130) a month on average, including overtime."

- A toy factory in impoverished Guangxi province, according to China Labor Watch, "hired 1,000 junior high school students."

- Taiwan's Hon Hai Precision Industry Company was "found to have made employees work more than 60 hours a week" to supply iPod music players for Apple Computer. To its credit, Apple forced an end to the practice.

- In Guangdong province, where many U.S.-bound toys are made, the monthly wage of toy factory workers "is around $100. They have no contracts and no social security." A study of twenty-six factories found "that employees often work eighty-hour weeks, with no holidays." Of course, underage workers are common.

These unscrupulous Chinese companies that supply American toy companies are particularly dependent on child labor. According to China Labor Watch, most of the child workers are girls, reflecting the low priority given to educating them in China. Their report noted, "Children earn salaries of as little as $40 per month. Along with receiving poor pay, bad food, and cramped living quarters, child workers are susceptible to violence and abuses such as forced overtime. Loneliness and a longing for lost school days contribute to their misery."

The United Nations International Children's Emergency Fund (UNICEF) estimates that more than 200 million child laborers are employed in Asia—60 percent of the global total.

The Associated Press reported that "most child workers have left school," though some are so-called work-study students, who are transported to factories or farms during school holidays. "Although technically legal, that practice is poorly regulated and widely abused," the AP noted.

Li Qiang of China Labor Watch is unequivocal in placing the blame on American toy companies. He charges that the working conditions result directly from the profit-minded demands of Western manufacturers and toy importers, which exploit competition among Chinese firms to keep prices down. "These companies only think about making money," Li says. "They keep pushing down the price. Now labor cost is at its lowest, manufacturers are starting to cut down on their material costs. Therefore, they're beginning to use unreliable or defective material." The exploitation of workers and the use of cheap but hazardous materials are two sides of the same coin—and pressure for lower costs by American toy companies causes them both.

While American consumers worry about exposing their children to chemicals used in the manufacture of Chinese-made toys, China Labor Watch's Li reports that "the manufacturers rip off the warning signs from the chemicals used at their factories. The workers have no idea that their health might be affected. Many of them get sick from the work." Qiang noted that "now Western customers are complaining that their kids might be harmed by Chinese toys. The fact is that, while producing them, tens of thousands of Chinese workers have already been exposed to such danger." He reports that each year in Guangdong province, more than ten thousand toy workers lose fingers in industrial accidents.

Disney and Hasbro vigorously defend their conduct. Disney said in a statement "that it and its affiliates take allegations of unfair labor practices seriously, investigate them thoroughly and take remedial action." Alannah Goss, a spokesman for Disney, said that the company has "a firm commitment to the safety and well-being of workers, and fair and just labor standards." Hasbro said it "has an excellent record in the arena of product safety and, in light of the recent news from China, we have increased the intensity of our ongoing safety review efforts when it comes to any of our products." It promised to "conduct a thorough investigation" into the issues raised by the China Labor Watch report and to "act swiftly and decisively in making any necessary changes."

However, as *The New York Times* noted, "some workers' rights groups say tainted and defective products are a result of a factory system that allows big corporations to outsource to contractors here who routinely violate Chinese labor laws and cheat workers to reduce costs and increase profits. China Labor Watch assigned part of the blame to multinational corporations that focus on keeping costs low."

The same companies that exploit workers and use child labor are also likely to turn out products that are safety hazards. The drive to cut costs—

triggered by the demands of U.S. toy companies—leads to both results: exploited workers and unsafe toys. Their promises to inspect their factories to find unsafe toys or exploitive labor conditions deliberately miss the point: it's their economic pressure that is causing these practices in the first place.

Until American consumers start making themselves heard, letting toy companies such as Disney and Hasbro know that they won't tolerate the exploitation of human beings in the manufacture of toys, these labor practices will likely continue.

ACTION AGENDA

Who Will Police the Consumer Police?

Congress is actively considering legislation to give the Consumer Product Safety Commission some teeth and some staff. Despite Nancy Nord's opposition, it's likely to pass in some form—and it's unlikely that President Bush would take the risk of vetoing it.

The House has been working on legislation aimed at improving toy safety by decreasing allowable lead levels, improving laboratory testing, and requiring outside testing of all imported and domestic children's products. The proposed legislation would also improve crib and child car seat safety standards. The Senate is considering a similar bill, one that would mandate more safety inspectors, double the agency's budget over seven years, and require that more agents be dispatched to the ports and airports where the toys enter the country. With luck, the two chambers will agree on one bill and pass it. And with luck Bush will sign it.

To help the process along, you can write the committee chairmen who are pushing the legislation: Bobby Rush (D-Ill.) in the House and Daniel Inouye (D-Hawaii) and Mark Pryor (D-Alaska) in the Senate. Here's how to reach them:

Congressman Bobby Rush
2416 Rayburn House Office Building
Washington, DC 20515
Phone: 202-225-4372
Fax: 202-226-0333

Senator Daniel Inouye
722 Hart Building
Washington, DC 20510-1102
Phone: 202-224-3934
Fax: 202-224-6747

Senator Mark Pryor
255 Dirksen Senate Office Building
Washington, DC 20510
Phone: 202-224-2353
Fax: 202-228-0908

The hard part will be getting President Bush to sign the bill after it passes. Write him (at the White House, 1600 Pennsylvania Avenue, Washington, DC 20500) and tell him that a child eating lead paint off a toy is a child left behind—something he promised would not happen in his administration.

Who Will Stop the Parade of Tainted Toys?

Until American consumers demand an end to the inhumane labor practices in China, they will not improve. And until they insist that product safety must come before lower prices and higher profits, nothing will change. American parents need to recognize that the toys they buy are made with the blood, tears, and forfeited futures of Chinese children. They need to demand that toys for children not be made by children.

The best way to apply pressure is through American toy companies that seek to preserve their child-friendly reputations. If Americans circulated online the reports of abusive labor conditions at factories that supply Disney with its toys, Mickey and Donald would quickly get the message. Concerns over toy safety have already shaken up the industry, but the message needs to be broadcast clearly that cutting corners on safety and exploiting low-cost child workers are both caused by the same reliance on cut-rate contractors. As long as American companies demand ever-lower costs, there will be no way to stop the abuses.

But will Americans tolerate slightly higher prices for toys? Recent public opinion surveys suggest that they would. In the summer of 2006, we conducted a national survey for a business client asking American consumers if they would be willing to pay more for products like toys and clothing if it meant that the workers who produced them "would not be children and would be paid adequate wages, health benefits, and work in safe and sanitary conditions."

The results were encouraging: 63 percent of consumers said they would be willing to pay at least 10 percent more and 53 percent said they would pay as much as a quarter more for products if they could be certain that they were made according to these humane standards.

Starbucks has pioneered the idea of charging more for coffee made under better working conditions. In countries such as Colombia, Honduras, and Costa Rica, the company pays 25 percent more for its coffee and makes sure the benefits of the higher prices are passed on to the workers and coffee growers. Called "Fair Trade Coffee," it sells for more in Starbucks stores but appears to more than make the money back in increased revenues.

Disney, Hasbro, and other multinational companies should follow Starbucks' lead. In the Clinton White House, Labor Secretary Robert Reich proposed that companies sew "no sweat" labels into their imported textiles as a way of certifying that the products were not made by children or exploited adults. His thought was that the private organization that would run the program would charge five cents for each "no sweat" label. The revenue would fund investigations of the labor standards of their contractors, on the one hand, and advertising in the United States to encourage consumers to buy only "no sweat" products, on the other.

His proposal could transform the current race to the bottom in world trade—where the cheaper the product, the larger the market share and the bigger the profit—into a race to the top, where humane treatment of the workforce would be rewarded.

Our survey data suggest that Americans would be enthusiastic about spending their money on products made under humane conditions even if they cost more. The inevitable consequence of the rising American consciousness of unsafe products for children and the labor abuses that lie behind their manufacture is further embarrassment for American companies. If Disney and the others led the way in this trend, taking the lead in assuring consumers that their products were made under conditions that were safe for both producers and consumers—even at the price of higher costs—they would profit nicely from their foresight.

Only by structuring their retail operations to give consumers the alternative of paying a slight premium for "safe" products can Disney and the other companies bring these problems to an end. No amount of increased inspection or enforcement can possibly substitute for this fundamental re-working of their business models.

So let Mickey Mouse and Donald Duck know how you feel: email Disney's senior vice president for corporate communications, Gary Foster, at gary.foster@disney.com.

Or contact Hasbro at 1-800-2HASBRO (1-800-242-7276), by e-mail at customersupport@hasbro.com, or by mail:

Hasbro, Inc.
P.O. Box 200
Pawtucket, RI 02862

HOW THE COMPANY BILL CLINTON WORKS FOR FLEECES THE VULNERABLE ELDERLY

There's something about infoUSA, the direct-marketing company Bill Clinton works for, that the former president doesn't want us to know: that it specializes in selling lists of vulnerable elderly people to solicitation companies, which then hound them and fleece them out of their savings.

In Bill Clinton's latest book, *Giving*, he extols the virtues of infoUSA, an Omaha, Nebraska, company he inaccurately describes as a "mass-mailing operation." Calling that company a mass-mailing operation is like calling the Stealth Bomber a "fast package delivery system." It's a whole lot more than that.

Here's a better way to describe infoUSA: as a company that's been identified as a key creator and distributor of databases that enable criminals to fleece the unsuspecting elderly.

The company and its founder, Vinod "Vin" Gupta, can also be described accurately as extremely generous benefactors to Bill and Hillary Clinton—including $900,000 the company allegedly spent flying them around on the company's private plane—and much more!

In *Giving*, Bill Clinton generously praises the company's participation in his administration's Welfare to Work policy and its hiring of more than a thousand former welfare recipients and disabled people. "A couple of years ago," he says, "I had a chance to visit infoUSA's employees, and they seemed happy and self-confident, clearly enjoying their work."

But Clinton's account leaves out as much as it tells about the company. It ignores widely published allegations of and reports of state criminal investigations of infoUSA. He never mentions that the reason he had the chance to see all those happy workers in Omaha was that he was there to give a $200,000 speech—paid for by infoUSA in July 2001.

What Clinton also leaves out is that he's been on the payroll of only two companies since he left office—and infoUSA is one of them. The company has paid him $3.3 million as a consultant since 2001. And he never mentions the rest of the largesse the Clintons have received from infoUSA and Gupta. Could those large payments have anything to do with his very positive outlook about the company?

In another section of the book, Clinton makes a downright false statement concerning his relationship with the Yucaipa Companies, a California investment company. "When I left office, the opportunity to work with Yucaipa was the only private sector offer I accepted, because I wanted to continue to work to bring economic opportunities to low-income communities, and I thought that Yucaipa could prove they're good investments."

That's not what Hillary Clinton's Senate financial disclosure statements show. In fact, she disclosed that her husband was working for infoUSA in 2001, a year before he revealed any financial relationship with Yucaipa. Had he already forgotten about the $500,000 annual consulting fee he was paid by infoUSA?

Hillary's May 15, 2002, Senate financial disclosure form, which covered payments made to the couple in 2001, simply indicates that Bill Clinton was paid "more than $1,000" by infoUSA in 2001 for "non-employee compensation." (The disclosure rules require no more specificity about the size of such payments.) Since then, however, the former president has admitted that he made $3.3 million from infoUSA. Yucaipa doesn't even show up on the disclosure forms until the following year.

Doesn't it seem as if Clinton should have been up front about his financial ties to infoUSA in his book—instead of pretending he was just talking about an arm's-length company whose policies he admires?

By not revealing the fact that he's been on infoUSA's payroll since he left the White House—and by failing to describe the true nature of the shady business—Bill Clinton has hoodwinked us all.

So what's so bad about infoUSA?

Here's the problem.

As *The New York Times* has reported, infoUSA compiled and sold contact lists of elderly men and women—the kinds of targets who would be especially susceptible to unscrupulous scams. The company advertised lists such as "Elderly Opportunity Seekers" (a list of 3.3 million older people "looking for ways to make money"); "Suffering Seniors" (4.7 million people with cancer or Alzheimer's disease); "Oldies but Goodies" (500,000 gamblers over age fifty-five). The words it used to describe one list, according to the *Times* report, were chilling: "These people are gullible. They want to believe that their luck can change."

The lists left no doubt about the vulnerability of infoUSA's elderly targets. And the company sold the lists to a number of dubious companies— including firms that were under investigation or have since been closed down by courts because of their criminal activity. The company's internal e-mails show that employees were aware that the investigation for elderly fraud involved their customers but sold the lists anyway.

The *Times* profiled one unfortunate ninety-two-year-old man who entered a sweepstakes sponsored by infoUSA. The information he innocently provided was then sold to the predator marketers. After responding to their telemarketing calls seeking financial information, he saw his entire life savings stolen from his bank account. Such scams, using lists supplied by infoUSA, were repeated all over the country.

The extent of Bill Clinton's windfall from the company was revealed only because of a lawsuit by disgruntled stockholders against the company management.

The relationship between Bill Clinton and Vinod "Vin" Gupta, the CEO and chairman of infoUSA, is both long-standing and deep.

A frequent donor to the Clinton camnpaigns, Gupta has stayed in the Lincoln Bedroom, admitted to donating *$1 million* to the Clinton Library, and told the press he'd consider making an additional donation. It's possible that he already has.

Since the Clintons refuse to disclose who donated how much money to the library, we don't know the total amount he actually gave. But we do know this: in late 1999, Gupta gave *$2 million* for Hillary Clinton's Millennium New Year's Eve bash. (The party, which cost *$16 million* to throw, was closed to the press!)

The links between Gupta and the Clintons are extensive:

- Gupta raised more than $200,000 for Hillary's Senate campaigns and has contributed thousands to the Democratic National Committee and to Democratic House and Senate campaigns.

- InfoUSA was one of the sponsors of the Aspen Festival of Ideas in 2006, where Bill and Hillary Clinton both spoke.

- Gupta built the Bill Clinton Science & Technology Center and the Hillary Clinton Mass Communications Center in his hometown of Rampur, India.

- Bill Clinton traveled to India with Gupta.

- Gupta reportedly paid for a golf outing for Bill at a legendary Scottish course.

- InfoUSA appointed Terry McAuliffe, the Clintons' longtime campaign strategist and fund-raiser, to the board of directors of its subsidiary company videoyellowpagesusa.com.

- Clinton appointed Gupta to the Kennedy Center board of trustees only a few days before he left office.

- Clinton also nominated Gupta as consul general of Bermuda and U.S. ambassador to Fiji, but Gupta was never confirmed.

- Gupta's company cosponsored the 2006 Clinton Global Initiative.

- Gupta sent a $7,000 treadmill to Chappaqua days after the Clintons left the White House. After the *New York Post* disclosed the gift, the Clintons returned it.

Gupta's generosity to the Clintons is matched only by his generosity to himself. InfoUSA has lately been attacked by some of its shareholders—particularly by the Greenwich, Connecticut, company Cardinal Capital, which also went after Conrad Black, the press mogul who was recently convicted of corporate fraud. Cardinal objected to Gupta's purchase of a $600,000 skybox at the University of Nebraska; to Gupta's family's $13.5 million in private jet fees; and to $2.5 million for the long-term lease of a yacht—all with corporate funds.

This connection between the Clintons and infoUSA only underscores the necessity of full disclosure of income sources and amounts by all the presidential candidates and the release of their income tax returns—a step Mrs. Clinton has thus far refused to take.

Outsized consulting fees have been only part of the largesse infoUSA has showered on the former president. Vinod Gupta has lent the Clintons the company's jet to use in traveling to places such as Switzerland, Hawaii, Jamaica, and Mexico. The jet service they were provided was worth a staggering $900,000.

In November 2007, the SEC announced that it had begun an investigation of infoUSA. All we can say is . . .

Happy hunting!

FROM MOVIE LIGHTS TO LIGHTING UP:
How Films Induce Teens to Smoke

Who's putting cigarettes in the hands of all the great movie stars?

It's a mystery.

No one wants to take the credit. Or the blame.

But there are really only two possible culprits: the movie industry and the tobacco companies. And the tobacco companies say they have nothing to do with it.

The timing is odd. Just as our culture seems to have reached a national consensus on the need to prevent teen smoking and teach kids about the serious health dangers caused by smoking, Hollywood is suddenly pushing Big Tobacco's poison.

Just as millions of dollars from the mandated tobacco settlement are slated to be put to use to help curb teen smoking, Big Tobacco is suddenly starring in films and movies *directed at kids,* showcasing glamorous actors and actresses and Hollywood role models with one big thing in common—they all smoke.

What's wrong with this picture?

Fifty-four percent of American smokers begin their addiction to smoking before they're eighteen, joining what the bioethics professor Laura M. Purdy calls "the lottery which kills 400,000 people a year." Hollywood and Big Tobacco seem to have come up with a clear message: smoking is cool, acceptable, a proper thing for role models—and thus the rest of us—to do.

Oh, it also kills? No matter.

Here's a shocking statistic: Eighty-five percent of all popular films depict people smoking. Even some G-rated films—made especially for kids—have shown actors lighting up: recent examples include *102 Dalmatians*, *Tarzan*, and *Muppets from Space*.

And in 2008, a surprising number of the Academy Award–nominated films for Best Picture showed smoking, usually in an unnecessary or even positive light. Perhaps it's no surprise that smoking was so prevalent on the screen in a gritty period film like *There Will Be Blood*—but was it really *necessary*? Worse yet, was it really a good idea for the makers of *Juno*, the comedy about teen pregnancy, to show its eccentric lead character (a prospective teenage mother) smoking a pipe—even if it was a prop?

Wait, you may be saying. It's only the movies. What's wrong with showing the occasional character taking a drag? Well, there's an undisputed correlation between the incidence of teen smoking and the exposure to stars and role models who smoke. Voluminous scientific evidence shows that movies featuring stars smoking cigarettes induce kids to light up, fleecing them of their health. Yet, despite this frightening evidence, more and more films show actors smoking. While tobacco use is down in the United States (only 24 percent of Americans smoke), the portrayal of smoking in American films is up. Way up.

Shrouding themselves in the cloak of creative liberty, film producers, writers, studios, and directors are doing the dirty work of the tobacco companies by including smoking scenes in more films. And it's not just adults who are shown smoking. Some films go completely over the top and actually depict children smoking! Here's a list of a dozen flicks that show kids lighting up.

FILMS SHOWING KIDS SMOKING

- *Bad Santa* (R; Disney, 2003): Teen skateboarders smoke.

- *The Butterfly Effect* (R; Time Warner, 2004): Evan, as a boy, and his friends smoke.

- *The Emperor's Club* (PG-13; Universal, 2002): Unnamed schoolgirls smoke.

- *How to Deal* (PG-13; Time Warner, 2003): Seventeen-year-old Halley smokes and coughs.

- *Insomnia* (R; Time Warner, 2002): Best friend and boyfriend of a murdered seventeen-year-old girl smoke.

- *It Runs in the Family* (PG-13; MGM, 2003): Middle school student Abby smokes.

- *Monster* (R; Newmarket, 2003): Eileen smokes as a teenager.

- *Raising Helen* (PG-13; Disney, 2004): Fifteen-year-old Audrey smokes.

- *Saved!* (PG-13; MGM, 2004): High school students Cassandra and Roland smoke.

- *Secondhand Lions* (PG; Time Warner, 2003): Fourteen-year-old boy takes chewing tobacco, gags, and spits it out.

- *Swimfan* (PG-13; News Corporation, 2002): High school swimmer Josh and his friends smoke.

- *The Weather Man* (R; Viacom, 2005): Twelve-year-old Shelley buys cigarettes and smokes with her friends.

Source: University of California at San Francisco.

Why is Hollywood so eager to show people smoking in films? It doesn't really make sense for the film companies to adopt a prosmoking policy—unless they see some advantage in it for them. But the tobacco industry *definitely* has an interest in doing so. They've known for years that smoking in movies translates into lots of new smokers, who become addicted to their poisonous product. That means the bottom line looks better and better.

A 1989 Philip Morris marketing plan said it all:

We believe that most of the strong, positive images for cigarettes and smoking are created by cinema and television. . . . If branded cigarette advertising is to take full advantage of these images . . . it has to feed off and exploit the image source.

The tobacco company's plan noted that "we have seen the heroes smoking in 'Wall Street,' 'Crocodile Dundee,' and 'Roger Rabbit.' Mel Gibson and Goldie Hawn are forever seen with a lighted cigarette. It is reasonable to assume that films and personalities have more influence on consumers than a static poster of letters."

Indeed they do.

Of course, that marketing plan was written a while ago. But the effects of smoking on screen haven't wafted away. A recent study by the Dartmouth Medical School found that "watching popular movies is the No. 1 factor leading nonsmoking teens to light up." The study determined that "film character smoking [was] more persuasive than traditional advertising, peer pressure or parents" when it came to encouraging kids to smoke. According to the study, "the more smoking children saw in the movies, the more likely they were to try smoking. Researchers studied more than 6500 children, and found that 38 out of 100 who tried smoking do so because of exposure to smoking in movies."

The study found that teenagers whose favorite stars smoked in three or more films were 2.6 times more likely than other teenagers to start smoking or to see smoking as socially acceptable.

That's reason enough to keep smoking out of kids' films.

The research tracked 2,600 children for two years. All the kids were between ten and fourteen years old, and none of them had ever smoked. The researchers correlated their moviegoing habits with whether they started smoking or not. In all, 31 percent of teens who saw more than 150 instances of smoking in movies had tried smoking—compared to only 4 percent of teens who had seen fewer than fifty occurrences.

So movies are definitely influential when it comes to enticing kids to start smoking: the more they see it, the more they do it. Other academic sources have made the same point. *The Lancet,* a British medical journal, noted that "health advocates point to the Marlboros smoked by Sam Rockwell in the 2003 film *Confessions of a Dangerous Mind,* Sissy Spacek's Marlboros in *In the Bedroom,* Russell Crowe's Winstons in *A Beautiful Mind,* or John Travolta's Skoal in *Basic*" among recent examples of apparently benign tobacco use in movies.

And the promotion of particular brands seems deliberately planned and targeted. The physician Michael Beach, who worked on the Dartmouth study, cited a good example of cigarette promotion in the popular movie *Men in Black II.* "You see the stars with a Marlboro carton. But when they open a refrigerator to get a jar of mayonnaise, the label on the mayonnaise is covered."

That's no accident.

Another study, by Stanton Glantz and Annemarie Charlesworth of the University of California at San Francisco, published in the journal *Pediatrics,* reports that "the science is very solid. Smoking in the movies has a very substantial effect on the risk that kids will get addicted to nicotine."

Glantz and Charlesworth analyzed the results of fifty-nine studies on smoking in movies and on teen smoking to assess the impact of film images on young people. They found that:

- Eighty percent of PG-13 films depicted smoking, usually by a major character.

- The depictions of smoking in top-grossing films dropped in half from 1950 to 1982 and now has soared back to 1950 levels.

- Teenagers "see [the] behavior [of on-screen smokers] as sophisticated and something to emulate. And while smokers in real life tend to be of lower socioeconomic status, smokers on-screen are primarily white males from upper income brackets."

Increasingly, Glantz found, smokers shown in movies are wealthy characters for whom tobacco is an indication of a luxurious lifestyle, one to which we are all supposed to aspire. In the 1960s, '70s, and '80s, more than half the characters who smoked in films were poor. But in the 1990s, only 21 percent were poor and half were upper middle class or rich.

The presence of smoking in Hollywood is ubiquitous. Even an animated hit such as *The Incredibles* featured characters who smoked, as did Disney's

G-rated *Hercules,* whose hero smokes a cigar. As the San Jose *Mercury News* has reported, "even aliens pack Marlboros in *Men in Black* and *Men in Black II,* both of which are rated PG-13."

Among the films singled out by the study's leader, Stanton Glantz, was the Oscar-winning musical *Chicago,* whose glamorous lead actresses offered potentially dangerous examples to impressionable teenage girls. In that film, Glantz noted, "you have very high-profile actresses [smoking] in a tremendously successful movie." (In *Chicago,* Queen Latifah, Catherine Zeta-Jones, and Richard Gere all smoke.) To those who argue that smoking was appropriate to the film's historical setting, Glantz responds that in the 1920s only 5 percent of women smoked and they tended not to be the kind of characters depicted in *Chicago.* He concludes, "There's a lot of girls who are smoking now because of that movie and girls will start smoking for years because of that movie."

When Thumbs Up! Thumbs Down!, a project devoted to smoking in the movies, studied the top ten movies each week from June 2003 through May 2004, it found that three quarters of all films studied contained some tobacco use. And half of those films were rated PG-13!

FILMS AIMED AT KIDS THAT SHOW SMOKING

- 39 percent of all PG movies
- 79 percent of all PG-13 films
- And 82 percent of all R flicks

Source: *National Catholic Reporter.*

In all, 53 percent of the lead characters lit up on screen in the films studied—more than double the percentage of us who smoke in real life.

And the smoke in these films kept on coming. In PG-13 films, the study found that there were ten smoking incidents per hour; in R films, there were sixteen. And when smoking was depicted, it was generally shown in a positive light. Thumbs Up! Thumbs Down! found that 56 percent of the films had actively protobacco messages, while only 23 percent had antismoking content.

SIXTY 2005 TEEN-RATED FLICKS
THAT SHOW SMOKING

PG-Rated Films

The Chronicles of Narnia: The Lion, the Witch, and the Wardrobe (Disney)

The Gospel (Disney)

The Greatest Game Ever Played (Sony)

The Hitchhiker's Guide to the Galaxy (Touchstone)

Kicking & Screaming (Disney)

The Legend of Zorro (Disney)

The Sisterhood of the Traveling Pants (Sony)

Son of the Mask (Time Warner)

Yours, Mine and Ours (Viacom/Sony)

Zathura (Disney)

PG-13-Rated Films

A Lot like Love (Disney)

An Unfinished Life (Disney)

The Bad News Bears (Viacom)

Batman Begins (Time Warner)

Be Cool (Sony)

Bee Season (Fox Searchlight)

Bewitched (Sony)

Cinderella Man (Universal)

Coach Carter (Viacom)

D.E.B.S. (Sony)

Dark Water (Disney)

Diary of a Mad Black Woman (Lions Gate)

The Dukes of Hazzard (Time Warner)

Elizabethtown (Viacom)

The Exorcism of Emily Rose (Sony)

Fever Pitch (Fox 2000)

Fun with Dick and Jane (Sony)

The Honeymooners (Viacom)

Hotel Rwanda (Sony)

In Good Company (Universal)

In Her Shoes (Fox 2000)

In the Mix (Lions Gate)

The Interpreter (Universal)

Into the Blue (Sony)

King Kong (Universal)

King's Ransom (Time Warner)

The Longest Yard (Viacom/Sony)

Lords of Dogtown (Sony)

Man of the House (Sony)

Melinda and Melinda (Fox Searchlight)

Miss Congeniality 2 (Time Warner)

Monster-in-Law (Time Warner)

Mr. and Mrs. Smith (20th Century Fox)

The Phantom of the Opera (Time Warner)

Prime (Focus Features)

Proof (Disney)

(continued)

Red Eye (DreamWorks)

Rent (Sony)

Sahara (Viacom)

Serenity (Universal)

The Skeleton Key (Universal)

Stealth (Sony)

Supercross (20th Century Fox)

Transporter 2 (20th Century Fox)

Underclassman (Disney)

Undiscovered (Lions Gate)

Walk the Line (Fox 2000)

The Wedding Date (Universal)

XXX 2 (Sony)

Source: Smoke Free Movies, University of California at San Francisco.
http://smokefreemovies.ucsf.edu/

What makes tobacco use in films especially dangerous is how easily kids can become hooked on tobacco. Corinne Husten, the chief of epidemiology for the Office on Smoking and Health at the U.S. Centers for Disease Control and Prevention in Atlanta, points out that "[young] people probably get addicted much faster than we used to think. I think the power of addiction has been underestimated, and adolescents underestimate the likelihood that they themselves will become addicted.

"To some extent," she adds, "tobacco companies preach that [smoking] is a choice, but if you're addicted to something, it's not really a choice. Most of the time people try to quit they're not successful. They find they're unable to quit. That points to a strong need to help adolescents understand it's dangerous to dabble."

This is a problem with a history. For decades, smoking in films filled a huge marketing void for tobacco companies that was created when Congress stopped them from advertising on television. Unable to put beguiling images of cool waterfalls, thin women, and rugged cowboys on television in the service of selling cigarettes, they did the next best thing: they paid moviemakers to include these images in their films. The industry spent millions for product placement in top-ranked motion pictures, mandating that stars smoke in their productions.

In these bad old days, tobacco companies were willing to shell out lavish fees to have actors and actresses promote smoking in general and their brands in particular. Among the worst offenders were action films with superheroes in starring roles. As the public health group Action on Smoking and Health (ASH) notes, in 1980's Superman II, "the Marlboro brand name appeared some 40 times in the film," and even Lois Lane—a nonsmoker in the original comic—smoked in the film. That highly visible bit of product placement cost Philip Morris $40,000. In the appropriately named 1989 James Bond flick *License to Kill,* the producers took a $350,000 payment to have Bond smoke Larks in the movie.

In the 1998 settlement of the attorneys general's lawsuit against Big Tobacco, however, the cigarette companies agreed to stop paying filmmakers to use their products. The agreement slowed the tobacco companies' efforts to promote their poisonous products—but it didn't defeat them. Soon cigarettes reappeared in films—and today they've returned as a common sight in your local multiplex.

How do tobacco companies get their products into films now that paid product placement for tobacco is illegal? No one seems to know. The tobacco companies say they haven't paid for product placement, since they promised the nation's attorneys general not to do so.

"If producers or directors use or depict our brands, they do so without seeking or obtaining our permission," said spokesperson Jennifer Golisch of Philip Morris USA. "Our policy for over a decade has been to deny requests for use of our cigarette brands, name or packaging in motion pictures or television shows for the general public, irrespective of whether that audience is adults or minors."

So why do Marlboros and other Philip Morris cigarettes pop up in the movies so frequently? Apparently, the film companies use the Philip Morris product without permission. Obviously, this hasn't given Philip Morris a moment's pause.

But even if you are gullible enough to believe the tobacco companies' denials, they are not completely innocent. ASH reports that it knows "of one instance in which a tobacco company helped finance a film and then put its products prominently in it. U.S. Tobacco, which makes most of the chewing tobacco, had a movie production division which made a movie, *Pure Country,* in which handsome, good-old-boy cowboys chew."

M. Bridget Aherns, one of the authors of the Dartmouth study on the impact of films on teen smoking, asked whether money may still be passing hands between tobacco companies and producers and actors. "We don't have any proof of how the cigarettes got there [in the films]—be it clandestine payments, free samples to a particular set designer, or an actor who just happens to smoke that brand. But now that we see it and we know what the effect is, we need to answer the question of why it is there."

In the Dartmouth study, Aherns and her fellow researchers found that after the tobacco companies promised to end paid product placement in films, the percentage of times that an actor actually endorsed a specific brand of cigarettes actually jumped from only 1 percent before the ban to 11 percent after the ban.

However cigarettes get into films, their influence is extremely bad and dangerous for the health of their teen audiences.

We need to save our kids' lives by stopping this nefarious product placement—no matter who's behind it.

ACTION AGENDA

The most important step we could take to stop teens from smoking would be for Congress to pass, and the president to sign, a bill now making its way through the Senate that would allow federal regulation of cigarettes.

In one of his most important acts as president, Bill Clinton backed the Food and Drug Administration (FDA) when it sought to regulate tobacco. But the Supreme Court overruled his decision, insisting on direct statutory authorization by Congress before it would permit FDA regulation—hence this bill.

On August 1, 2007, the Senate Health, Education, Labor and Pensions Committee voted 13 to 8 to put tobacco under FDA regulation. The bill directs the FDA "to restrict tobacco advertising, regulate warning labels, and remove hazardous ingredients." With more than fifty cosponsors in the Senate, the bill stands a good chance of passing. In 2004, the Senate passed a similar bill but the Republican-controlled House killed it. Now, with Democrats in control of both houses, it may pass and Bush may sign it.

To his everlasting credit, GOP presidential nominee Senator John McCain has led the efforts to extend federal regulation to tobacco.

One of the key catalysts for passing the bill this time is a switch by Philip Morris, which originally opposed the bill but backs it now. Philip Morris hasn't gotten religion: it's just achieved such a dominant share of the U.S. cigarette market that it wants to stop all promotions that might give its competitors a chance to horn in.

Leading the bad guys in opposing this bill is Senator Richard Burr, Republican of North Carolina. Choosing to side with R. J. Reynolds, based in his home state, over the concerned parents and teenagers who are his constituents, Burr has threatened to hold up the bill on the Senate floor. So far he's been successful: there has been no vote on this important legislation.

How much did the senators who voted against FDA regulation of tobacco—all Republicans—receive in contributions from Big Tobacco? Plenty. Here's the list of those who voted no—and how much they received from the tobacco lobby:

THEY TOOK THE MONEY AND DID TOBACCO'S BIDDING

Senator	Tobacco Contributions (2001–2007)
Wayne Allard (R-Colo.)	$27,750
Orrin Hatch (R-Utah)	$26,000
Pat Roberts (R-Kans.)	$17,500
Richard Burr (R-N.C.)	$16,378
Lamar Alexander (R-Tenn.)	$16,000
Michael Enzi (R-Wyo.)	$2,000
Norm Coburn (R-Okla.)	$1,000

Source: Public Citizen.

Then there are the intrepid souls who took tobacco's money—but then voted *against* the cigarette companies and supported FDA regulation:

THEY TOOK THE MONEY AND RAN

Senator	Tobacco Contributions (2001–2007)
Christopher Dodd (D-Conn.)	$41,700
Hillary Clinton (D-N.Y.)	$18,550
Ted Kennedy (D-Mass.)	$7,500

(continued)

THEY TOOK THE MONEY AND RAN *(continued)*

Senator	Tobacco Contributions (2001–2007)
Judd Gregg (R-N.H.)	$5,000
Lisa Murkowski (R-Alaska)	$5,000
Tom Harkin (D-Iowa)	$4,000
Jeff Bingaman (D-N.M.)	$3,000
Barbara Mikulski (D-Md.)	$1,000

Source: Public Citizen.

For the Democrats, who voted unanimously in favor of FDA regulation and against the interests of Big Tobacco, this was an easy vote. Despite any individual campaign contributions from tobacco they may have received, tobacco is still a Republican industry and the Democrats don't need to cut the Republicans any slack.

But a special note of thanks is due to two Republicans who resisted the party trend and didn't sell out to Big Tobacco even though they took campaign contributions from the industry. Senator Judd Gregg (R-N.H.) took a $5,000 contribution from tobacco in the 2001–2002 election cycle but voted to regulate the industry anyway. And Lisa Murkowski (R-Alaska) voted right even though she, too, soaked the industry for $5,000.

Apart from FDA regulation, however, can Congress do more to stop portrayals of tobacco use in movies? Could Congress ban tobacco use in films, for example, as it has already banned cigarettes on television? Probably not. The congressional ban on tobacco on television is based on the fact that TV stations broadcast over public airwaves, which are under the government's control. The FCC can regulate television but not films because there are no public airwaves involved in the showing of movies at theaters or on DVDs.

Constitutional protections of commercial speech—as opposed to political speech—are not absolute. But they might still make it possible for tobacco company lawyers to challenge any congressional ban on smoking in films.

Because of this legal obstacle, the public health community has focused on ratings by the Motion Picture Association of America (MPAA). Researchers Stanford Glantz and Karen Kacirk want Hollywood to give R ratings to all "smoking movies." "If an actor says the 'F-word' twice in a film, or once in a sexual context (versus a single profanity exclamation), that film [should get] an R rating. I want tobacco treated as seriously as they treat the F-word."

Ratings would, of course, help to keep teenagers out of theaters where tobacco use was portrayed. But by reducing teen attendance at films, it would also cut sharply into the studios' revenues. Just as movie studios work to screen out sex scenes so as to avoid an R rating, they would presumably work overtime to delete tobacco use if it would trigger such a rating.

The problem lies with the MPAA. Though the association's representatives claim they oppose tobacco use in films, their actions belie their words.

The motion picture industry has been slow—to say the least—to take up the challenge of banning smoking in its products. Former liberal Democratic congressman Dan Glickman, the new head of the MPAA, is trying to talk the talk. "Any effort to address tobacco's influence on kids in this country is welcome," he says. In May, the MPAA "announced that portrayals of smoking would be considered alongside sex and violence in assessing the suitability of movies for young viewers. Films that appear to glamorize smoking will risk a more restrictive rating."

We'll see. Health advocacy groups charge that the MPAA's threat to change the ratings of films based on smoking is just so much public relations bluster. The American Lung Association and Smoke Free Movies, a group at the University of California at San Francisco, said that of 433 "movies with smoking in the past four years, only one box-office film included tobacco use in its rating description."

The public should put increasing pressure on the MPAA to impose R ratings on films that feature smoking. As Americans concerned about our children's health, we need to press stars and studios to keep tobacco off their screens. If stars like Richard Gere, Julia Roberts, Brad Pitt, and others were lighting up marijuana joints as opposed to cigarettes, they'd be subject to massive public criticism and scorn. But the problem of teen smoking is truly a national emergency. About half of the teenagers who start smoking every year are heavily influenced by what they see in films. That amounts to 390,000 teenagers each year who embark on the path to tobacco addiction under the influence of films.

The stars who smoke and the studios that glamorize them must be held accountable—and made to suffer for it financially.

Among the major studios, only Disney has taken the lead. On July 26, 2007, it announced that it would "ban cigarettes in its family films and discourage it in others." In a letter to Representative Edward J. Markey (D-Mass.), who has been pioneering the battle against tobacco, Disney CEO Robert A. Iger said the historically family-friendly company would not only ban smoking in its branded films but would "discourage depictions of cigarette smoking" in pictures produced by its Touchstone and Miramax units.

That's a big step. But we should demand that other studios stop their stars from smoking on screen. The health of our children is at stake.

The new president of the MPAA is Dan Glickman, who took the job after Lyndon Johnson's former adviser Jack Valenti passed away. Before he took the MPAA job, Glickman was a liberal Democratic congressman from Kansas and Bill Clinton's second secretary of agriculture. He was consistently in the antismoking camp in Congress—but now that the studios are paying his salary he appears to have become a bit more tepid on the subject. So reach out to him at www.mpaa.org. We're sure he'll be glad to hear from you!

CONCLUSION

So that's a brief, by no means exhaustive, survey of some of the ways we're getting fleeced in America today—by government officials, market forces, foreign interests, and worse.

What can we do about it?

Don't despair. There are actually some concrete things we *can* do.

The only way to avoid being fleeced by our own government is to pay attention to what our elected and appointed representatives are doing—or not doing—in Washington. We've got to make them accountable. How can we do that?

One simple reform we should demand immediately is that every member of Congress and every upper-level bureaucrat post his or her schedule on the Internet. It wouldn't be hard to do: they all have Web sites, and they all have people who keep their calendars. They're working on our dime, so we should be able to know how they spend their time.

But don't expect many of them to do it anytime soon. If we could see their daily schedules, we'd know which of our elected officials are meeting with which lobbyists; which ones are spending most of their time raising money; and which ones are spending most of their workday running for office—instead of meeting with and working for their constituents.

It's a small demand, but it would bring big results. And it might even encourage some of our elected and appointed officials to spend more time doing the job they were elected to do.

The American people deserve more transparency and accountability from our leaders. We need to send our congressmen—and the president—e-mails whenever we approve or disapprove of something they do. And when they fail to act on an important issue—such as subprime mortgages or credit card abuse—we need to let them know that we're paying attention and we're angry.

The Internet has made the democracy Thomas Jefferson dreamed of much more possible. With up-to-the-minute news, an intelligent electorate, and the ability to start a conversation with decision makers, we can truly make a difference. And with YouTube, it's easier than ever to catch politicians who lie and exaggerate—as Hillary Clinton did when she repeatedly claimed that she was on a dangerous mission in Bosnia and landed under sniper fire. The video of her calmly attending a welcoming ceremony and accepting flowers from a young Bosnian girl demonstrated her lie more decisively than any newspaper story could ever do.

So use the Internet to make your voice heard. E-mail your senators and representatives, telling them to make their schedules public and post them on the Internet.

The demand for accountability shouldn't stop with government. Let the corporations that take advantage of you know how unhappy you are. And if a union exploits you, let it know, too.

The injustices we've tracked down, here and in *Outrage,* generally arise when government action—or inaction—allows a few people to get rich by exploiting the rest of us. In fact, sometimes the government even rewards such conduct.

Political debate in America is often discussed in terms of two camps: those who want more government and those who want less. But these distinctions are too theoretical and abstract. What we *should* want is good government that punishes those who do us harm, in order to discourage others from following their example, and that rewards those who do us good.

In some instances, government policy itself causes the ripoffs that make us angry: Our tax laws, which allow hedge fund partners to get rich without paying the same taxes as the rest of us. Defense spending that rewards Halliburton for fleecing us as we try to create a free Iraq. Federal disaster relief policies that give people money to rebuild their million-dollar flooded homes again and again in the same place. Weak federal regulatory policies that coddle companies who sell us unsafe products.

But some problems are so severe that we *need* more government action, not less. The government needs to step up and discipline the subprime lenders, stopping them from getting away with their sleazy frauds. It needs to stop credit card companies from robbing us and charging more than 30 percent in interest.

We need political leaders who will use government to police the marketplace in our interests—the interests of the many, not the few.

But that will be no easy task. Behind each of these ripoffs are hundreds of millions of dollars in special interest money—payoffs to our political leaders in the form of "contributions" that are nothing more than thinly disguised bribes.

But with public action and a participatory democracy in which the decision makers know that we're watching—and that there are consequences for their actions—we can definitely make a difference.

Free-market capitalism is morally neutral. It's possible to accumulate great wealth by curing cancer or by selling cocaine. We can do good or evil and be well paid for either or both.

The role of government should be to ensure that those who hurt others in pursuit of wealth are punished and that those who help others along the way are encouraged. By translating society's attitudes into action in this way, government helps us as a nation to preserve our shared values.

Cleaning up the government, and policing private business, can be a bit like trying to eradicate cockroaches: every year or two a new generation appears, immune to last year's preventive measures. It's up to us to come up with new, improved ways to kill the bugs we can catch—and keep the rest on the run.

In a year full of political promises, is a roach-free kitchen really too much to ask?

ACKNOWLEDGMENTS

Thanks to Morgan Beuhler, Tom Gallagher, and Irma Cruz for their help in making this book possible.

And special thanks to our friends and neighbors Beverley and Stan Platt for their proofreading skills, endless patience, and ideas.

Cal Morgan, our editor, is an old teammate. This is our seventh book together. We work well together and he was, as always, a pleasure to work with.

Sandy Frazier, who is handling publicity for the book, is a gem who seems not only to know everybody but to be liked by all as well.

Maureen Maxwell made sure the trains ran on time in the rest of our lives so that we could write and write and write.

At HarperCollins, thanks also to Jonathan Burnham, Kathy Schneider, Christine Boyd, Tina Andreadis, Campbell Wharton, Brittany Hamblin, Susan Kosko, Cindy Achar, and John Jusino.

NOTES

INTRODUCTION

1 Stripped of money: Oxford English Dictionary, http://dictionary.oed.com/cgi/entry/ 50086057?query_type=word&queryword=fleeced&first=1&max_to_show=10&sort_type= alpha&result_place=1&search_id=j24Y-TTpb89–4760&hilite=50086057se1.

1 deprived of money: Dictionary.com, http://dictionary.reference.com/browse/fleece.

1 "avoid using word combinations": Diversity Guidelines, Society of Professional Journalists, http://www.spj.org/dirguidelines.asp.

2 "30 billion in profits": Stephen Labaton, "Bankruptcy Bill Set For Passage: Victory For Busy," *The New York Times,* March 9, 2005.

2 collect a hidden fee: "Congress To Credit Card Companies: Play Fair; Retailers Applaud Introduction of Fair Credit Card Fee Act, reuters.com, March 7, 2008.

2 One third of all: Ruth Mantell, "Cardholders Caught in Credit 'Trap': Report," Market Watch.com, August 1, 2007, www.marketwatch.com/news/story/%20cardholders-caught-credit-trap-report/story.aspx?guid=%7b3995C83B-77A5–4DBB-83F1–04B07771CD52%7 d&print=true&dist=printTop.

3 was paid $100 million: Claudia H. Deutsch, "Despite the harsh spotlight, CEO pay rises," *International Herald Tribune,* April 6, 2008, www.iht.com/articles/2008/04/06/business/06 comp.php?page=3.

3 more than $60 million: Alex Veiga, "Countrywide's Mozilo Forgoing $37.5M," Associated Press, January 27, 2008, www.sfgate.com/cgi-bin/article.cgi?f=/n/a/2008/01/27/financial/ f211557S93.DTL&feed=rss.business.

3 $1.2 billion loss: Associated Press, "Panel Grills CEOs Involved in Mortgage Crisis," MSNBC, March 7, 2008, www.msnbc.msn.com/id/23522531/.

3 laid off 12,000 workers: Jonathan Stempel, "Countrywide Says Foreclosures Highest on Record," Reuters, January 9, 2008, www.reuters.com/article/businessNews/idUSN08497 66020080109.

3 The FBI is investigating: Robert Schmidt and David Mildenberg, "Countrywide Is Probed by FBI for Possible Fraud, Person Says," Bloomberg.com, March 9, 2008, www.bloomberg .com/apps/news?pid=20601103&sid=atU2Uy.lOsyw&refer=news.

5   $30 billion: Stephen Labaton, "Bankruptcy Bill Set for Passage; Victory for Bush," *The New York Times,* March 9, 2005, www.nytimes.com/2005/03/09/business/09bankruptcy.html? pagewanted=print&position=.

6   $161 million: Associated Press, "Panel Grills CEOs Involved in Mortgage Crisis," March 7, 2008, www.msnbc.msn.com/id/23522531/.

6   with $68 million: Jenny Anderson, "Chiefs' Pay Under Fire at Capitol," *The New York Times,* March 8, 2008, www.nytimes.com/2008/03/08/business/08pay.html.

6   Countrywide was eventually sold: Christopher Palmeri and Dean Foust, "Bank of America Bags Countrywide," *BusinessWeek,* January 11, 2008, www.businessweek.com/bwdaily/ dnflash/content/jan2008/db20080111_790414.htm?campaign_id=rss_daily.

6   45 percent more foreclosures: Melinda Fulmer, "More Americans Are Losing Their Homes," MSNBC, http://realestate.msn.com/buying/articlenewhome.aspx?cp-document id=338165.

7   as high as $875 billion: Chip Cummins, "Abu Dhabi Sets Investment Code for Sovereign Fund," *The Wall Street Journal,* March 18, 2008.

8   "While I am": Stephen Labaton and Julia Werdiger, "Mild Reaction in Capitol to a Dubai Nasdaq Stake," *The New York Times,* September 20, 2007, www.nytimes.com/2007/09/21/ business/worldbusiness/21exchange.html?partner=rssnyt&emc=rss.

CHAPTER 1

15   "end welfare as we know it": Douglas J. Besharov, "End Welfare Lite as We Know It," *The New York Times,* August 15, 2006, www.nytimes.com/2006/08/15/opinion/15besharov.html?n =Top/Reference/TimesTopics/Organizations/D/DemocraticParty.

15   "like a laser beam": "William Jefferson Clinton," PBS.org, www.pbs.org/wgbh/amex/presi dents/42_clinton/index.html.

15   "bold, persistent experimentation": "Bill Clinton: First Inaugural Address," January 21, 1993, www.bartleby.com/124/pres64.html.

17   Barack Obama, he has: Richard E. Cohen, Brian Friel, and Kirk Victor, "Obama: Most Liberal Senator in 2007," *National Journal,* January 31, 2008, http://nj.nationaljournal.com/vote ratings/.

18   The United States already: "Only the Rich Pay Taxes," RushLimbaugh.com, October 10, 2003, www.rushlimbaugh.com/home/menu/top_50__of_wage_earners_pay_96_09__of_ income_taxes.guest.html.

19   "for the wealthy": " 'Meet the Press' Transcript for Nov. 11, 2007," MSNBC.com, November 11, 2007, www.msnbc.msn.com/id/21738432/.

20   Individual stock market: "U.S. Institutional Investors Boost Control of U.S. Equity Market Assets," The Conference Board, October 10, 2005, www.conference-board.org/utilities/press PrinterFriendly.cfm?press_ID=2726.

20   "capital gains tax": "Americans for Prosperity Says Edwards' Plan to Hike Capital Gains Taxes 87% Would Smash Middle-Income Retirement Nest Eggs, Bring in Less Money than Current Lower Rate," Americans for Prosperity, EarthTimes.org, July 26, 2007, www.earth times.org/articles/show/news_press_release,147381.shtml.

22   Since 52 percent: "A Capital Gains Primer," *The Wall Street Journal,* October 15, 2007, tax-prof.typepad.com/taxprof_blog/2007/10/wsj-a-capital-g.html.

22 "Well, Charlie": "Transcript: Obama and Clinton Debate," ABC News, April 16, 2008, *http://abcnews.go.com/Politics/DemocraticDebate/story?id=4670271&page=1.*

23 "If we kept": Teddy Davis, "Obama Floats Social Security Tax Hike," ABCNews.com, September 22, 2007, http://abcnews.go.com/Politics/Story?id=3638710&page=1.

23 The Cato Institute: "2007 Democratic Primary Debate in Las Vegas, Nevada, Nov. 15, 2007," OnTheIssues, www.ontheissues.org/2007_Dems_Las_Vegas.htm.

23 "Understand," he said: Ibid.

24 When it was: "S.AMDT.471," Library of Congress, March 23, 2007, http://thomas .loc.gov/cgi-bin/bdquery/z?d110:SP471.

25 Obama wants their children: Ibid.

27 "Before any guestworker," Jeralyn E. Merritt, "How the Candidates Differ on Immigration," TalkLeft, February 15, 2008, www.talkleft.com/story/2008/2/15/134236/391.

27 "would strengthen the requirement": Ibid.

27 "if they are illegal": Ibid.

27 "When I was": Jeralyn E. Merritt, "How the Candidates Differ on Immigration," www .uslaw.com/law_blogs/TalkLeft?blog=2.

28 But the United States already: "N.H. Debate: the Dems' Turn," *Newsweek,* January 7, 2008, www.newsweek.com/id/84794/page/5.

30 "If you're starting": "Democratic Presidential Debate Sponsored by CNN and the Congressional Black Caucus Institute on January 21, 2008," OnTheIssues, www.ontheissues.org/ 2008_CBC_Dems.htm.

30 "National Health Insurance Exchange": Barack Obama, "Blueprint for Change," pp. 6–9, www.barackobama.com/pdf/ObamaBlueprintForChange.pdf.

32 "get our troops": 2008 Democratic Debate in Las Vegas, January 15, 2008.

32 "the only troops": 2007 Democratic Primary Debate at Dartmouth College, September 26, 2007.

32 "We know right now": "2007 AFL-CIO Democratic Primary Forum, August 8, 2007," OnTheIssues, www.ontheissues.org/2007_AFL-CIO_Dems.htm.

33 "go into western Pakistan": "2008 Democratic Primary Debate, Sponsored by ABC News, Facebook, and ABC Affiliate WMUR-NH; Jan. 5, 2008; Final Debate Before New Hampshire Primary; at St. Anselm College in Manchester," OnTheIssues, www.ontheissues.org/2008 _Dems_Facebook.htm.

33 "we strengthened judicial review": "Floor Statement of Senator Barack Obama on S.2271-USA PATRIOT Act Reauthorization," February 16, 2006, http://obama.senate.gov/speech/ 060216-floor_statement_2/.

34 "provide specific evidence": "USA PATRIOT Act Reauthorization: Differences Between House and Senate Bills," August 18, 2005.

35 "to see stronger": Obama Speech on the Senate Floor, February 16, 2006.

36 "sanctuaries of learning": Carla K. Johnson, Associated Press, "Obama's Stand Against Patriot Act Cheered By Librarians," *Free Republic,* June 25, 2005, www.freerepublic.com/focus/ f-news/1430799/posts.

36 "federal agents to get": Carla K. Johnson, "Obama's Stand Against Patriot Act Cheered By Librarians," June 25, 2005, www.freerepublic.com/focus/f-news/1430799/posts.

37 "identify with particularity": "USA PATRIOT Act Reauthorization: Differences Between House and Senate Bills."

38 "We've got to make": 2007 Democratic Primary Debate at Howard University, June 28, 2007.

38 In the Illinois state senate: "On the Issues," ObamaForIllinois.org, September 28, 2004.

38 "if you excel": Ruth Marcus, "From Barack Obama, Two Dangerous Words," *The Washington Post*, July 11, 2007, www.washingtonpost.com/wp-dyn/content/article/2007/07/10/AR 2007071001304_pf.html.

38 "an experienced": Barack Obama, *The Audacity of Hope* (New York: Crown, 2006), 161.

38 "It may not": Marcus, "From Barack Obama, Two Dangerous Words."

39 "Don't tell us": Ibid.

39 "will continue to": "Chairman Miller: While Maintaining Accountability in Schools, We Must Make the Law Fair, Flexible, and Funded; Announces Six Key Features of Bill to Reauthorize No Child Left Behind," Committee on Education and Labor, July 30, 2007, www.house.gov/apps/list/speech/edlabor_dem/rel073007nclb.html.

40 "his plan means": Paul Steinhauser, "Obama Tax Plan: $80 Billion in Cuts, Five-Minute Filings," CNN, September 18, 2007, www.cnn.com/2007/POLITICS/09/18/obama.taxplan/ index.html.

41 "effectively eliminate": Ibid.

41 For families making: "Barack Obama on Social Security," OnTheIssues, www.ontheissues .org/2008/barack_obama_social_security.htm.

41 President Obama would: "Education," BarackObama.com, www.barackobama.com/issues/ education/.

41 "Democrats and Republicans": "Democrats and Republicans": Author's conversation with President Bill Clinton, June 1996.

CHAPTER 2

46 WHAT AMERICANS WORRY ABOUT: www.albany.edu/sourcebook/pdf/t212007.pdf.

47 attack army recruiting centers: John Miller, "Law Enforcement, American Style," *The New York Times*, September 14, 2006, www.nytimes.com/2006/09/14/opinion/14miller.html.

47 travel to Iraq: Ibid.

47 attack the U.S. Capitol: Ibid.

47 blow up the Sears Tower: Scott Shane and Andrea Zarate, "F.B.I. Killed Plot in Talking Stage, a Top Aide Says," *The New York Times*, June 24, 2006, www.nytimes.com/2006/06/24/us/ 24terror.html.

47 bomb the New York City subways: Miller, "Law Enforcement, American Style."

47 attack Fort Dix, New Jersey: Kelli Arena and Kevin Bohn, "Official: Radicals Wanted to Create Carnage at Fort Dix," CNN.com, May 9, 2007, http://edition.cnn.com/2007/US/05/08/ fortdix.plot/index.html.

47 blow up fuel lines: Michael Powell and William K. Rashbaum, "Papers Portray Plot as More Talk than Action," *The Boston Globe*, June 4, 2007, www.boston.com/news/nation/ articles/2007/06/04/filings_portray_plot_as_more_talk_than_action/.

48 "Avoid using word combinations": Diversity Guidelines, Society of Professional Journalists, http://www.spj.org/divguidelines.asp.

51 "nearly 70 percent": Noel Sheppard, "Almost 70% Believe Traditional Media Out of Touch With their News Needs," Reuters, March 1, 2008.

51 "it is too hot": Author's interview with New York Police Commissioner Raymond W. Kelly, June 2007.

51 When the feds captured: Eric Lichtblau, "Threats and Responses: Terror, U.S. Cites Al Qaeda in Plot to Destroy Brooklyn Bridge," *The New York Times,* June 20, 2003, http://query.ny times.com/gst/fullpage.html?res=9B02EEDF1F38F933A15755C0A9659C8B63.

52 "prosecutors said Mr. Faris": Ibid.

52 FARIS AND AL QAEDA: Ibid.

52 more than 140,000: "Brooklyn Bridge History," AAMCAR.com, http://aamcar.com/ brooklyn-bridge.php.

53 "seemed pathetically amateurish": "A Chilling Reminder," *The New York Times,* June 21, 2003, http://query.nytimes.com/gst/fullpage.html?res=9901E1DC163BF932A15755C0A96 59C8B63&n=Top/Reference/Times%20Topics/Subjects/B/Brooklyn%20Bridge%20(NYC).

53 "the alleged plan": Patrick Healy, "Terrorists on the Brooklyn Bridge? Fans Say It's Still the Best Way to Get to the Other Side," *The New York Times,* June 21, 2003, http://query.ny times.com/gst/fullpage.html?res=9F01E1D6163BF932A15755C0A9659C8B63&sec=&spon =&pagewanted=print.

54 "Justice Department officials": Lichtblau, "Threats and Responses."

54 "[A]n F.B.I. official": Ibid.

54 "a senior law enforcement official": Randy Kennedy, "Threats and Responses: The Brooklyn Bridge; A Conspicuous Terror Target Is Called Hard to Topple," *The New York Times,* June 20, 2003, http://query.nytimes.com/gst/fullpage.html?res=9A0DE0D71E38F933A15755C0A96 59C8B63.

54 "another senior law enforcement official": Ibid.

54 "Several engineers interviewed": Ibid.

55 "think of the time": Ibid.

55 "The thought of losing": Ibid.

56 "We captured Khalid": Ankush Khardori, "Stage Wright: His Trip to Al Qaeda, And Why Lawrence Wright Is Still Very, Very Scared," The Huffington Post, March 9, 2007, www .huffingtonpost.com/eat-the-press/2007/03/09/stage-wright-his-trip-to_e_42942.html.

56 "Prosecutors say": "All Ten Democratic Presidential Candidates Debate; Report Indicates U.S. Sources Have Found No Signs of Weapons in Iraq," CNN.com, September 25, 2003, http://transcripts.cnn.com/TRANSCRIPTS/0309/25/acd.00.html.

56 "a man of wild dreams". Larry C. Johnson, "What George Bush Didn't Say About Guantanamo," The Huffington Post, September 7, 2006, www.huffingtonpost.com/larry-c-johnson/what-george-bush-didnt-s_b_28873.html.

56 "Maybe they're tired": Peter Baker and Dan Eggen, "Bush Tells of Terror Plot on LA Tower," *The Washington Post,* February 10, 2006, www.azcentral.com/arizonarepublic/news/articles/ 0210bush-terror0210.html.

57 "I have a plot": Clay Waters, "Times Watch Presents the Quotes of Note for 2006," TimesWatch.org, December 19, 2006, www.timeswatch.org/articles/2006/20061219090814 .aspx.

58 "In the years since 9/11": Noel Sheppard, "NYT Answers Questions Concerning Placing JFK Terror Plot Story off Front Page," NewsBusters, June 6, 2007, http://newsbusters.org/ node/13259.

58 "the plot involved": Powell and Rashbaum, "Papers Portray Plot as More Talk than Action."

58 "had the plot": Ibid.

58 "suggests a less": Michael Powell and William K. Rashbaum, "Papers Portray Plot As More Talk than Action," *The New York Times,* June 4, 2007, http://www.nytimes.com/2007/06/04/nyregion/04plot.html.

58 "the public was never at risk": Ibid.

60 "home-grown Islamic terrorist": Ibid.

60 "some law enforcement officials": Ibid.

60 "Papers Portray Plot": Ibid.

61 "a convicted": Ibid.

61 "one man with": "Liberal Minds and Homegrown Terrorism: Disbelief and Disrespect," Newsvine.com, June 4, 2007, http://purelypolitical.newsvine.com/_news/2007/06/04/754214-liberal-minds-and-homegrown-terrorism-disbelief-and-disrespect.

61 "a broader risk": Powell and Rashbaum, "Papers Portray Plot as More Talk than Action."

61 "Its ring leader": Arianna Huffington, "The JFK Pipeline 'Plot': Another 'Chilling' Example of Political and Media Hyperbole," UndertheCarpet.com, June 6, 2007, www.underthecarpet.co.uk/Pages/NewsArticle.php?num=2465.

62 "In order to foil": Nora Ephron, "How to Foil a Terrorist Plot in Seven Simple Steps," The Huffington Post, June 4, 2007, www.huffingtonpost.com/nora-ephron/how-to-foil-a-terrorist-p_b_50474.html?view=print.

63 "inspiring a new round": Eric Lipton, "Recent Arrests in Terror Plots Yield Pre-Emptive Action by Government," *The New York Times,* July 9, 2006, www.nytimes.com/2006/07/09/us/09plot.html?r=1&oref=slogin.

63 "We don't wait": Ibid.

64 "There is some": Ibid.

64 "Plotting for this": Ibid.

64 "When they go": Ibid.

64 "the people you": Ibid.

64 "We are dangerously": Ibid.

65 "one defendant": Dan Eggen and Dale Russakoff, "Six Charged in Plot to Attack Fort Dix," *The Washington Post,* May 9, 2007, www.washingtonpost.com/wp-dyn/content/article/2007/05/08/AR2007050800465_pf.html.

65 "men firing assault weapons": David Kocieniewski, "6 Men Arrested in a Terror Plot Against Fort Dix," *The New York Times,* May 9, 2007, www.nytimes.com/2007/05/09/us/09plot.html?_r=1&oref=slogin&pagewanted=print.

65 The group had scouted: Ibid.

65 "one of the terrorists": Ibid.

65 "the women and children": Eggen and Russakoff, "Six Charged in Plot to Attack Fort Dix."

65 "Today we dodged": Kocieniewski, "6 Men Arrested in a Terror Plot Against Fort Dix."

66 "would-be terrorists": Eggen and Russakoff, "Six Charged in Plot to Attack Fort Dix."

66 "law enforcement source": Ibid.

66 "prosecutors described a complicated": Kocieniewski, "6 Men Arrested in a Terror Plot Against Fort Dix."

66 "Circuit City where": Anthony Kaufman, "Why Wasn't the Headline 'Bombers Not Smart Enough to Bomb JFK'?" The Huffington Post, June 4, 2007, www.huffingtonpost.com/anthony-kaufman/why-wasnt-the-headline-_b_50696.html.

67 "boobs" who got caught: Arianna Huffington, "The JFK Pipeline 'Plot': Another 'Chilling' Example of Political and Media Hyperbole," The Huffington Post, June 6, 2007, www.huffing tonpost.com/arianna-huffington/the-jfk-pipeline-plot-_b_51051.html.

67 "plan" that Padilla presented: Amanda Ripley, "The Case of the Dirty Bomber," Time, June 16, 2002, www.time.com/time/printout/0,8816,262917,00.html.

68 "In response": Ibid.

68 "hinted to his FBI": Ibid.

68 "FBI officials, including": Ibid.

68 "an unlikely attacker": Ibid.

69 "known terrorist": Ibid.

69 But the Nuclear Regulatory Commission: "Fact Sheet on Dirty Bombs," www.nrc.gov/reading-rm/doc-collections/fact-sheets/dirty-bombs.html.

69 "mass death or injury": Ripley, "The Case of the Dirty Bomber."

69 "enemy combatant": Ibid.

69 "the fundamental question": Stephen I. Vladeck, "The Lost Padilla Verdict," Los Angeles Times, August 17, 2007, www.latimes.com/news/printedition/suncommentary/la-oe-vladeck17aug17,1,6337844.story?coll=la-headlines-suncomment.

69 "the key piece": Laura Parker, "Padilla Trial to Begin, Minus the 'Dirty Bomb' Talk," USA Today, www.usatoday.com/news/nation/2007–05–13-padilla_N.htm.

70 "Mr. Padilla was added": Abby Goodnough and Scott Shane, "Padilla Is Guilty on All Charges in Terror Trial," The New York Times, August 17, 2007, www.nytimes.com/2007/08/17/us/17padilla.html?_r=1&oref=slogin.

70 "the government knew": "Legal Limbo," PBS, June 12, 2002, www.pbs.org/newshour/bb/law/jan-june02/limbo_6–12.html.

71 "The government's dilemma": Ibid.

71 "The problem here": Ibid.

71 "elaborating on the": Jerry Markon, "U.S. Defends Conduct in Padilla Case," The Washington Post, December 29, 2005, www.washingtonpost.com/wp-dyn/content/article/2005/12/28/AR2005122801463.html.

72 "conspiracy to levy war": Carol J. Williams, "Are They Terrorists or 'Naïve Losers'?" Los Angeles Times, October 3, 2007, www.latimes.com/news/nationworld/nation/la-na-sears3oct03,1,3777335.story?track=rss&ctrack=1&cset=true.

72 "kill all the devils": Shane and Zarate, "F.B.I. Killed Plot in Talking Stage."

72 "these defendants came": Williams, "Are They Terrorists or 'Naïve Losers'?"

72 "more aspirational": Shane and Zarate, "F.B.I. Killed Plot in Talking Stage."

72 "a construction odd-jobs worker": Williams, "Are They Terrorists or 'Naïve Losers'?"

73 "painted a picture": Ibid.

73 "the conspirators gave": Shane and Zarate, "F.B.I. Killed Plot in Talking Stage."

73 "delusions of grandeur": Williams, "Are They Terrorists or 'Naïve Losers'?"

73 "wait to see": Shane and Zarate, "F.B.I. Killed Plot in Talking Stage."

74 "learn the identity": Philip Bobbitt, "The Warrantless Debate over Wiretapping," The New York Times, August 22, 2007, www.nytimes.com/2007/08/22/opinion/22bobbitt.html.

74 "it became difficult": Ibid.

75 "German officials": Eric Schmitt, "New U.S. Law Credited in Arrests Abroad," The New York Times, September 11, 2007, www.nytimes.com/2007/09/11/washington/11terror.html.

75 "50 percent": Ibid.
76 "confront a generation-long challenge": Jane Perlez, "British Leader Seeks New Terrorism Laws," *New York Times,* July 26, 2007, www.nytimes.com/2007/07/26/world/europe/26 britain.html.
76 "biometric": Ibid.
76 "staffed by 375 lonely souls": Nina Bernstein, "Without Guns or Raids, a Tiny Squad of Officers Homes In on Visa Fraud," *The New York Times,* July 17, 2007, www.nytimes.com/2007/07/17/nyregion/17fraud.html.

CHAPTER 3

77 "reasonable opportunity": Dante Chinni, "Is the Fairness Doctrine Fair Game?" Pew Research Center Publications, July 19, 2007, http://pewresearch.org/pubs/546/fairness-doctrine.
77 "stations . . . had to carry": Ibid.
78 54 percent of Americans: "Where Do We Get Our News?," PBS, July 30, 2006, www.pbs.org/wgbh/pages/frontline/newswar/part3/stats.html.
78 "based on the idea": Chinni, "Is the Fairness Doctrine Fair Game?"
78 "the FCC revisited": Ibid.
79 "bailed out of bankruptcy": Kara Rowland, "Senate Democrats Foil Attempt to Bar 'Fairness Doctrine,' " *Washington Times,* July 20, 2007, http://washingtontimes.com/apps/pbcs.dll/article?AID=/20070720/BUSINESS/107200052&SearchID=73287732798441&template=printart.
79 360 news/talk radio stations: Chinni, "Is the Fairness Doctrine Fair Game?"
79 "The major reason": Ibid.
80 by 9 to 1: Rowland, "Senate Democrats Foil Attempt to Bar 'Fairness Doctrine.' "
80 "days after the": Ibid.
80 "the current Republican-led": Ibid.
80 margin of 309 to 115: Chinni, "Is the Fairness Doctrine Fair Game?"
80 "we live in an": Rowland, "Senate Democrats Foil Attempt to Bar 'Fairness Doctrine.' "
81 "It's time to reinstitute": Ibid.
81 And a recent victim: Ibid.
81 "For citizens who value": Monisha Bansal, "Dems Will Reinstate Fairness Doctrine, Some Say," CNSNews.com, February 08, 2008, http://www.cnsnews.com/ViewCulture.asp?Page=/Culture/archive/200802/CUL20080208a.html.
81 But there may be: Mark Lloyd, "Forget the Fairness Doctrine," Center for American Progress, July 24, 2007, www.americanprogress.org/issues/2007/07/lloyd_fairness.html.
81 "ownership rules": Ibid.
82 "underlying market control": Ibid.
82 "afford reasonable opportunity": Ibid.
82 "the public": Ibid.
82 "Strengthened limits": James L. Gattuso, "Fairness Doctrine, R.I.P.," National Review Online, July 5, 2007, http://article.nationalreview.com/?q=NmYzNGU0ZjAxNWFlOWE2Nm UzYWFjMmEwNWM1OTgyZjQ=.
82 "Shortening broadcast": Ibid.

82 "Requiring radio broadcasters": Ibid.

83 "Imposing a fee": Ibid.

83 "the goal of the": Ibid.

83 "public interest requirements": Ibid.

85 "If anyone ever": Alexander Bolton, "Battle Lines Are Drawn over Conservative Radio," *The Hill*, October 3, 2007, http://thehill.com/leading-the-news/battle-lines-are-drawn-over-conservative-radio-2007–10–03.html.

85 "We are getting": Author's conversation with President Bill Clinton, 1995.

CHAPTER 5

106 "could be important": Interview with the author, June 2007.

106 "the world's first": Frank J. Gaffney, Jr., "Invest Terror Free," *Washington Times,* November 13, 2007, www.washingtontimes.com/article/20071113/COMMENTARY03/111130012/1012.

112 "involved companies doing": Ibid.

112 California: Governor Arnold: Ibid.

112 "I couldn't be more": "California Governor Schwarzenegger Issues Statement on California's Divestment from Iran," September 24, 2007, www.allamericanpatriots.com/48733057_california_california_governor_schwarzenegger_issues_statement_california_s_divestment_iran.

112 "My office has": "Thompson Statement on DiNapoli Plan for Iran-Linked Investments," November 14, 2007, www.r8ny.com/node/14400.

113 "fiduciary duty": Authors interview with spokesman for office of Tim DiNapoli, New York State comptroller, September 23, 2007.

113 But pension funds: Eli Lake, "World Bank Vows a Big Loan to Iran," *The New York Sun,* November 5, 2007, www.nysun.com/article/65833.

114 Only part of this: Ibid.

114 "When I initially": Ibid.

115 "The bank adheres": Ibid.

CHAPTER 6

118 human rights violations: "2007 Country Reports on Human Rights Practices," U.S. State Department, www.state.gov/g/drl/rls/hrrpt/2007/.

119 43 percent of: "Members of Congress Increasingly Use Revolving Door to Launch Lucrative Lobbying Careers," Public Citizen, July 27, 2005, www.citizen.org/pressroom/release.cfm?ID=1999.

120 "How is it that": Ken Silverstein, "Their Men in Washington: Undercover with D.C.'s Lobbyists for Hire," *Harper's Magazine,* July 2007, www.harpers.org/archive/2007/07/0081591.

120 "stunning upset": Leslie Wayne, "U.S.-Europe Team Beats Out Boeing on Big Contract," *The New York Times,* March 1, 2008, www.nytimes.com/2008/03/01/business/01tanker.html?fta=y.

121 "breaks a relationship": Ibid.

121 "sustain employment in": Ibid.

121 "production of the": Ibid.

121 "the creation of": Ibid.

122 U.S.-Airbus trade dispute: Michael D. Shear and Matthew Mosk, "McCain's Role in Plane Pact Spotlights Ties to Lobbyists," *The Washington Post,* March 12, 2008; www.washington post.com/wp-dyn/content/article/2008/03/11/AR2008031103134.html?hpid=topnews.

123 AIRBUS LOBBYING FIRMS CLOSE TO JOHN McCAIN: David M. Herszenhorn, "McCain Advisers Lobbied for Europeans to Win Air Force Tanker Deal," *The New York Times,* March 28, 2008, www.nytimes.com/2008/03/12/us/politics/12tanker.html?ref=politics.

123 headed by Thomas Loeffler: Ibid.

124 Boeing PAC contributed $525,500: Eric Rosenberg, "Boeing, Rival Lobby for U.S. Tanker Contract," Seattlepi.com, October 31, 2007, http://seattlepi.nwsource.com/business/337612_contract01.html.

124 "I had nothing": Ibid.

125 "The planet's most": David Lynch, "Has CITGO Become a Political Tool for Hugo Chavez?" *USA Today,* January 11, 2006, www.usatoday.com/money/industries/energy/2006–01–11 -citgo-cover-usat_x.htm.

125 "first enemy": Russ Buettner, "Hugo Chavez Is Tied to Giuliani Firm," *The New York Times,* March 15, 2007, www.nytimes.com/2007/03/15/us/politics/15rudy.html?ref=politics.

125 "nearly total lack ": Ibid.

125 "[T]o prevent U.S.": U.S. Department of Justice, Foreign Agent Registration 5609, 2004, by Venezuelan Information Office, LLC.

126 at about $30,000: Ibid.

127 $3 million by Citgo: "Major Romney Donors Lobby for Venezuelan Government Linked Oil Company," The Huffington Post, September 28, 2007, www.huffingtonpost.com/2007/09/28/major-romney-donors-lobby_n_66290.html.

127 $280,000 in 2007: "Lobbying Report, Kelley, Drye on Behalf of Petroleos de Venezuela, S.A.," August 14, 2007, www.opensecrets.org.

127 "fuel supply, foreign oil": Ibid.

128 "This bill raises": Dina Cappiello and Richard Rubin, "Renewable-Energy Tax Breaks Pass House Despite Dispute over CITGO," *Congressional Quarterly,* February 27, 2008, http://public.cq.com/docs/cqt/news110–000002677810.html.

128 more than $15,000: "Major Romney Donors Lobby."

128 was paid $150,000: "Giuliani's Law Firm Tied to Venezuela's Chavez," CNN, March 15, 2007, www.cnn.com/2007/POLITICS/03/15/giuliani.chavez/index.htm.

128 "state oil company": Profile of Citgo, "Petróleos de Venezuela, S.A.," Citgo.com, www.citgo .com/AboutCITGO/PDVSAprofile.jsp.

129 "Airbus Industrie and": Lobbying Registration, Glover Park Group and Airbus Industrie and Airbus Industrie North America Holdings, Inc., document #00000042861, 00000042852, filed with the Secretary of the Senate, February 14, 2005.

129 "Unified Energy System": "History of the Company," RAO UESR, www.rao-ees.ru/en/info/history/show.cgi?history.htm.

130 "security officials": "2006 Country Report on Human Rights Practices in Turkmenistan," U.S. Department of State, March 6, 2007, www.state.gov/g/drl/rls/hrrpt/2006/78845 .htm.

131 $120,000 per month: Contract letter between Cassidy & Associates, Inc., and Equatorial Guinea, filed with the U.S. Department of Justice on December 24, 2005.

131 "No one is": Silverstein, "Their Men in Washington."

134 Howard Paster: Beth Fouhy, "Clinton Camp Adds Operating Officer," Associated Press, March 20, 2008, http://abcnews.go.com/Politics/wireStory?id=4490865.

134 "I have found": Timothy J. Burger and Kristin Jensen, "Clinton Aide Penn Mixes Campaign Role, Advocacy for Companies," Bloomberg.com, May 24, 2007, www.bloomberg.com/apps/news?pid=20601070&sid=aYaUqMqpWpW4&refer=home.

135 $40,000 a month contract: U.S. Department of Justice, Foreign Agent Registration, Glover Park Group, www.usdoj.gov/criminal/fara/links/search.html.

135 Bill himself made $800,000: Arianna Huffington, "The Clinton-Colombia Connection: It Goes Back a Long Time," The Huffington Post, April 8, 2008, www.huffingtonpost.com/arianna-huffington/the-clinton-colombia-conn_b_95929.html.

135 $25,000 a month: U.S. Department of Justice, Foreign Agent Registration, Glover Park Group, www.usdoj.gov/criminal/fara/links/search.html.

136 for $1.2 million: U.S. Department of Justice, Foreign Agent Registration, Quinn & Gillespie, www.usdoj.gov/criminal/fara/links/search.html.

136 BKSH, was retained: U.S. Department of Justice, Foreign Agent Registration, BKSH, www.usdoj.gov/criminal/fara/links/search.html.

136 Burson-Marsteller signed: U.S. Department of Justice, Foreign Agent Registration, Burson-Marsteller, www.usdoj.gov/criminal/fara/links/search.html.

136 "share information with": U.S. Department of Justice, Foreign Agent Registration, BKSH, www.usdoj.gov/criminal/fara/links/search.html.

137 "endanger our national": Glenn Kessler, "White House and Turkey Fight Bill on Armenia," The Washington Post, October 10, 2007, www.washingtonpost.com/wp-dyn/content/article/2007/10/09/AR2007100902347.html.

137 Penn & Schoen, contracted: U.S. Department of Justice, Foreign Agent Registration, Penn & Schoen, www.usdoj.gov/criminal/fara/links/search.html.

138 "lobby the [Clinton] Administration": Ibid.

139 a "temporary" engagement: Ben Smith, "Penn-Blackwater Link Puts HRC on Defense," Politico.com, October 5, 2007, www.politico.com/news/stories/1007/6219.html.

140 The group was indicted: Sylvia Moreno, "3 DeLay Workers Indicted in Texas," The Washington Post, September 22, 2004, www.washingtonpost.com/ac2/wp-dyn/A39563-2004Sep21?language=printer.

142 $25,000 a month: "Father & Son," Time, July 23, 1934, www.time.com/time/magazine/article/0,9171,747539,00.html?promoid=googlep.

142 "corporate monster into": Ibid.

144 "death squad responsible": Colum Lynch, "Ivory Coast First Lady Leads Death Squad, Report Alleges," The Washington Post, January 29, 2005, www.washingtonpost.com/wp-dyn/articles/A45644–2005Jan28.html.

144 "Their victims have included": James Astill, "Ivory Coast Death Squads Sow Terror," The Guardian, February 12, 2003, www.guardian.co.uk/world/2003/feb/12/westafrica.jamesastill.

144 "credible reports of": "2006 Country Report on Human Rights Practices in Cote d'Ivoire," U.S. Department of State, March 6, 2007, www.state.gov/g/drl/rls/hrrpt/2006/78730.htm.

145 "Security forces continued": Ibid.

145 "hate messages": "Analysis: Ivory Coast's hate media," BBC News, November 16, 2004, news.bbc.co.uk/2/hi/africa/4017069.stm.

145 "marred by violence": "2006 Country Report on Human Rights Practices in Cote d'Ivoire."

146 The agreement, filed: Contract letter between Quinn Gillespie & Associates LLC and République de Côte d'Ivoire, filed with the U.S. Department of Justice on December 22, 2004, www.fara.gov/docs/5662-Exhibit-AB-20041222-IBAYAM04.pdf.

147 For the most part: Supplemental Statement 2005 made by Quinn Gillespie to the Department of Justice under the Foreign Agent Registration Act, February 12, 2003, www.fara.gov/docs/5662-Supplemental-Statement-20050801–1.pdf.

150 $550,000 per year: U.S. Department of Justice, Foreign Agent Registration, Whitaker Group, www.usdoj.gov/criminal/fara/links/search.html.

CHAPTER 7

152 flooded the track: Glen Carey, "Dubai's $21 Million Horse Race Spurs Dress Sales, Lures Bankers," Bloomberg.com, March 28, 2007, www.bloomberg.com/apps/news?pid=20601081&sid=awvyv4oUcdyI&refer=australia.

153 Some of the money: "Statement for the Record: FBI Director Robert S. Mueller III Joint Intelligence Committee Inquiry," www.fas.org/irp/congress/2002_hr/092602mueller.html.

154 "a source of concern": John R. Emshwiller, "Bill Clinton May Get Payout of $20 Million," The Wall Street Journal, January 22, 2008, online.wsj.com/public/article/SB120097424021905843.html?mod=blog.

155 "indentured servants": Associated Press, "Emirates Labor Law Enshrines Abuses, Human Rights Watch Says," International Herald Tribune, March 25, 2007, www.iht.com/articles/ap/2007/03/25/africa/ME-GEN-Emirates-Labor-Abuse.php.

155 more than 250,000 employers: "UAE: Address Abuse of Migrant Workers," Human Rights Watch, March 30, 2006, www.hrw.org/english/docs/2006/03/28/uae13090.htm.

156 "low-skilled employees": "2006 Country Report on Human Rights Practices in United Arab Emirates," U.S. Department of State, March 6, 2007, www.state.gov/g/drl/rls/hrrpt/2006/78865.htm.

156 "Since 1995 the": Simon Henderson, "High Rises and Low Wages: Expatriate Labor in Gulf Arab States," The Washington Institute, March 27, 2006, www.thewashingtoninstitute.com/print.php?template=C05&CID=2456.

159 "boys as young": Jim Popkin and the NBC Investigative Unit, "NBC: Boys Forced to Be Camel Jockeys in UAE," MSNBC, September 12, 2006, www.msnbc.msn.com/id/14803248/.

159 "U.S. State Department": Ibid.

CHAPTER 8

163 $850 billion in consumer debt: "Senators Grill Bank Execs on 'Unfair' Credit Card Fees," USA Today, March 7, 2007, www.usatoday.com/news/washington/2007–03–07-credit-hearing_N.htm.

163 690 million credit cards: Marcy Gordon, "Study: Credit Card Late Fees Much Higher," The

Boston Globe, October 11, 2006, www.boston.com/business/articles/2006/10/11/study
_credit_card_late_fees_much_higher/.

163 more than tripled: "Fee Harvester Credit Cards Scam Vulnerable Consumers," *USA Today*,
November 16, 2007, http://blogs.usatoday.com/oped/2007/11/our-view-on-pre.html.

164 "$30 billion in 2004": Stephen Labaton, "Bankruptcy Bill Set for Passage; Victory for Bush,"
The New York Times, March 9, 2005, www.nytimes.com/2005/03/09/business/09bankruptcy
.html?pagewanted=print&position=.

164 half of all card users: Gordon, "Study: Credit Card Late Fees Much Higher."

164 average balance of $13,000: Ibid.

164 average late fee in 2005: Jeanne Sahadi, "Credit Card Fees Head Higher," CNNMoney.com,
October 18, 2006, http://money.cnn.com/2006/10/17/pf/gao_creditcard_bankruptcy/index
.htm.

165 Over-the-limit fees: Ibid.

165 average 30 percent: Ibid.

165 Card companies often charge: Ibid.

165 three different interest rates: Ibid.

165 A cardholder charges: Ibid.

165 "universal default": " 'It's Always Christmas Time' for Credit Card Companies but
Consumers Can Get Trapped by Abusive Fees and Practices," CommonDreams.org, November
20, 2006, www.commondreams.org/cgi-bin/newsprint.cgi?file=/news2006/1120–10
.htm.

165 "if you have problems": Herb Weisbaum, "GAO Report Lifts Lid on Credit Card Industry,"
MSNBC.com, October 23, 2007, www.msnbc.msn.com/id/15292149.

165 sometimes the higher interest rate: Ibid.

166 "chances are you'll find": " 'It's Always Christmas Time.' "

166 "What business": Weisbaum, "GAO Report Lifts Lid on Credit Card Industry."

166 "it would no longer": Ibid.

166 "if you pay the minimum": " 'It's Always Christmas Time.' "

166 "are systematically mailing": Ibid.

166 "Does the punishment": Herb Weisbaum, "Credit Card Companies Come Under Attack,"
MSNBC.com, June 11, 2007, www.msnbc.msn.com/id/19178133/.

167 double-cycle billing: " 'It's Always Christmas Time.' "

167 two of the six largest card issuers. Weisbaum, "GAO Report Lifts Lid on Credit Card
Industry."

167 Cash advance interest rates: " 'It's Always Christmas Time.' "

167 as high as $39: Ibid.

167 "a fee to issue": Ibid.

167 Many credit card companies: Mantell, "Cardholders Caught in Credit Card Trap."

167 one third of active: " 'It's Always Christmas Time.' "

167 "credit card companies must be stopped": Weisbaum, "Credit Card Companies Come
Under Attack."

167 "cardholders [with] household incomes": Mantell, "Cardholders Caught in Credit Card
Trap."

167 "credit limit of up to $1,500": "Fee Harvester Credit Cards Scam Vulnerable Consumers."

168 "with a collective": "Congress to Credit Card Companies: 'Play Fair'; Retailers Applaud In-

troduction of 'Credit Card Fair Fee Act.' " Merchants Payments Coalition, Reuters.com, March 7, 2008, www.reuters.com/article/pressRelease/idUS144604+07-Mar-2008+PRN 20080307.

168 "interchange fees are": Ibid.

169 "At first, no one": Steve Diggs, "Why are Credit Card Interest Rates So High?" Crosswalk .com, www.crosswalk.com/finances/11550138/print/.

169 contributed literally millions of dollars: "Member Money: Top Committee-Related Industries for Committee Members—Banking, Housing, and Urban Affairs, 109th Congress, 2006 Cycle Data," Center for Responsive Politics, www.opensecrets.org/cmteprofiles/profiles.asp? cycle=2006&CmteID=S06&Cmte=SBAN&CongNo=109&Chamber=S.

169 "to improve the disclosures": Mantell, "Cardholders Caught in Credit Card Trap."

170 "Stop Unfair Practices in Credit Cards Act": Weisbaum, "Credit Card Companies Under Attack."

171 In 2004, six credit card issuers: Gordon, "Credit Card Late Fees Much Higher."

171 "In 2007, Citigroup" : Gerri Willis, "Sidestep Credit Card Fees," CNN, April 2, 2007, http://money.cnn.com/2007/03/08/pf/saving/toptips/index.htm.

172 "check your cardholder": Ibid.

172 "average daily balance": Ibid.

172 Chase pledged: Ibid.

172 "more often credit card companies": Ibid.

172 "If you're transferring $10,000": Ibid.

172 "you can even set up": Ibid.

173 "The legislation now pending": Ibid.

CHAPTER 9

177 The U.S. Department: Sam Dillon, "With Turnover High, Schools Fight for Teachers," *The New York Times*, August 27, 2007, www.nytimes.com/2007/08/27/education/27teacher .html?_r=1&oref=slogin.

177 "The problem is not": Ibid.

177 "leave the profession": Ibid.

178 "scored higher": Sam Dillon, "Report Finds Better Scores in New Crop of Teachers," *The New York Times*, December 12, 2007.

178 Forty percent of the: Ibid.

178 We spend about: "Health Care Spending to Double by 2016," March 27, 2007, http:// myhealthinsurancenews.blogspot.com/2007/03/health-care-spending-to-double-by-2016 .html.

178 $500 billion on education: Eleanor Chute, "Back to School: Education Booms into an $850 Billion Enterprise," *Pittsburgh Post-Gazette*, August 30, 2006, www.post-gazette.com/pg/ 06242/717293–298.stm.

178 In 1989, we paid: "Estimated Average Annual Salary of Teachers in Public Elementary and Secondary Schools: Selected Years, 1959–60 Through 2004–05," IES, National Center for Education Statistics, http://nces.ed.gov/programs/digest/d05/tables/dt05_076.asp.

179 spending on schools has doubled: "Public Education Spending Has Doubled in the Last 15

Years," Education Portal, August 29, 2007, http://education-portal.com/articles/Public _Education_Spending_Has_Doubled_in_the_Last_15_Years.html.

179 $7 billion a year: Ibid.

179 "midcareer professionals": Ibid.

179 Los Angeles offers: Ibid.

179 In Guilford County: Ibid.

180 "three quarters of": Michael Alison Chandler, "Schools Pinched in Hiring," *The Washington Post,* June 24, 2007, www.washingtonpost.com/wp-dyn/content/article/2007/06/23/AR 2007062301394.html.

180 Three times as many: Ibid.

180 "widespread research that shows": Ibid.

180 These new, higher: Ibid.

180 "California is projecting": Dillon, "With Turnover High, Schools Fight for Teachers."

181 WHY THEY QUIT: "Teacher Turnover 1997–98," NCPublicSchools.org, www.dpi.state .nc.us/cte/teacher-education/nccvte/turnover_index.html.

182 "For years": Sam Dillon, "Long Reviled, Merit Pay Gains Among Teachers," *The New York Times,* June 18, 2007, www.nytimes.com/2007/06/18/education/18pay.html.

183 "As a Republican governor": Ibid.

183 "a consensus is building": Ibid.

183 "It's looking like": Ibid.

183 Denver has one: Nancy Zuckerbrod, "Many Teachers Dubious of Merit Pay," July 4, 2007, www.boston.com/news/education/k_12/articles/2007/07/04/many_teachers_dubious_of _merit_pay/.

183 The program was approved: "Merit Pay for Teachers Begins to Earn High Grades," *USA Today,* www.usatoday.com/printedition/news/20070913/edit13.art.htm.

183 "system works in Denver": Ibid.

184 "greater collaboration": Ibid.

184 "We never sat down": Ibid.

184 "We realized we": Dillon, "Long Reviled, Merit Pay Gains Among Teachers."

184 "only after reshaping": Ibid.

185 "The Milken Family Foundation": Ibid.

185 "Increasingly, cafeteria workers": "Education: Merit Pay for Teachers Begins to Earn High Grades," *USA Today,* September 13, 2007, http://blogs.usatoday.com/oped/2007/09/ our-view-on-e-1.html.

185 "And when test scores": Ibid.

185 "poor and urban": Ibid.

185 The NEA, the larger: Dillon, "Long Reviled, Merit Pay Gains Among Teachers."

185 "schoolwide bonuses": Ibid.

186 "when school children": "Albert Shanker Quotes," ThinkExist.com, http://en.thinkexist .com/quotation/when-school-children-start-paying-union-dues-that/570022.html.

186 "opposes plans that": Ibid.

186 "stems partly from": Nancy Zuckerbrod, "Education Groups Consider 'Merit Pay' Tied to Scores," *The Olympian,* August 19, 2007, www.theolympian.com/news/story/194168 .html.

186 "often had no basis": Ibid.

186 "When I look": Zuckerbrod, "Many Teachers Dubious of Merit Pay."
187 " 'Can you account' ": Ibid.
187 "looking at this": Ibid.
187 "In most professions": Ibid.
189 "fundamentally flawed": Diane Ravitch, "Get Congress Out of the Classroom," *The New York Times,* October 3, 2007, www.nytimes.com/2007/10/03/opinion/03ravitch.html.

CHAPTER 10

191 "our reports indicate": Donald W. Shepard, "Gitmo, In and Out," *National Guard,* July 2005, http://findarticles.com/p/articles/mi_qa3731/is_200507/ai_n14824218.
192 "possibly as many as fifty": Josh White and Robin Wright, "Guantanamo Splits Administration," *The Washington Post,* June 22, 2007, www.washingtonpost.com/wp-dyn/content/article/2007/06/21/AR2007062102341.html.
192 "We build up": Shaun Waterman, "Afghans Released from Gitmo Return to Terrorism," *Insight,* July 6, 2004, www.papillonsartpalace.com/afgthans.htm.
192 Abdullah Mehsud: "Pakistani Taliban Leader Refuses to Be Taken Alive," CNN, July 24, 2007, www.cnn.com/2007/WORLD/asiapcf/07/24/pakistan.taliban.reut/index.html.
192 In December 2001: Salman Masood, "Taliban Leader Is Said to Evade Capture by Blowing Himself Up," *The New York Times,* July 25, 2007, www.nytimes.com/2007/07/25/world/asia/25pakistan.html.
193 "while in custody": John Mintz, "Released Detainees Rejoining the Fight," *The Washington Post,* October 22, 2004, www.washingtonpost.com/wp-dyn/articles/A52670-2004Oct21.html.
193 "took up arms again": Masood, "Taliban Leader Is Said to Evade Capture."
193 "We would fight America": Mintz, "Released Detainees Rejoining the Fight."
193 "a counter-terrorism squad": "Pakistani Leader Refuses to Be Taken Alive."
193 "We asked them to surrender": Ibid.
193 "a senior Taliban commander": John J. Lumpkin, Associated Press, "7 Ex-Detainees Return to Fighting: Guantanamo Release Process Called Imperfect," *The Boston Globe,* www.boston.com/news/world/articles/2004/10/18/7_ex_detainees_return_to_fighting/.
193 "ambushed and killed": Mintz, "Released Detainees Rejoining the Fight."
194 "has not led to": Lumpkin, "7 Ex-Detainees Return to Fighting."
194 "released detainee killed a judge": Ibid.
194 "appears to have become active": Waterman, "Afghans Released from Gitmo Return to Terrorism."
194 "is still at large": Mintz, "Released Detainees Rejoining the Fight."
194 "another returned [Guantánamo] captive": Ibid.
195 "[W]e've already had instances": Waterman, "Afghans Released from Gitmo Return to Terrorism."
195 process is "pretty meticulous": Ibid.
195 at least 425 detainees: William Glaberson, "6 at Guantánamo Said to Face Trial in 9/11 Case," *The New York Times,* February 9, 2008 http://www.nytimes.com/2008/02/09/us/09gitmo.html.
195 "included fighters of Al Qaeda": William Glaberson, "Pentagon Study Sees Threat in Guan-

tanamo Detainees," *The New York Times,* July 26, 2007, www.nytimes.com/2007/07/26/washington/26gitmo.html.

195 "We could have said": Mintz, "Released Detainees Rejoining the Fight."

196 "It would be a gross": Phillip Carter, "To Fight Another Day: The Real Reason Guantanamo Detainees Have Returned to the Battlefield," Slate.com, October 25, 2004, www.slate.com/id/2108634/.

196 "In response to this blowback": Ibid.

196 "usually with assurances": Ibid.

197 "the ruling in France": "France convicts ex-Gitmo inmates of terrorism ties," MSNBC.com, December 19, 2007, http://www.msnbc.msn.com/id/22330283/.

197 "By refusing to give": Waterman, "Afghans Released from Gitmo Return to Terrorism."

197 "began work on a more": Ibid.

197 "an avalanche of litigation": Ibid.

197 "process of sorting": Ibid.

198 "International law": Carter, "To Fight Another Day."

198 "worst of the worst": Ibid.

198 "it would have been wiser": Waterman, "Afghans Released from Gitmo Return to Terrorism."

198 "It makes much more sense": Ibid.

198 "There were very": Carter, "To Fight Another Day."

199 "More important": Ibid.

199 "to disclose virtually": Willaim Glaberson, "Officials Cite Danger in Revealing Detainee Data," *The New York Times,* September 12, 2007, www.nytimes.com/2007/09/12/washington/12gitmo.html?ex=1347249600&en=ebc4b029d82182a6&ei=5088&partner=rssnyt&emc=rss.

199 "exceptionally grave damage": Ibid.

199 "that it was not possible": Ibid.

199 "would reveal counterterrorism": Ibid.

199 "information about virtually": Ibid.

CHAPTER 11

203 Stephen A. Schwarzman: Jenny Anderson and Andrew Ross Sorkin, "Bill Is Offered to Increase Tax on Private Equity," *The New York Times,* June 23, 2007, www.nytimes.com/2007/06/23/business/23tax.html?ei=5070&en=6e17e3f29f436cd0&ex=1189915200&adxnnl=1&adxnnlx=1189807230-OgsM/LDckLKQcu8kKPL+mg.

203 James Simons: Robert H. Frank, "A Career in Hedge Funds and the Price of Overcrowding," *The New York Times,* July 5, 2007, www.nytimes.com/2007/07/05/business/05scene.html?ex=1189915200&en=dd41977be697488a&ei=5070.

204 "Let them eat cake": Ibid.

204 In the first half: Patrick Martin, "Democrats Back Down on Ending Tax Windfall for Hedge-Fund Billionaires," World Socialist Web site, August 4, 2007, www.wsws.org/articles/2007/aug2007/hedg-a04.shtml.

204 "guardian of America's": Ibid.

204 "In another era": Nina Easton, "Democrats: We Hate the Rich, We Love the Rich," *Fortune,*

August 3, 2007, money.cnn.com/2007/08/02/news/economy/powerplay_dems.fortune/index.htm.

204 "June was a busy": Raymond Hernandez and Stephen Labaton, "In Opposing Tax Plan, Schumer Breaks with Party," *The New York Times,* July 30, 2007, www.nytimes.com/2007/07/30/washington/30schumer.html?ei=5090&en=59c40a9b43932760&ex=1343448000&partner=rssuserland&emc=rss&pagewanted=all.

204 "But there is another": Ibid.

205 Schumer has considerable: Ibid.

205 "he was torn": Ibid.

205 "unintended consequences": Ibid.

205 "They [private equity firms]": Ibid.

206 "We did think": Jessica Holzer, "Once targets of tax hikes, hedge funds now unscathed," *The Hill,* December 20, 2007, http://thehill.com/the-executive/once-targets-of-tax-hikes-hedge-funds-now-unscathed-2007–12–20.html.

206 "Meanwhile": Ibid.

206 "from investors": Frank, "A Career in Hedge Funds and the Price of Overcrowding."

206 The managers of these funds: Martin, "Democrats Back Down on Ending Tax Windfall for Hedge-Fund Billionaires."

206 "Under the law": Frank, "A Career in Hedge Funds and the Price of Overcrowding."

207 "there is little": Alan Rappeport, "Senate Debates Tax for Private Equity," CFO.com, July 31, 2007, www.cfo.com/article.cfm/9572028?f=related.

207 Paul Krugman: Ibid.

208 "Private equity and": Lisa Lerer, "Hedge Fund Lobby Wants to Know 'Score,' " Politico.com, September 11, 2007, http://www.politico.com/news/stories/0907/5771.html.

209 "I don't buy it": Jenny Anderson and Stephen Labaton, "Testimony Counters Private Equity's Tax Argument," *The New York Times,* September 6, 2007, www.nytimes.com/2007/09/06/business/06cnd-equity.html?dlbk.

209 "would significantly affect": Ibid.

209 "The United States": Ibid.

CHAPTER 12

211 Just as the worst: *Inferno* was one of the three parts of *The Divine Comedy* by Dante. According to Dante, the ninth—and last—circle of Hell was reserved for those who had betrayed someone in a special relationship.

211 3.2 million members: Gretchen Morgenson, "Lawsuit Says Teachers Are Overcharged on Annuities," *The New York Times,* July 17, 2007, www.nytimes.com/2007/07/17/business/17suit.html?_r=1&oref=slogin.

211 along with a number: Ibid.

213 "Teacher A contributes": Kathy M. Kristof, "Union's Advice Is Failing Teachers," *Los Angeles Times,* April 25, 2006, www.latimes.com/business/la-fi-retire25apr25,0,132341,full.story?coll=la-home-headlines.

213 Art Dawe: Ibid.

213 "By comparison": Ibid.

214 "he paid ING": Ibid.

214 "plan with a low-cost": Ibid.

214 "the most recent disclosure": Ibid.

215 "local unions that help": Ibid.

215 "7 million public school": Margaret E. Haering, "403(b) Excess Fees a Drag on Investment Growth," NewHavenRegister.com, August 5, 2007, www.nhregister.com/site/printer Friendly.cfm?brd=1281&dept_id=592272&newsid=18665134.

215 "originally, insurance company products": Ibid.

215 "participants who invest in annuities": Ibid.

216 "retirement plan participants": Morgenson, "Lawsuit Says Teachers Are Overcharged on Annuities."

216 "Dan D. Otter": Ibid.

216 "he couldn't understand": Kristof, "Union's Advice Is Failing Teachers."

216 "good for members": Ibid.

216 "pays the salaries": Ibid.

216 "A lot of our members": Ibid.

217 "ING offers a lower-cost": Ibid.

217 "overwhelmingly, the teachers": Ibid.

218 Their suit, filed in: Ibid.

218 "NEA, through its": Ibid.

218 "by taking fees": Ibid.

218 "a recent Security Benefit": Ibid.

218 "competitive criteria": Ibid.

218 The lawsuit charges: Ibid.

218 "The NEA-endorsed": Ibid.

218 "the fees levied": Morgenson, "Lawsuit Says Teachers Are Overcharged on Annuities."

219 THE VALUEBUILDER/NEA RIPOFF: Kristof, "Union's Advice is Failing Teachers." Amounts based on actual fund returns for the five years ended December 31. Return and cost data based on return calculator at www.sec.gov.

219 "got almost $3 million": Haering, "403(b) Excess Fees a Drag on Investment Growth."

220 "change the way": Kathy M. Kristof, "New York Teachers Union Settles Retirement Probe," Los Angeles Times, June 14, 2006, www.nyfera.org/originals/6.16.06/NYSUTScandal_LA Times_2006-06-14.pdf.

220 "carried fees and expenses": Ibid.

220 "under the guise": Ibid.

220 "to hire an independent": Ibid.

220 "your exposure": Ibid.

221 "has also begun": Ibid.

221 "said it had [also] begun": Ibid.

CHAPTER 13

225 "properties with repetitive flood losses": Kathy Chu, "Katrina Renews Calls for Change in Rebuilding Rules," USA Today, www.usatoday.com/money/economy/housing/2007-08-21 -repeat-losses_N.htm.

226 "the median value": Bill Swindell, "Budget Office Paints Grim Fiscal Portrait of Flood Insurance Program," *Congress Daily,* June 28, 2007, www.govexec.com/dailyfed/0607/062807 cdam2.htm.

226 40 percent of the homes: Ibid.

227 "four or more losses": Rawle O. King, "Federal Flood Insurance: The Repetitive Loss Program," Congressional Research Service, June 30, 2005.

227 "that has already": Chu, "Katrina Renews Calls for Change in Rebuilding Rules."

227 But the storm: Ibid.

227 Another couple who had: Ibid.

227 From the homeowners': Ibid.

228 "a well-known problem": Bernard Wasow, "Ensuring Flood Damage by Insuring Flood Damage," Century Foundation, March 16, 2007, www.tcf.org/list.asp?type=NC&pubid =1532.

228 "the problem with": Ibid.

228 "with the idea that": "Our View on Coastal Insurance: Help Gulf Recover, but Don't Subsidize the Next Disaster," *USA Today,* August 29, 2007, http://blogs.usatoday.com/oped/ 2007/08/our-view-on-coa.html.

229 "uniquely vulnerable undeveloped land": Ibid.

229 "federal flood insurance": Wasow, "Ensuring Flood Damage by Insuring Flood Damage."

229 The flood insurance program: Bill Walsh, "Flood Insurance Measure Advances," *The Times-Picayune,* May 26, 2006, www.nola.com/news/t-p/washington/index.ssf?/base/news-1/ 114862450118280.xml&coll=1.

229 Coverage goes up: Ben Evans, "Flood Insurance Overhaul Stalls," Associated Press, www1.pressdemocrat.com/article/20070827/NEWS/708270351/1033/NEWS0.

229 $23 billion in claims: Walsh, "Flood Insurance Measure Advances."

229 "a typical homeowner's policy": Chu, "Katrina Renews Calls for Change in Rebuilding Rules."

229 On July 27, 2007: "Flood Insurance," Credit Union National Association, www.cuna.org/ gov_affairs/legislative/issues/2007/flood_ins.html.

230 "Why should the people": Matthew Mogul, "Federal Flood Insurance Is on the Rocks," Kiplinger.com, June 19, 2006, www.kiplinger.com/businessresource/forecast/archive/ federal_flood_insurance_is_on_the_rocks.html.

230 STATES WITH REPETITIVE FLOOD LOSSES: Chu, "Katrina Renews Calls for Change in Rebuilding Rules."

230 "Two Floods and You": Swindell, "Budget Office Paints Grim Fiscal Portrait of Flood Insurance Program."

231 "It is both wasteful": Wasow, "Ensuring Flood Damage by Insuring Flood Damage."

231 "economic reality is already": Chu, "Katrina Renews Calls for Change in Rebuilding Rules."

231 "people in Kansas or Colorado": Ibid.

231 "Gulf Coast residents": Ibid.

231 "Among the likely": Wasow, "Ensuring Flood Damage by Insuring Flood Damage."

232 "If we are going": Ibid.

232 "roll with nature's punches": Ibid.

232 Indeed, only about: Matthew Swibel, "Road Map to Disaster," *Forbes,* September 7, 2005,

www.forbes.com/services/2005/09/07/katrina-flood-insurance-cz_ms_0907beltway.html.

233 "when the storm surge": Ibid.

233 "greatly limits their value": Ibid.

233 "the flood maps": Ibid.

233 In 2004, FEMA: Wasow, "Ensuring Flood Damage by Insuring Flood Damage."

233 "developers and builders": Mogul, "Federal Flood Insurance Is on the Rise."

235 "We were 70 percent": Chu, "Katrina Renews Calls for Change in Rebuilding Rules."

CHAPTER 14

238 "In a March 2008 survey": "Credit Crisis Seen as Top U.S. Economic Threat," March 2, 2008, http://canadianpress.google.com/article/ALeqM5iI3sb9_ZesdwLSYBtDST70o8W-3A

238 "the credit crisis did not": Ibid.

239 About 20 percent: Jim Hightower, "The Subprime Mortgage Disaster: Loan Sharks Wreak Havoc on Main Street and Wall Street," August 22, 2007, www.infowars.com/articles/economy/subprime_mortgage_disaster_loan_sharks_wreak_havoc.htm.

240 More than 90 percent of subprime mortgages: Ibid.

241 By the first half of 2007: Joshua Rosner, "Stopping the Subprime Crisis," July 25, 2007, *The New York Times*, www.nytimes.com/2007/07/25/opinion/25rosner.html?_r=1&oref=slogin.

243 $1.2 trillion in subprime mortgage loans: Ibid.

243 But the $1.2 trillion: Ibid.

243 mortgage lenders have spent more than $3 billion: Ibid.

243 "This is a rate alert": Louise Story and Vikas Bajaj, "As Woes Grow, Mortgage Ads Keep Up the Pitch," August 25, 2007, *The New York Times*, www.nytimes.com/2007/08/25/business/25mortgage.html?pagewanted=print.

244 "estimates that mortgage companies": Ibid.

244 "prolific" and outrageous: Ibid.

244 "the [mortgage] advertising": Ibid.

244 $18 billion in lending commitments: Ibid.

245 Seventy-one percent: William Poole, "Reputation and the Non-Prime Mortgage Market," Federal Reserve Bank of St. Louis, July 20, 2007, http://stlouisfed.org/news/speeches/2007/07_20_07.html.

245 ninety percent of the time: Hightower, "The Subprime Mortgage Disaster."

245 "salespeople worked on commission": David Cho, "Pressure at Mortgage Firm Led to Mass Approval of Bad Loans," *The Washington Post*, May 7, 2007, www.washingtonpost.com/wp-dyn/content/article/2007/05/06/AR2007050601402_pf.html.

246 "brokers are on the front lines": Hightower, "The Subprime Mortgage Disaster."

246 "commonly hit with fees": Ibid.

246 "you could be dead": Ibid.

246 "feeding frenzy": Cho, "Pressure at Mortgage Firm."

246 "lenders also made a fortune": Ibid.

246 "automated underwriting software": Ibid.

247 "leads to borrower shock": Hightower, "The Subprime Mortgage Disaster."

247 Seventy percent of subprime loans: Ibid.

247 "What a system!": Ibid.

247 41 percent during the first half: Ibid.

247 550,000 American families: Clifford Krauss, "U.S. States Take Action on Predatory Lending," *International Herald Tribune,* August 23, 2007, www.iht.com/articles/2007/08/23/business/states.php.

247 some 2 million: Cho, "Pressure at Mortgage Firm."

247 "conspired with a bank," Catherine Tomasko, "Bank, Mortgage Company Sued for Elder Abuse, Fraud," AndrewsPublications, September 6, 2007, news.findlaw.com/scripts/printer_friendly.pl?page=/andrews/bf/bll/20070906/20070906_porter.html.

247 "took advantage of him": Ibid.

248 Porter says that: Tomasko, "Bank, Mortgage Company Sued For Elder Abuse, Fraud."

248 "he was shocked": Ibid.

248 "This year's markets": Poole, "Reputation and the Non-Prime Mortgage Market."

248 "my attitude is entirely": Ibid.

248 "People of color": Carlo Albano, "The Subprime loan crisis a lot worse than Hurricane Katrina," February 11, 2008, http://uwmpost.com/article/52/19/3058-The-Subprime-loan-crisis.

249 "to purchase and restructure": "Investment management firms, former Countrywide exec start new mortgage firm," *Wichita Business Journal,* March 25, 2008.

249 "An examination of regulatory": Edmund L. Andrews, "Fed Shrugged as Subprime Crisis Spread," *The New York Times,* December 18, 2007, www.nytimes.com/2007/12/18/business/18subprime.html?hp.

250 "Congress to the Rescue?": http://speaker.gov/issues?id=0053.

251 North Carolina recently passed: Krauss, "U.S. States Take Action on Predatory Lending."

251 "If Washington isn't": Ibid.

251 "about a dozen states": Ibid.

252 "rolled out mortgage programs": Ibid.

252 "prohibit brokers and lenders": Jessica Holzer, "Sen. Dodd Shifts Plans to Unveil Predatory Lending Bill," *The Hill,* September 6, 2007, http://thehill.com/business—lobby/sen.-dodd-shifts-plans-to-unveil-predatory-lending-bill-2007—09–06.html.

254 "would for the first time": Edmund L. Andrews, "Bill Allowing Mortgage Lawsuits Expected to Stir Fierce Opposition," *The New York Times,* October 23, 2007, www.nytimes.com/2007/10/23/business/23lend.html?fta=y.

254 "require any mortgage lender": Ibid.

254 "people who can show": Ibid.

254 "people who package": Ibid.

CHAPTER 15

257 "Corruption has long plagued": Deborah Hastings, "Americans Who Report Iraq Corruption Pay a Price," *International Herald Tribune,* August 27, 2007, www.iht.com/articles/2007/08/27/asia/fraud.php.

257 "In [this] combat environment": Eric Schmitt and Ginger Thompson, "$6 Billion in Con-

tracts Reviewed, Pentagon Says," *The New York Times,* September 21, 2007, www.nytimes
.com/2007/09/21/washington/21contract.html.

258 "Pentagon auditors found": Committee on Oversight and Government Reform, "Iraq Reconstruction," http://oversight.house.gov/itsyourmoney/iraq.html.

258 "The company charged": Ibid.

258 "Halliburton truck drivers": Ibid.

258 "Halliburton procurement officials": Ibid.

258 "A Halliburton manager": Ibid.

259 "A Halliburton subsidiary": Matt Kelley, "Largest Iraqi Contract Rife with Errors," *USA Today,* July 16, 2007, www.usatoday.com/news/world/iraq/2007–07–16-iraq-auditors_N
.htm.

259 "A former manager": Charles R. Babcock, "Ex-KBR Worker Tied to Iraq Contract Fraud," *The Washington Post,* March 18, 2005, www.washingtonpost.com/ac2/wp-dyn/A45442
-2005Mar17?language=printer.

259 "including [charging] for meals": Kelley, "Largest Iraqi Contract Rife with Errors."

259 "shipping containers": Ibid.

259 "by far the largest": Ibid.

259 "the Defense Contract Audit Agency": Ibid.

260 "auditors turned up": Babcock, "Ex-KBR Worker Tied to Iraq Contract Fraud."

260 "federal investigators": James Glanz, "Bribery Network to Bloat War Costs Is Alleged," *The New York Times,* July 21, 2007, www.nytimes.com/2007/07/21/washington/21contract
.html?ex=1342670400&en=d4cd7dee4bd170d8&ei=5088&partner=rssnyt&emc=rss.

260 "hired by KBR": Ibid.

260 "operated by a rival": Ibid.

261 "nearly $34,000": Ibid.

261 "there have been": Richard Lardner, "Army Combs for Abuses in Iraq Contracts," Associated Press, *USA Today,* August 29, 2007, www.usatoday.com/news/washington/2007-08-29
-1196366105_x.htm.

261 $20 million retirement package: "Cheney Violates Ethics Law," HalliburtonWatch.org, www.halliburtonwatch.org/about_hal/ethics.html.

261 "severed all [his] ties": Associated Press, "Cheney's Halliburton Ties Remain," September 26, 2003, CBSNews.com, www.cbsnews.com/stories/2003/09/26/politics/main575356.shtml.

261 Between 2001 and 2004: Frank R. Lautenberg, "Congratulations Halliburton and Vice President Cheney!" September 15, 2005, http://lautenberg.senate.gov/newsroom/record
.cfm?id=254548.

261 "are among those": Ibid.

262 "Halliburton, largely through": Daniel Politi and Andre Verloy, "Halliburton Contracts Balloon," Center for Public Integrity, August 18, 2004, www.publicintegrity.org/wow/report
.aspx?aid=366.

263 "in 1998": Ibid.

263 "They're already in": Maud S. Beelman, "Halliburton Lobby Costs See Big Drop," *The Boston Globe,* March 27, 2004, www.boston.com/news/nation/articles/2004/03/27/halliburton
_lobby_costs_see_big_drop/.

263 During 2004: "Halliburton Spent $770,000 Lobbying Washington in First Half of 2004, a

400% Increase from 2003," Halliburton Watch, www.halliburtonwatch.org/news/lobbying.html.

263 "in February 2003": Timothy J. Burger and Adam Zagorin, "Beyond the Call of Duty," *Time,* October 24, 2004, www.truthout.org/docs_04/102504V.shtml.

263 "several representatives": Ibid.

263 "When the contract": Ibid.

264 the Halliburton contract was divided: Ibid.

264 "now sits": Hastings, "Americans Who Report Iraq Corruption Pay a Price."

264 "one after another": Ibid.

264 "a Wal-Mart for guns": Ibid.

265 "imprisoned by the U.S. military": Ibid.

265 "[U.S.] government officials": Matthew Jaffe, "Senate Dems Promise Action on Contractor Abuse," ABCNews.com, September 21,2007, http://abcnews.go.com/Politics/story?id=3636447&page=1.

265 "cheated the U.S. government": Hastings, "Americans Who Report Iraq Corruption Pay a Price."

265 "you will be destroyed": Ibid.

266 "The only way": Ibid.

266 "the Justice Department: Lara Jakes Jordan, "Plan to Curb Contract Fraud Doesn't Apply Overseas," Associated Press, February 12, 2008, http://www.usatoday.com/news/washington/2008-02-12-contract-fraud_N.htm.

266 "specifically exempt": Ibid.

CHAPTER 16

269 one full-time: "Playing Games with Toy Safety," *The New York Times,* November 4, 2007, www.nytimes.com/2007/11/04/opinion/04sun1.html.

270 "Ms. Nord": Ibid.

270 "In November 2007": Ibid.

271 the Consumer Product: Ibid.

271 "more than 21 million": Associated Press, "Consumer Safety Chief Says She Won't Quit," CBSNews.com, October 31, 2007, www.cbsnews.com/stories/2007/10/31/national/main3434914.shtml.

271 "one hundred field investigators": David Barboza and Eric S. Lipton, "As More Toys Are Recalled, Trail Ends in China," *The New York Times,* June 19, 2007, www.nytimes.com/2007/06/19/business/worldbusiness/19toys.html?n=Top/Reference/Times%20Topics/Organizations/C/Consumer%20Product%20Safety%20Commission.

271 "it is very clear": Associated Press, "Consumer Safety Chief Says She Won't Quit."

271 "could have the unintended": Ibid.

271 Nord opposed provisions: Stephen Labaton, "Bigger Budget? No, Responds Safety Agency," *The New York Times,* October 30, 2007, www.nytimes.com/2007/10/30/washington/30consumer.html?_r=1&ref=business&oref=slogin.

272 "13 million toys": Ibid.

272 "may have the": Ibid.

273 Nord also opposed: Stephen Labaton, "Strengthening of Consumer Agency Opposed By Its Boss," *The New York Times,* October 29, 2007, www.nytimes.com/2007/10/30/washington/30cnd-consumer.html.

273 "dramatically drain": Ibid.

273 Nord was not: Steve Crickmore, "Bush Acting Head of the Consumer Product Safety Commission Accepts Free Corporate Trips but Not an Increase in Budget to Pay for Them," November 4, 2007, wizbangblue.com/2007/11/04/bush-acting-head-of-the-consumer-product-safety-commision-accepts-free-corporate-trips-but-not-an-increase-in-budget-to-pay-for-them.php.

273 "have taken dozens": Elizabeth Williamson, "Industries Paid for Top Regulators' Travel," *The Washington Post,* November 2, 2007, www.washingtonpost.com/wp-dyn/content/article/2007/11/01/AR2007110102732.html.

273 "nearly 30 trips": Ibid.

274 eleven-day visit: Ibid.

274 "urged the commission": Ibid.

274 Nord's China trip: Ibid.

274 "the meetings drew": Ibid.

274 Could the largesse: Ibid.

274 "My view was": Ibid.

275 In February 2007: Ibid.

275 "would cause a reasonable": Ibid.

275 "does not accept": Ibid.

275 organizations "engaged in": Ibid.

275 "a blatant violation": Ibid.

276 Four out of five toys: Jose Qian, "Poor Conditions in Chinese Factories," Deutsche Welle, August 23, 2007, www2.dw-world.de/southasia/East_Asia/1.227920.1.html.

276 more than 21 million: Associated Press, "Consumer Safety Chief Says She Won't Quit," CBSNews.com, October 31, 2007, www.cbsnews.com/stories/2007/10/31/national/printable3434914.shtml.

276 twice in one month: Barboza, "U.S. Group Accuses Chinese Toy Factories of Labor Abuses."

277 "Some children as young": Sandra Williams, "Child Slaves in China Freed," Suite101.com, June 21, 2007, poverty.suite101.com/article.cfm/child_slaves_in_china_freed.

278 "adding three hours every day": Ibid.

278 "hired 1,000 junior high": David Barboza, "U.S. Group Accuses Chinese Toy Factories of Labor Abuses," *The New York Times,* August 22, 2007, select.nytimes.com/gst/abstract.html?res=F00B1EFA3D550C718EDDA10894DF404482.

278 "found to have": Allen T. Cheng, "Price Cuts Worsen China's Toy Quality," http://www.bloomberg.com/apps/news?pid=20601101&sid=aXd6pwh2TqSE&refer=japan.

278 "is around $100": Qian, "Poor Conditions in Chinese Factories."

278 child workers are girls: Associated Press, "Report: Child Labor Use Rises in China," *USA Today,* September 3, 2007, www.usatoday.com/news/world/2007–09–03-china-labor_N.htm.

278 "Children earn salaries": Ibid.

278 more than 200 million: Ibid.

278 "most child workers": Ibid.

279 "the manufacturers rip off": Qian, "Poor Conditions in Chinese Factories."

279 "that it and its affiliates": Barboza, "U.S. Group Accuses Chinese Toy Factories of Labor Abuses."

279 "has an excellent record": Ibid.

279 "conduct a thorough": Ibid.

279 "some workers' rights groups": Ibid.

280 "the House has been": "Reform and Consumer Safety," *The New York Times*, November 19, 2007, www.nytimes.com/glogin?URI=www.nytimes.com/2007/11/19/opinion/19mon4 .html&OQ=_rQ3D1&OP=5b986323Q2FQ2AvkRQ2AbmCVgmm,EQ2AEuuXQ2A44Q2 A4Q2BQ2Amo5Q7D5mQ7DQ2A4Q2B@mQ7DQ5BaF,@d.

CHAPTER 17

285 "mass-mailing operation": Bill Clinton, *Giving* (New York: Alfred A. Knopf, 2007).

286 "A couple of years ago": Ibid. at 176.

286 "When I left office": Ibid. at 176.

286 "she disclosed that": Hillary Rodham Clinton, Financial Disclosure Form, May 15, 2002; Hillary Rodham Clinton, Financial Disclosure Form, May 15, 2003.

286 "more than $1,000": Ibid.

287 "These people are gullible": Charles Duhgs, "Bilking the Elderly, with a corporate Assist," *The New York Times*, March 20, 2007.

CHAPTER 18

292 "the lottery which kills": http://books.google.com/books?id=xIX7cnk4hJwC&pg=PA136 &lpg=PA136&dq=lottery+kills+400000&source=web&ots=IQdkDWZZU-&sig=9bpnik PxMPkVfzBGgyZmUV7fw94.

292 Eighty-five percent: James D. Sargent, Jennifer J. Tickle, Michael L. Beach, Madaline A. Dalton, M. Bridget Ahrens, and Todd F. Heatherton, "Brand Appearances in Contemporary Films and Contribution to Global Marketing of Cigarettes," *The Lancet*, January 6, 2001, www.thelancet.com/journals/lancet/article/PIIS0140673600035686/abstract.

292 Even some G-rated: www.scenesmoking.org/frame.htm.

292 Wait, you may be saying: "Increasing Evidence Points to Link Between Youth Smoking and Exposure to Smoking in Movies," Associated Press, 2005, www.cancer.gov/newscenter/ pressreleases/TeenSmokingMovies.

292 Some films go: Stanton A. Glantz, "MPAA Misleads Parents, Press on Tobacco Movie Ratings," University of California at San Francisco, Press Office, December 21, 2005, www.ucsf.edu/its/listserv/smokefreemov/0116.html.

294 We believe that: C. Mekemson and Stanton A. Glantz, "How the Tobacco Industry Built Its Relationship with Hollywood," 2002, http://tobaccocontrol.bmj.com/cgi/content/full/11/ suppl_1/i81.

294 "we have seen": Ibid.

294 "watching popular movies": Suzanne Batchelor, "Movie Smoking Hooks Teens, Experts Say," *National Catholic Reporter*, February 6, 2004, http://ncronline.org/NCR_Online/ archives2/2004a/020604/020604a.php.

294 "the more smoking": "Increasing Evidence Points to Link Between Youth Smoking and Exposure to Smoking in Movies," Associated Press, 2005, www.cancer.gov/newscenter/press releases/TeenSmokingMovies.

294 The study found: "Teen Smoking Strongly Linked to Tobacco Use in Movies," National Cancer Institute, December 13, 2001, www.cancer.gov/newscenter/Tobaccomovies.

294 "health advocates point": Batchelor, "Movie Smoking Hooks Teens."

295 "You see the stars": Ibid.

295 "the science is very solid": Lisa M. Krieger and Glennda Chui, "Smoke Thickens on Silver Screen, Researchers Warn of Copycat Teens," *Mercury News,* December 5, 2005, www.ucsf.edu/its/listserv/smokefreemov/0113.html.

295 Eighty percent of PG-13: Ibid.

295 The depictions of smoking: Ibid.

295 "see [the] behavior": Ibid.

295 Increasingly, Gantz found: "Study Says Smoking in Movies is Increasing, in Contrast to Real Smoking Rates," University of California at San Francisco, Press Office, March 2, 1998, www.tobaccofree.org/films.htm.

296 "even aliens pack": Krieger and Chui, "Smoke Thickens on Silver Screen."

296 "you have very high-profile": Batchelor, "Movie Smoking Hooks Teens."

296 three quarters of all films: Ibid.

296 FILMS AIMED AT KIDS: Batchelor, "Movie Smoking Hooks Teens."

297 SIXTY 2005 TEEN-RATED: Ibid.

298 "[Young] people probably": Ibid.

298 "To some extent": Ibid.

298 "the Marlboro brand name": "Placing Cigarette Brands in Films," ASH—Action on Smoking and Health, www.tobaccofree.org/films.htm.

299 In the appropriately: Ibid.

299 "If producers or directors": Ibid.

299 "of one instance": "Placing Cigarette Brands in Films."

299 "We don't have": Sargent et al., "Brand Appearances in Contemporary Films".

300 In the Dartmouth study: Ibid.

300 "to restrict tobacco advertising": "Senate Panel OK's FDA Regulation of Tobacco," CBS News, August 1, 2007, www.cbsnews.com/stories/2007/08/01/health/main3124038.shtml?source=RSSattr=Business_3124038.

303 "If an actor says the 'F-word' ": Batchelor, "Movie Smoking Hooks Teens."

303 "Any effort to address": Brooks Barnes, "Bowing to Pressure, Disney Bans Smoking In Its Branded Movies," *The New York Times,* July 26, 2007, query.nytimes.com/gst/fullpage.html?sec=health&res=9F02E2D91E3FF935A15754C0A9619C8B63.

303 "announced that portrayals": Ibid.

303 "movies with smoking": Glantz, "MPAA Misleads Parents."

304 That amounts to 390,000 teenagers: Kreiger and Chui, "Smoke Thickens on Silver Screen."

304 On July 26, 2007: Barnes, "Bowing to Pressure."